GIFTS
of the
SPIRIT

Living the Wisdom of the Great Religious Traditions

PHILIP ZALESKI AND PAUL KAUFMAN

DANIEL GOLEMAN, EXECUTIVE EDITOR

HarperSanFrancisco
A Division of HarperCollinsPublishers

Board of Advisers for *Gifts of the Spirit:*

GIFTS OF THE SPIRIT: *Living the Wisdom of the Great Religious Traditions.* Copyright © 1997 by The Nathan Cummings Foundation, the Fetzer Institute, Philip Zaleski, and Paul Kaufman. All rights reserved. Printed in the United States of America. No part of this book may be used or reproduced in any manner whatsoever without written permission except in the case of brief quotations embodied in critical articles and reviews. For information address HarperCollins Publishers, 10 East 53rd Street, New York, NY 10022.

HarperCollins books may be purchased for educational, business, or sales promotional use. For information please write: Special Markets Department, HarperCollins Publishers, 10 East 53rd Street, New York, NY 10022.

HarperCollins Web Site: http://www.harpercollins.com

HarperCollins®, ▦®, and HarperSanFrancisco™ are trademarks of HarperCollins Publishers Inc.

FIRST HARPER COLLINS PAPERBACK EDITION PUBLISHED IN 1998

Designed by Laura Lindgren

Library of Congress Cataloging-in-Publication Data
Zaleski, Philip.
    Gifts of the spirit : living the wisdom of the great religious traditions / Philip Zaleski and Paul Kaufman ; Daniel Goleman, executive editor. — 1st ed.
        p.   cm.
    Includes bibliographical references.
    ISBN 0–06–069701–6 (hardcover). — ISBN 0–06–069702–4 (pbk.)
    1. Spiritual life. 2. Religions. 1. Kaufman, Paul, 1935–   . 11. Goleman, Daniel. 111. Title.
BL624.Z34   1997
291.4'4—dc21   97-018419

        00 01 RRD(H) 10 9 8 7 6 5 4 3 2

CONTENTS

To my mother, Jean Busuttil Zaleski
and
in memory of my father, Thaddeus Peter Zaleski (1918–1991)

To Libby, Karen, Jennifer, and the Colman-Kaufman clan

PREFACE

by Daniel Goleman

At the heart of spiritual traditions are methods for bringing stillness and contemplation into life. In moments of quiet and peace we more readily open ourselves to the spirit; contemplation is the grand pathway to the inner life. For Christians, methods have included the Jesus prayer and the Practice of the Presence of God; for Hasidic Jews, blessings that recognize and proclaim the presence of God in life's small moments. In Buddhism, it is mindfulness—a careful, meditative attention to life's activities.

In modern times, such contemplative practices are all the more valuable, offering an antidote to our hurried pace by reminding us of the deeper significance of our lives and activities. Yet even as the contemplative life has become an invaluable counterbalance to the hollowness of modern life, many people are at a loss to find ways to bring this stillness into their own lives.

For some—this is particularly true of many Christians and Jews—the difficulty stems in part from having lost sight of the connection to the ancient contemplative paths of their own traditions. For others the problem lies in finding a contemplative path that has meaning for them or that can be adapted to their own worldview. For most people, no matter what their faith, the dilemma is to find their way to contemplative practices that offer both authenticity and effectiveness.

Contemplation, in its most profound sense, connotes awareness directed toward a sacred end. In Latin the word's roots, *con* and *templum,* indicate the act of thoughtful observation involved in marking out the grounds for a temple. Contemplation sacralizes the ordinary, divining its deepest dimensions. Contemplation ranges from thoughtful reflection to meditative states that transcend all thought. It includes every mode of prayer in its deepest dimensions, including adoration, thanksgiving, petition, and surrender to or union with a higher presence. It also covers the many meditative modes, such as heightened awareness of the flow of experience; rapt attention, absorption, and one-pointed concentration; and immersion in inner silence and stillness. Today, many of us seek a way of weaving these contemplative modes into the fabric of daily existence, of bringing the highest aspects of the spiritual into the ordinary moments of life.

Gifts of the Spirit speaks directly to this need. It presents the wisdom of the world's major spiritual traditions and shows how that wisdom can help us live healthier and more fruitful lives.

AUTHORS' NOTE

The spiritual life is both personal and communal. Because it is personal, we have written this book in our own voices, using the first-person singular throughout. Because it is communal, we have written this book as a team. Philip Zaleski is responsible for the principal text; wherever Paul Kaufman's essays, interviews, and profiles appear, they are clearly identified as such and enclosed by the following symbols ⌒⚬⌒ at the beginning and ⌒⚬⌒ at the end.

The photographs were selected by Paul Kaufman.

A NOTE ON BIBLE TRANSLATIONS

Most biblical quotations in the text come from the King James Version Bible. However, now and then we have turned to other translations to highlight the traditional meaning of a teaching or practice. These translations include the Revised Standard Version Bible (copyright © 1946, 1952, 1971, Division of Christian Education of the National Council of the Churches of Christ in the United States of America), and the New Revised Standard Version Bible (copyright © 1989, Division of Christian Education of the National Council of Churches of Christ in the United States). All such instances are noted.

INTRODUCTION

At the dawn of the fourteenth century, the great Venetian explorer Marco Polo, along with other members of his merchant family, recast the cultural map of the world by pioneering the first trade routes between Europe and the Far East. Suddenly, the vast riches of Cathay—spices, silks, porcelain, paper currency, ink paintings, rare ointments—poured across the Yangtze and Amur rivers, over the Himalayan and Caucasus mountains, through the Gobi and Persian deserts, and into the eager hands of European consumers. China, in turn, reveled in the textiles, tools, and manufacturing methods, as well as the tales of exotic folklore and folkways, that the Polos exported from home on their camel caravans. The world's two most powerful civilizations shook hands, and nothing has been the same since.

Seven hundred years after the Polo expeditions, a new series of trade routes are being pioneered, signaling what may well be a comparable—or even more dramatic—cultural transformation. Unlike the goods carried on Renaissance caravans, the products of this modern cross-cultural exchange are not material but spiritual: the teachings of the great wisdom traditions of the world. All the major religions—Judaism, Christianity, Islam, Hinduism, Buddhism, Native American and African religions, and more, with all their immense cultural lore and learning—have joined in this exchange, for the most part with exuberance and goodwill.

One can never say with certainty why spiritual revolutions take place, as they may spring from forces both natural and supernatural. But we can pinpoint three concrete sources for the current ferment. One is the spread into the West of Asian religions, initiated by the work of Sri Vivekananda at Chicago's World Parliament of Religions in 1895, accelerated by the writings of Zen scholar D. T. Suzuki in the middle of the twentieth century, and propelled still further by the diaspora of meditation masters, manuals, and methods in 1959 from the Himalayan jewel box of Tibet. The second is the rediscovery by the West of its own rich contemplative and mystical heritage—for many centuries available only to monks and scholars— prompted by the popular writings of such figures as Thomas Merton and Abraham Heschel. The third, still in its initial stages of growth, has been the attention paid by the industrialized world, both West and East, to the practices of the primal traditions, especially those of Africa and the Americas.

Coptic monastery, Egypt   Linda Connor

This troika of events has changed forever the religious face of the world. Whether we live in California or Calcutta, we find ourselves heirs to an immense treasury of new (but often very old) spiritual teachings, embracing everything from esoteric cosmology to prayers of adoration to techniques for mindful walking. The response to this windfall has been remarkable. The religion shelves bulge in the neighborhood bookstore, prayer and meditation groups sprout in every urban center, Gregorian chant tops the hit parade, and angels flutter on the bestseller list. These extraordinary events, unthinkable a generation ago, bespeak an intense hunger for the sacred that seems to grow more acute from year to year.

Amid all this hullabaloo, one aspect of the spiritual revolution catches our attention above all others—or, one could say, behind all others, for this dimension, the most exalted of all, also exists as a stabilizing drumbeat, the ground of all human encounters with the sacred. Coauthor Paul Kaufman and I call it the contemplative dimension, or simply *contemplation*. As we define it, contemplation embraces such diverse practices as prayer, meditation, and mindfulness, as well as the wordless absorption in God's presence that the Western traditions mean by the term. In every tradition, East or West, contemplation serves as the royal road to the divine. It lies at the heart of the practices described in every chapter of *Gifts of the Spirit*.

All contemplative disciplines share a love of stillness, silence, and attention. They lead us out of destructive emotions like envy, jealousy, and hatred and into clear thinking and lovingkindness. They lead us out of fantasy and into reality, and thus they confer on us wisdom. As the Christian philosopher Josef Pieper writes, "a man is wise when all things taste to him as they really are."[1] Contemplative practices appeal because they offer a practical method for collecting our scattered energies, for remembering the deeper significance of our lives, for encountering the sacred. In many cases, they can be used in the most ordinary passages of life: washing the dishes, diapering the baby, driving a bargain or a car. Given our tangled lives of sound bites and megabytes, of hurry up and one-upmanship, we need—and we crave—this contemplative dimension more than ever.

Marco Polo called the record of his discoveries *The Book of the Marvels of the World*. The aim of *Gifts of the Spirit* is to serve as a new "book of the marvels of the world," an open-sesame and guide to this vault of treasures, this bounty of ways to stillness and serenity, peace and thanksgiving.

Many years ago, a young man named Raoul turned up at my college dormitory. He arrived with no explanation, not an uncommon experience in the late 1960s, when people rolled around America like tumbleweed, stopping wherever they found a roof or reefer or rock 'n' roll. Raoul haunted our college halls for a month or so, amusing us with his charming aspect. He spoke with a Moroccan accent; he played guitar divinely well; and he responded to any event large or small, good or bad, with a shrug and a declaration that "everything is everything." If he burned his breakfast toast, it didn't matter, for "everything is everything." If he met a beautiful woman, well, fortune smiled on him today but after all, "everything is everything." A tramp at heart, Raoul exhibited a remarkable degree of self-knowledge and predicted that one day he would end up in the gutter. But so what? He really didn't mind, for "everything is everything."

This breezy indifference to fate marked Raoul as a holy fool—a noble office in many religions—and it came as no surprise when he developed an interest in spiritual practice, or even when he offered to teach my roommates and me how to meditate. We should have known better. Raoul's first class met, I recall, on the stroke of midnight one Friday night. We sat cross-legged on the floor, in a semi-circle facing our teacher. He began to hyperventilate at top speed. We followed suit. Just when the room began to spin, he started to moan in a loud, undulating voice. We followed suit. For a while we alternated fits of heavy breathing with moans and groans. After five minutes, our stomachs heaved; after ten, our aggrieved neighbors threatened to call the police.

Thus ended Raoul's one and only evening as a guru. As my roommates left the room, I went up to him to express my puzzlement. "Raoul," I said, "I've read about Zen sittings, about the Jesus prayer. I've talked with priests and lamas, rabbis and monks. But I've never run across panting and wailing as spiritual practice. Do you really know what you're doing?"

"Well," Raoul replied, "maybe, maybe not."

"But are you sure that this is meditation?"

"Of course it is," he said. "Everything is everything."

A quarter of a century later, I think often of Raoul and pray that he wound up on a silver-lined cloud rather than in a gutter. He did many things well; above all, he taught some college kids how to live with a pinch of daring and a pound of insouciance. In his clumsy guruship, I believe, we catch a glimpse of genuine spiritual search. That is why Raoul appealed to us so: he scoffed at money and sneered at fame; he had overcome the allurements that ensnare us in lives that Thoreau describes as of "quiet desperation." Even Raoul's moanings and groanings, inarticulate though they were, spoke of a desire for *something more*; they bring to mind St. Paul's reminder that "the whole creation groaneth and travaileth . . . we ourselves groan within ourselves, waiting for the adoption, to wit, the redemption of our body. For we are saved by hope" (Rom. 8:22–24).

But I've come to realize that, when it comes to the nuts and bolts of spiritual practice, Raoul was hardly the most reliable of teachers. Everything is not everything, even in the spiritual life. Distinctions matter. In the early years of polar exploration, when all equipment had to be hauled by man or dog, the problem of how to transport sufficient food plagued many an expedition. The solution came in the form of pemmican, an unappetizing, greasy, compressed concoction of walrus meat, fat, and carbohydrates. Year after year, explorers munched their pemmican three times a day and then fell asleep to dreams of roasted turkey, sizzling plum pudding, and tumblers brimming with single-malt whiskey. Raoul's spiritual pemmican satisfied none of us; we craved genuine spiritual cuisine.

This is precisely what we find in the great religions of the world. Over centuries or millennia, each has developed a rich array of principles and practices—solid food for the spirit—to guide human beings toward an authentic encounter with the sacred. That is to say, each has evolved a living *tradition*.

Tradition lies at the heart of *Gifts of the Spirit*. All the material that you will meet in these pages springs from tradition, from the cumulative wisdom of humankind, gathered by men and women living in close proximity to the sacred, and then sifted, clarified, and refined from one era to the next. "Tradition" derives from the Latin *tradere*, "to hand over"; each generation hands over its knowledge and understanding to the next. In the Western traditions of Judaism, Christianity, and Islam, many of the practices that Paul and I present harken back to Abraham and his descendants, the first Hebrew prophets; the material from Eastern traditions bears a pedigree at least as venerable. Everything you will find in this book is tried and true.

At the same time, Paul and I have included many contemporary adaptations of traditional practices. We have no wish to guide you through a museum of mummified wonders; our aim is to offer material that speaks to the ordinary conditions of ordinary people (here G. K. Chesterton's observation may be in order, that "all men are ordinary men; the extraordinary men are those who know it"). You will discover, we believe, that the contemporary material offered here, while couched in modern vocabulary and method, retains a profound sense of sacred realities; it too demonstrates the outer plasticity and inner steel that have always characterized the world's great religious traditions.

To ensure that *Gifts of the Spirit* presents the best available contemplative material, Paul and I have assembled a special board of advisers for our book. The members of the board include distinguished representatives of most of the world's great religious traditions. They are listed on the copyright page. All have influenced, through their counsel and their living example, the ideas and practices presented here.

The wealth of contemplative practices in the world's religions dazzles the mind. Many of us will be familiar with the Jesus prayer of Christianity, Buddhist walking meditation, the Native American vision quest, or the Islamic *dhikr*; a thousand others could be named. We may enter the contemplative dimension through meditation, mindfulness, ritual, or prayer; in dance or a martial art or a sequence of bows and prostrations; with the help of cushions or incense, bells or drums; on a lonely hilltop or in a crowded cathedral; at birth, marriage, or death. We find it in every nation and in every walk of life. A vendor telling her beads in the Lhasa marketplace, a fisherman singing a sacred chantey as he hauls in his nets off the Comoro Islands, a nun praying the Divine Office in a Brazilian monastery; each represents one facet of the contemplative life. It is just this glorious variety that we wish to highlight through our title, *Gifts of the Spirit*.

In the process of researching and writing this book, Paul and I have discovered a few core contemplative principles that are held in common by all traditions. In that college dormitory so long ago, Raoul and his pupils tried to build an ark in the dark, without blueprint or tools. The principles of which I speak are the blueprint and tools, the laws that govern all contemplative practice. We may call them the three fundamental truths of the contemplative life:

Parvati Markus

Sitting—contemplation is nourished by attention, stillness, and silence

1. Contemplation is nourished by attention, stillness, and silence.

A mind lost in daydreams knows only its own fantasies. But in the contemplative life, we wish to know the world as it really is. Our task is to attend to reality, that is, to *cultivate attention*.

In a sense, we all know what attention means, if only through its absence. How many times have we have failed to pay attention and suffered as a consequence! In this curious phrase, "to pay attention," however, we learn something important: that attention carries a price tag. We pay for it with our efforts. This has nothing to do with stress or strain. Whether we attend to our breath, or our walk, or the presence of God, our effort is that of relaxing the mind, emptying it of noise and distraction. It is essentially an act of letting go. The Christian philosopher Simone Weil describes the process as one of "suspending our thought, leaving it detached, empty, and ready to be penetrated by the object."[2] Polished through attention, our minds become mirrors, ready to gather and reflect whatever light may come their way. Attention is then an act of love; when I attend to my son, I see him as he really is, and not as I wish him to be; I awaken to his real needs, and not to those that I superimpose on him from my overcrowded den of desires.

In the search for attention, stillness and silence prove invaluable allies. This truth is powerfully conveyed by the biblical account of Elijah's search for God on Mt. Horeb:

> Now there was a great wind, so strong that it was splitting mountains and breaking rocks in pieces before the Lord, but the Lord was not in the wind; and after the wind an earthquake, but the Lord was not in the earthquake; and after the earthquake a fire, but the Lord was not in the fire; and after the fire a sound of sheer silence. When Elijah heard it, he wrapped his face in his mantle and went out and stood at the entrance of the cave. Then there came a voice to him. . . .
>
> *1 Kings 19:11–13, NRSV*

Neither in wind nor earthquake nor fire does Elijah discern God's summons, but in the "sound of sheer silence." I'd like to add, however, that this "sheer silence" needn't depend upon outward circumstance. While many beginners require an atmosphere of exterior quiet—that of a hermitage, a *zendo,* or a remote country path—more experienced contemplatives report that silence can be found anywhere. There exists, they say, a cloistered room at the heart's center to which one can retreat even in Times Square or Piccadilly Circus. Many is the saint who has achieved holiness in the midst of the city's clamorings.

2. Contemplation thrives in the midst of everyday life.

In water, as every survivor of high-school chemistry remembers, hydrogen and oxygen join in holy matrimony. So it is with the sacred and the profane, in the fluid realm of everyday life. Contemplation is not a special state reserved for special occasions, for births and deaths, for church or synagogue; contemplation belongs in the grit and grind of quotidian existence.

Perhaps this sounds grandiose to those of you drowning in the drudgery of the daily round, diapering babies or clerking at the supermarket or perched all day before the baleful blue screen of an office computer. What do these activities have to do with contemplation or the inner life? Paul and I wrote *Gifts of the Spirit* to answer this question. We worked with a single aim: to demonstrate that every human act, from eating to working to going to bed, from giving birth to comforting the dying, offers the opportunity for contemplative practice, that an awakened inner life can be ours always and everywhere.

Consider, for example, the Jewish practice of *berakot,* or blessings. These blessings bring God's goodness and glory into the world, as one source writes:

A person who enjoys the pleasures of this world without a blessing is called a thief because the blessing is what causes the continuation of the divine flow into the world.[3]

The *berakot* bridge earth and heaven; they unite us to the source of all being and thus constitute a quintessential contemplative act. Now, the extraordinary thing is that these blessings are not restricted to "holy" occasions, to sabbath meals or bar mitzvahs. Almost every conceivable event offers the chance to bestow a blessing. There are blessings to be said upon wearing new clothes:

Blessed are you, O Lord our God! King of the universe, who clothes the naked.

Upon seeing lightning:

Blessed are you, O Lord, our God! King of the universe, whose power and might fill the universe.

Upon smelling sweet herbs:

Blessed are you, O Lord, our God! King of the universe, who creates aromatic herbs.

Upon learning that someone has recovered from a severe illness:

Blessed are you, O Lord our God! King of the universe, who has given you back to us, and has not given you to the dust.

The world is drenched in the divine presence, and the attentive soul responds by offering blessings with the eagerness of a beggar and the liberality of a king.

3. Contemplation includes a moral dimension.

At a recent national conference on contemplation, one participant raised the issue of "the navy frogman." He was referring to the unsettling practice, adopted by at least one Middle Eastern militia, of teaching navy commandos to meditate in order to make them more effective combatants. The rationale seems difficult to refute: meditation induces calm, which steadies one's hand with knife or gun.

The story of the navy frogman can knock a contemplative right off his *zafu*. It raises troubling, perhaps unanswerable questions about the manipulation of

The essential bond between morality and contemplation—
service in front of burned church, Alabama

religious practices in a secular world. It also demonstrates, in rather chilling terms, that to be worthy of its name contemplation must include a moral dimension. At the end of his life, when he was blind and penniless, the great Sioux holy man Black Elk spoke eloquently of the essential bond between morality and contemplation:

> I am blind and do not see the things of this world; but when the Light comes from Above, it enlightens my heart and I can see, for the Eye of my heart sees everything. The heart is a sanctuary at the center of which there is a little space, wherein the Great Spirit dwells, and this is the Eye. This is the Eye of the Great Spirit by which He sees all things and through which we see Him. If the heart is not pure, the Great Spirit cannot be seen. . . . In order to know the center of the heart where the Great Spirit dwells you must be pure and good, and live in the manner that the Great Spirit has taught us. The man who is thus pure contains the Universe in the pocket of his heart.[4]

How can we "purify the heart," as Black Elk asks us to do? You will find various suggestions in the pages that follow; for now, I merely mention the possibility of an examination of conscience, of the sort recommended in the famous Fourth Step of Alcoholics Anonymous, the "searching and fearless inventory of ourselves." Such a self-examination may prove to be of enormous and lasting help, no matter where we stand on the contemplative path. I may discover, for example, that

I need to change my behavior in order to advance in the spiritual life. Serious problems like drug addiction require immediate attention. But a host of other vices, many of which we like to dismiss as harmless peccadilloes, may also need to be addressed. Gluttony, procrastination, sloth, and similar habits can wreak havoc with the best intentions. To recognize my faults will spur me on to greater efforts; in addition, it teaches tolerance for the failures of others.

How to Seek the Gifts of the Spirit

To cultivate an inner life; to rise, toil, and retire with attention and love; to "contain the Universe in the pocket of [our] heart," as Black Elk puts it: this is a lofty goal and in many cases a distant one. Along the way, a number of obstacles will surely arise, some of them peculiar to the conditions of life on the verge of the third millennium. Our fast-food, fast-paced, fast-fix culture offers little support for the contemplative way. This hectic pace afflicts us all. We live in the thick of things, and too often the thick of things turns into a thicket, a thorny tangle of plans, appointments, emergencies, and obligations through which we hack our way willy-nilly. Under such conditions, it may help to bear in mind a few basic guidelines:

We need patience. Very little happens overnight in the spiritual life. It takes time to learn to live the timeless life. Here we may turn to the idea of apprenticeship, the slow, steady accumulation of knowledge and insight that leads to mastery in any craft. No spiritual master comes by wisdom instantly; every satori, or sudden enlightenment, is preceded by years of suffering, study, and prayer. The way of contemplation is the way of apprenticeship; it is, if you will, the way of the tortoise (a common pet in Japanese monasteries). A tortoise never shouts or runs. A tortoise observes the world with equanimity, attending with intelligence and serenity to his humble tortoise needs. Yet, as you may remember, the tortoise always wins the race; it is the tortoise who sees the face of God.

We need courage. Contemporary society, as I've said, makes few allowances for the inner life. As a result, we may find that some contemplative practices feel embarrassing, at least at first. Consider, for example, grace before meals. Table grace unites the family and links it to the sacred. It fulfills the fundamental human need to give thanks for our existence. Perhaps for these reasons, after a period of attrition grace has again become a staple in many homes. At the same time, saying grace can be awkward at first. Uncle Bill and Aunt Coo will gawk at you mercilessly, as if you have taken leave of your senses. Your children won't stop giggling. You will feel exposed, as if caught with your zipper open. You will feel like a fool.

Rest assured, no blush lasts forever. With perseverance comes acceptance and then joyful participation. In time the entire family will welcome grace as an essential part of eating, the spiritual salt that brings savor to the meal. So it is with all contemplative practices.

We need to know that we cannot fail. An ancient saying has it that "if we take one step, God will take a thousand." All religions agree that the smallest effort brings in return an immense outpouring of divine assistance. We need only take the first step. If even this proves to be too much, take heart, for tradition teaches that the bare wish to take the first step will suffice. Any impulse of the heart, however faint, will bring a response; such is the generosity of God's love. As the medieval contemplative Julian of Norwich put it, "all will be well, and all will be well, and all manner of thing will be well."

Allied to this great truth is another: that our actions, no matter how frail, have their effect. Nothing is lost, nothing forgotten. As Simone Weil remarks:

> Never in any case whatever is a genuine effort of the attention wasted. It always has its effect on the spiritual plane and in consequence on the lower one of the intelligence, for all spiritual light lightens the mind.[5]

Our least effort of attention or mindfulness, compassion or love, alters the balance of forces in the world (alas, this applies to our sins as well). We see this

expressed in the art of bonsai, where a bit of wire here or a minute clipping there can dramatically change the growth of a tree; we see it too in the delicacy of ecological harmonics, where introducing a tiny beetle into a forest may upset the entire cycle of life from microbes to mountain lions. In the harmonics of the contemplative life, a moment of mindfulness may change the world—or at least ourselves.

How to Use This Book

Gifts of the Spirit is designed as a coherent narrative, to be read from cover to cover. It's certainly possible, however, to dip into the text at random, as if cruising a lavish buffet table. You might also wish to search an area of particular interest. A couple contemplating a wedding, for example, might turn to the chapter on marriage, to discover how this sacred state is celebrated in various

Walking meditation

traditions around the world. Someone looking for a way to make office routine more meaningful will find ample assistance in the chapter on working. If your children are growing horns and fangs, the chapter on childhood may help turn things around.

We have divided each chapter into three parts. The first part introduces the subject and provides background material. The second part, the "contemplative close-up," offers an in-depth look at one aspect of the subject or explores its place in a particular tradition. The third section provides a "contemplative harvest," an array of practices, reflections, interviews, and profiles that illuminate the subject from many directions. For example, chapter 3, "Eating," begins with a discussion of the general spiritual role of food, follows with a "contemplative close-up" that explores in detail how Zen monks prepare, cook, and consume their meals, and concludes with a variety of materials, including advice from Dr. Dean Ornish on eating mindfully, a profile of Buddhist cook Ed Brown, a discussion of Jewish, Hindu, and Native American table graces, and a look at a Japanese tea ceremony.

Much of what you read will be immediately applicable to your needs; some of it may seem far afield. Use what you wish, and squirrel away the rest for future reference. Bear in mind that the book in your hands is but a beginning. Only through regular practice will the prayers, exercises, rituals, and reflections in the following pages acquire their full weight and meaning.

PART I

Day

Introduction:

LIFE IN A DAY

I was clambering over a toppled oak when I caught the faint, acrid scent. Perhaps a patch of moldy mushrooms, I thought. I had spotted large clumps of brown fungi in the area a few weeks ago, before the late spring rains arrived. As I continued on my evening ramble down the rough trail toward the lake, the smell increased. Looking up, I noticed dark specks mottling the air. I broke through the brush, cutting my thumb on a bramble as I entered the waterside clearing.

Before me the air danced with fairies. I didn't notice the pain in my thumb, so entranced was I by the sight. The fairies were tiny, with pale green or yellow translucent wings, their torsos long, brown and curved as if in ecstasy. Clouds of them coagulated and burst apart, roiling up twenty feet or more, then thinning like mist and drifting toward the ground. I discerned individual threads in the shimmering tapestry, but only for a second or two before a wind gust or some herd instinct remixed the threads into a seething knot.

Right away, I recognized what I was seeing: a swarm of *ephemeroptera*, or mayflies—also known as fishfly, spinner, shadfly, and sandfly—dancing in erotic frenzy. The ground was slick with their carcasses; they coated the gravelly path and

Morning Light Lawrence Hudetz

the surrounding granite rocks. A faint scent of decay arose from the mass grave. But this insect cemetery couldn't hold my attention; I was far more captivated by the bedroom antics in the sky. There males danced, females pranced, happy couples mated, and a new generation of *ephemeroptera* was conceived before my eyes. It was a glorious sight. But what gave it special poignancy was the remarkable life cycle of these miniature creatures—also known, fittingly, as dayflies—for after a long somnambulistic stretch as nymphs, they burst into adulthood, make love, and die all in a single day.

If, as Matthew Arnold observed, the life that burns half as long burns twice as hard, then these mayflies blaze like the sun. To be born, procreate, and die in twenty-four hours! No wonder the mayfly has become an archetype of life's swift passage, beloved by poets, philosophers, and fishermen (who find them to be splendid bait for trout). Benjamin Franklin wrote a soliloquy from the viewpoint of a "venerable ephemera who had lived four hundred and twenty minutes," a hoary age. This mayfly, a prophet and visionary, shakes his head in wonder at his "great age," decides to spend his remaining seconds "in the reflection of a long life spent in meaning well," and surmises that the sun, whose arc he has traced across the sky, will soon "be extinguished in the waters that surround us, and leave the world in cold and darkness, necessarily producing universal death and destruction."[1]

I sat down on the shore, the low summer sun warming my neck, wondering idly how many mayfly Methuselahs reeled toward death within this great throng of life. I planned to watch the delicate ballet for five or ten minutes before resuming my hike. It didn't work out that way. Within a few seconds I was engulfed in mayflies. They clumped around me, flying into my ears and mouth, settling on my red shirt and blue pants like flecks of whitish-brown paint. I breathed shallowly, reluctant to draw a family—or an entire clan—into my lungs. They flew against my face, so thick at times that it seemed like a crystal veil was suspended before my eyes, through which the world shimmered, suddenly unknown.

Enveloped in mayflies, I held my ground for a minute or two—each minute a month from a mayfly's point of view—enraptured by this spectacle of life coming and going like ocean waves. Is this, I wondered, how God sees the rising and falling of generations, kingdoms, civilizations? Just for fun, I tried to switch lenses, to see this drama from the mayfly's point of view. Here was something new! It dawned on me that philosophers write from a human perspective when they pity the mayfly its brief moment in the sun. But from a mayfly's perspective—that is, from the profundity of a mayfly's experience of time—a moment can contain a lifetime. William Blake knew the secret:

To see a World in a Grain of Sand
And a Heaven in a Wild Flower,
Hold Infinity in the palm of your hand
And Eternity in an hour.

When Benjamin Franklin's mayfly rejoices in his "long life spent in meaning well," we laugh, but that laugh contains a secret assent, for on some level we know that the mayfly doesn't deceive himself; his day is indeed a lifetime, and he really has "lived long enough . . . to glory."

Well then, I thought, why not take the mayfly's wisdom as our own? Every day, our mayfly sage suggests, is a miniature life: we are born with the dawn, grow to full potency at noon, retire in the evening, and find oblivion with sleep. Here lies a deep truth. Whether we yearn for yesterday or pine for tomorrow, it is only in this day, this *now*, that our life unfolds. Thus the most famous slogan of the 1960s counterculture: "Be Here Now." Twelve-Step programs offer a close cousin in "one day at a time." Days do come one at a time, and so we must take them. "Carpe diem," goes a more ancient saying, and although we may reject the bitter-sweet despair that underlies that summons to pleasure, we in search of the spiritual life must also seize the day.

In religious cultures, people cherish an exalted view of the day—a view, one might say, commensurate with that of the learned mayfly. The very word *day* derives from the Indo-European *dhegwh*, meaning "burning" or "shining," the same root that gives rise to *deity, divinity,* and *divine.* Some traditional societies perceive the day—and time, its parent—as a god. In the *Bhagavad Gita,* Krishna, the supreme Lord, reveals himself as "time, the devourer of worlds." The ancient Romans, Greeks, and Babylonians all worshiped time and its offspring. In every traditional culture, the cycles of time, especially the year, month, and day, glow with a mysterious, numinous light. Listen to this Syrian Orthodox prayer, in which God, the day, all creation, and the human heart share, each in its own way, the same illumination:

> Lord of the morning and ruler of all seasons, hear our prayer and have
> mercy on our souls. Shine upon me, Lord, and I shall be light like the day; I
> will sing your praise in light while I marvel. The creation is full of light, give
> light also to our hearts that they may praise you with the day and the night.[2]

How many of us greet the day in this way, as if in the presence of a shining god (*dhegwh*)? Most of us, I suspect, wake up in a fog, go to work in a funk, come home in a fuss, and fall asleep in a fret. At best we shrug off each day with that magic mantra "mañana," reasoning that, after all, days are as plentiful as daisies in a meadow, with 30,000 in the average human life span. What does one more or less matter? At worst, we hate our days with a terrible passion. I still shudder when I think back some twenty-five years, to a time when my days seemed bled of meaning. Just out of college, I had landed a job in New York City manning an old-fashioned telephone switchboard, the kind that looks like a vertical plate of spaghetti, with cords running every which way. Whenever I inserted the wrong plug in the wrong hole, my boss would turn cherry red and scream his lungs out. I hated each day with a passion, and the highlight of my waking hours came when I slashed a big crimson X across the date on my desktop calendar, a stroke of the pen familiar to all prisoners. My aim, to put it bluntly, was to murder time.

Sad to say, this is a common story. Too many of us scorn our days; too few of us take a lesson from the mayfly and make use of every moment. Now, a bad job is a problem worth confronting (for more on this, see chapter 4, "Working"), but the crisis that I faced ran deeper than monotonous work and an intemperate boss. It was a crisis in how I approached the day, a crisis shared by the world at large. The historian Jacques Le Goff has traced the origins of this crisis to the rise of capitalism and the subsequent switch from what he dubs "church time," ruled by sacred patterns and rhythms, to "merchant's time," in which minutes, hours, days, and weeks are reduced to a mundane commodity, like crude oil or hog bellies, to be bought, sold, and hoarded ("time is money," as the expression goes).

The awful upshot of this transformation is clear to see: when it comes to time, we display all the clearheadedness of a punch-drunk boxer. We battle for every second of "free" time, yelp when some unexpected event—extra work at the office, an untimely visit from great-aunt Gertrude—steals our precious seconds, and then spend our hours on the beach stewing about the office. Time "hangs heavy on our hands": we get bored in a flash; we hunt desperately for diversions to escape the ticking of the clock. In the midst of this befuddlement, our sense of time as a sacred mystery has deserted us completely.

It doesn't have to be this way. We can claim our birthright. We can hallow time. The religious traditions of the world point the way, suggesting two complementary means by which to experience each moment as a divine gift: *we may see the sacred in every moment,* and *we may make every moment sacred.* Let us consider each of these in turn.

To See the Sacred in Every Moment

Throughout part 1 of *Gifts of the Spirit,* Paul and I explore the spiritual riches inherent in the mundane activities of daily life. To invest this wealth properly, we

need to cultivate that special disposition that we call "contemplation"
(which we discussed in the Introduction), which we can loosely define as a
loving openness toward the world. We
may put our task like this: *to be on our
sitting cushion in the midst of life.* Learning
how to do this comes not only through
prayer in the conventional sense, but
through an awakened attention in all
activities, from washing the dishes to
solving higher mathematical equations.
If we adopt this rule of life, we never
throw one hour away in favor of
another, never shrug our shoulders and
say, "Well, it's just one of those days."
We never settle for mediocrity.

Bill Aron

*Sunrise Hallel—a Jewish prayer of praise: "Blessed be his glorious kingdom
for ever and ever"*

The religions of the world offer
a cornucopia of practices aimed at
opening our eyes to the ever-present
reality of the sacred. Brother Lawrence
of the Resurrection, a seventeenth-
century Carmelite, brought to the world
the Practice of the Presence of God,
which entails pausing in the midst of the
daily whirl—perhaps while shining a
shoe or baking a cake—to renew oneself in the radiance of God's love. The
twentieth-century Quaker Thomas Kelly writes of immersing oneself in the
"eternal Now," which we experience as "a steadfast Presence, an infinite ocean of
light," by which we see all human beings in a new way, as brothers and sisters, as
children of God.[3] Buddhists everywhere practice the discipline of mindfulness,
wherein one strives to be engaged in the present moment "for the purification of
beings, for the overcoming of griefs and sorrows . . . for winning the right path,
for realizing Nirvana."[4]

There is one practice, found in every religion, that may justly be called the royal
road to wisdom. This discipline goes straight to the core of inner work, teaching us
to relish the life in every second, and yet reminds us that life itself is transient, a sign
of something greater still. I am speaking of the remembrance of death.

Several years ago, while living in France, my wife Carol and I took a train to Rome for a week of carefree tourism. We soon exhausted the familiar tourist spots—the Coliseum, the Vatican, the Spanish Steps—and found ourselves strolling down the Via Veneto. Suddenly we noticed on our right a double staircase leading to a church and crypt.

Inside, an astounding sight met our eyes. Six chapels stretched fifty yards underground, each ornately decorated in the best Italian fashion—not with frescoes or plaster statues, however, but with bones, hundreds of thousands of bones, the ossuary remains of 4,000 brothers of the Capuchin order (an offshoot of the Franciscans) who had died here during the past 300 years. One chapel held skulls arranged into great arches, circles, and crosses, watched over by four skeletons dressed in brown Capuchin robes. Another contained a clock made of foot and finger bones. Everywhere pelvises, shoulder blades, and arm and leg bones festooned doorways, windows, and alcoves. At the end of the passageway a trio of child skeletons, clutching hourglasses, stood guard near a plaque that read: YOU ARE WHAT WE WERE ONCE; YOU WILL BE WHAT WE ARE NOW.

This strange Capuchin museum of death is not a monkish variation on Grand Guignol; it is, rather, a memento mori, an oversized, insistent, and somewhat grotesque instance of the remembrance of death. No Capuchin who inhabits this property can fail to remember his mortality or that of everyone he meets. This example may be extreme, but the practice is universal. The fifth-century *Rule* of St. Benedict, which provides the template for daily life in Christian monasteries around the world, includes among its "tools for good works" the instruction "to hold death before one's eyes daily." A famous tantric exercise in Tibetan Buddhism involves the visualization of one's own rotting corpse, an application of the Buddha's observation that "of all mindfulness meditations, that on death is supreme."[5] The seventeenth-century samurai Daidoji Yuzan Shigesuki saw remembrance of death as the warrior's most important task:

> One who is a samurai must before all things keep constantly in mind, by day and by night, from the time he takes up his chopsticks to eat his New Year's breakfast to Old Year's night when he pays his yearly bills, the fact that he has to die. That is his chief business.[6]

Al-Ghazali, the great Muslim mystic, writes that "in the recollection of death there is reward and merit" and tells of a man putting to Muhammed the question, "Who is the most intelligent and generous of men?" to which the Prophet replies, "The most diligent in recalling death, and the one who is best prepared for it."[7]

The remembrance of death crops up repeatedly even in modern secular literature; my favorite example is E. M. Forster's superb aphorism, "Death destroys a man but the idea of death saves him."

The remembrance of death is a counsel of joy, not of sorrow; of hope, not of despair. It leads us to reappraise our lives, sifting wheat from chaff. It has inspired many people to change jobs, drop bad habits, seek new friends, find their heart's delight.

As our little mayfly knows, the approach of death also salts the taste of life. Sense with all your being the reality of your own death and that of everyone around you, and a stupendous transformation takes place, as radical as that of a leper whose flesh is restored or a paralytic who suddenly walks. In a flash, you see with the eyes of eternity; you discover a world illuminated not only by the sun's pale rays, but by Henry Vaughn's "ring of pure and endless light." This same principle, reduced a thousandfold, underlies the platitude that "absence makes the heart grow fonder." To remember death is to understand that absence is our common lot; in response, friendship grows into compassion, and fondness into love. Every person becomes precious, every thing shines forth in immaculate purity, every action acquires the severe beauty of a last will and testament.

There are many ways to practice the remembrance of death. A Tibetan Buddhist friend tells me that he never leaves home in the morning without reminding himself that he may not return in the evening. Millions of Christian children practice a rudimentary form of the remembrance of death through the following traditional nighttime prayer:

> *Now I lay me down to sleep,*
> *I pray the Lord my soul to keep.*
> *If I should die before I wake,*
> *I pray the Lord my soul to take.*

As an introduction to this discipline, you might designate a short period during the day—the lunch hour is a good choice—during which you remind yourself, whenever you talk to another person, that he or she is destined to die. You will find that old grudges and preoccupations melt away, replaced by a surge of compassion for all transient beings.

To Make Every Moment Sacred

A few months after our Rome adventure, Carol and I flew to Turkey on Bulgarian Airlines. Our choice of airline could have been better, as the trip featured seven suffocating hours in the Sofia transit room, air thick with the harsh smoke of Russian cigarettes, as well the dubious thrill of watching rivets pop from the plane's walls whenever we encountered the tiniest bit of turbulence. Things worsened when we arrived and ran into a barrage of taxi drivers demanding exorbitant fees for the short drive into town. But we successfully negotiated these adversities, and at 3:00 A.M. we settled down for a sweet night's sleep in an air-conditioned Western-style hotel a few blocks from the Hagia Sofia in downtown Istanbul.

Or so we thought. A few hours after putting head to pillow, I was awakened by a thin, high cry. At first the voice seemed so ethereal that I shook it off as a fragment of a half-digested dream. Then I realized that the sound came from outside my head; a glance at my wife, who was still sleeping, and I realized that it had originated from outside our room. *What kind of a country was this?* I stuffed the pillow over my ears, but the sound came again, a haunting voice, suggestive of high mountain peaks or undersea kingdoms. I threw open the window. To the east, the sun skirted the horizon, huge and red. Cold air rushed into the room. I followed the voice back to its source, a needlelike tower beside a domed structure about 500 yards away.

Then I realized what I was hearing, my irritation fled, and fascination rushed in. For this was the voice of a muezzin singing the call to prayer (*salat*), a summons answered five times each day by one billion Muslims around the world. If I had understood Arabic, I might have felt a twinge of conscience as well, for the muezzin was singing, among other things, that "prayer is better than sleep."[8]

During our stay in Turkey, Carol and I observed tens of thousands of people, even in this most secular of Islamic nations, pausing in their daily round to pray. We visited shrines, mosques, cemeteries, and centers of learning, and saw everywhere a people at prayer, a land suffused with a sense of the sacred. Five times a day—at daybreak, noon, midafternoon, sunset, and evening, a schedule established by Muhammad—the *salat* unfolds, in a precise sequence of words, bows, and prostrations through which body, mind, and heart participate fully in turning toward God. The prayer always includes the *Fatihah*, the opening chapter of the Koran, which begins, "In the Name of Allah, the Beneficent, the Merciful," and continues with a plea for divine guidance and help throughout the day. According to scholar Anne-Marie Schimmel, some early Sufi commentators traced the word *salat* to the root word *walasa*, meaning "to be united." Through *salat*, Muslims find union within themselves and unite themselves to God. Five times from dawn to dark, the believer reads the watermark of the sacred in the text of his or her day, a rhythmic reminder of the meaning and purpose of human existence. Moreover, the influence of these five periods of prayer spills over to flood the entire day with a sense of God's presence.

The *salat* thus represents a fully realized example of our second approach to the spiritual life: to sanctify each moment. With divine help, we deliberately set out to imprint the sacred upon our lives. Thus Orthodox Judaism carves three major prayer periods—the *Ma'ariv, Shaharith,* and *Minchah*—out of the day, while Catholicism celebrates the Divine Office (see chapter 2, "Waking Up") seven times daily. Hinduism, Buddhism, and several other religions offer their own variations on the theme.

But you needn't adhere to a particular religion to punctuate the day with spiritual practice. The principle is clear: to break at set intervals from the habitual routine for a moment of contemplation. Your approach may be as simple as saying grace before each meal, pausing for a moment of recollection whenever the phone rings, or offering a hasty prayer upon arising and before retiring. I urge you to try a number of alternatives, until you find one that meets your needs. The most important thing is to start without delay. Today is the summation of your life. Now is the time to begin.

When you wake up tomorrow morning, let this be among your first thoughts: *now is the time to begin.* Sleep has erased the past; I awake in the land of the "eternal Now," with the rest of my life before me, a path of unpredictable length and inconceivable wonder. How will I begin? The first steps of the day are the most important. Let us turn, then, to the study and practice of "Waking Up."

Women at prayer in a mosque, Jerusalem

Olema Window

Marty Knapp

WAKING UP

Swallowing goldfish, dressing up like Santa Claus, roller-blading around the world: human beings do many strange and wonderful things. But of all human doings, nothing approaches in strangeness or wonder that most ordinary of daily events, the simple act of waking up. We come to ourselves each morning, and each morning it seems like a miracle. Shamanistic traditions from Siberia to New South Wales teach that the soul quits the body during sleep to wander in unmapped dimensions of space and time; who knows what contortions our travel-weary soul must go through to reenter its human abode? I have a friend who kisses his bedroom wall each morning upon opening his eyes, so astonished is he at his good luck in making it back to the right address.

Personally, I believe that my soul is a stick-in-the-mud, a wallflower that never ventures afield. Still, awakening seems to me to be an astounding acrobatic feat. One moment I'm rocketing over the face of the moon, accepting an Academy Award from Sophia Loren, or slaying dragons in the fields of Middle Earth, and the next moment I find myself at home in western Massachusetts, sandwiched between my wife and the wall on a dark December morning. Or, conversely, I'll be enjoying eight hours of dreamless oblivion, only to awaken to the hunger cries of baby Andy, a wake-up whack from my older boy, John, or the sound of a plow rumbling down the street, warning me that it's time to pull on my long johns, grab a cup of coffee, and scoot outside to shovel the sidewalk. Whatever the sequence, waking up is a dramatic voyage from one world to another; it is truly a second birth.

Lately I've been puzzling over why we find this birth so difficult, despite a lifetime of daily practice. We wrestle with it, often unsuccessfully, on the rawest biological level. We make jokes about "coffee transfusions," we buy alarm clocks that screech like owls or clang like express trains, we see cartoons of Rube Goldberg–like contraptions that send the hapless, half-asleep victim sliding down a chute into an ice-cold wake-up bath and secretly think, *Maybe that's a good idea.*

The best advice I've gotten yet on how to wake up comes from a pair of gerbils named Nebula and Glaxoid. They live in our basement in a large glass cage, where I often catch them snoozing away a warm summer afternoon. When I tap on the glass, a tremble runs through the wall of their nest (a gerbilly concoction of wood shavings, burlap, and shredded gym sock). Then a tiny black nose pops out of the round hobbit-hole doorway, followed by a whiskered face. The gerbil blinks his eyes and pans around the cage, absorbing the scenery—water bottle, food bowl, chew-toy, giant human face looming in the sky. He mulls this over and then retreats. A minute later he reappears, reconnoiters, and vanishes again. This routine is repeated three or four times, until finally a brave paw ventures forth, followed—if all goes well, as it invariably does—by another paw and finally the whole animal: first Glaxoid, the more intrepid of the two, and then his retiring brother. The brothers Gerbil then circle their world, ever so cautiously, stopping at food bowl, water bottle, and all the major landmarks, giving each a cheerful good-morning bite.

Gerbils, it seems, know how to bridge the gap between sleep and wakefulness. Their method is simplicity itself: they meditate before they move; they scrutinize before they scamper. Gerbils are tiny souped-up creatures, with a metabolism as fast as the jet stream, but they take their time in the early morning. It's as if they awake on miniature sitting cushions, where they spend the first moments of the day in serene gerbil-meditation.

The same routine holds with other animals, if we make allowance for species variation. My family once owned a pet tortoise named Zeno that would cogitate for a quarter-hour, swiveling his head slowly east to west, before lumbering toward his morning snack. A dog I once loved, a mongrel named Spot, would circle his bed upon awakening, as if spiraling slowly out of the dream world into the bone world. All cats stretch long and languidly at first light, as if fitting into their cat outfits for the day.

This, I believe, is what human beings need to do as well. We need to come into our estate slowly each morning. We need to twitch our whiskers, poke our head out of the nest, pad around a little, and gradually grow reacquainted with ourselves and our world.

No doubt, this is even more true of human beings than it is of gerbils, for we can wake up physically yet remain spiritually asleep. Every religious tradition addresses this state of spiritual slumber: "Awake, O sleeper, and rise from the dead!" exclaims an ancient Christian morning prayer. To awake in body and soul, to steer a course through the day's reefs and shoals, we need the time to remember who we are, where we are, and what we seek. We need, in short, a chance for *orientation.*

Orientation

Every year the Huichol Indians of central Mexico go on pilgrimage in search of peyote, the psychotropic cactus that they associate with Elder Brother Deer and other deities, and around which their entire religious and social life revolves. On this quest, the Huichol trek across several hundred miles of mountain and plain to a semidesert landscape that they identify as Wirikuta, the mythical paradise where the ancestral gods and the sacred peyote still dwell. As the pilgrims near their destination, a magical transformation takes place, visible only to themselves: they are transformed into gods, while the surrounding desert becomes, to their deified vision, a fertile valley of deer, maize, and multicolored flowers.

When the Huichol arrive in Wirikuta, a crucial ritual unfolds. The *mara 'akame* (chief shaman) points a stick toward the six sacred directions of north, south, east, west, up, and down, reciting prayers as he marks the dimensions of the universe. The Huichol thus discover where they stand in relation to the cardinal directions, to the human and divine realms, to the present and the primordial past. Once stabilized in this way, they are ready to undertake the sacred peyote hunt.

As with the Huichol, so with each of us. Orientation is our first order of business each morning, whether we awake to find ourselves in paradise or in a familiar, rumpled bed. Through orientation, we reaffirm our identity in relationship to the wider world. We drop anchor in the universe, we find safe harbor at the beginning of the day. It is the same process that gerbils follow without fail. All the great religions recognize the supreme importance of orientation, and its effectiveness as an antidote to the poison of anxiety and confusion that mars so many of our mornings and often lingers throughout the day. During *salat,* no matter where they are on the planet, Muslims turn their faces toward Mecca, the sacred heart of the Islamic cosmos. It is toward Mecca that they fall to the ground in grateful prostration. From sunrise to dark, in each of the five daily periods of prayer, Muslims orient themselves toward the sacred, surrendering their will to that of God. Similarly, Catholics often begin the day with the sign of the cross, touching fore- and middle fingers of the right hand to forehead, chest, left shoulder, and right shoulder. This gesture not only sketches out the cross on which Christ died but traces the four cardinal directions, with Christ at the center. By making the sign, Catholics imprint a cosmic map upon their flesh, thus consecrating their bodies—and by inference, their total being—to a holy life.

The significance of this morning process cannot be overstated. One doesn't build a temple on quicksand; a day, too, needs a firm foundation. By beginning the morning with a period of contemplation—be it prayer, meditation, or listening to gentle music that brings life into a deadened room—we ensure not only that we wake, but that we wake *up*, that our hearts and souls rise with our bodies.

A Morning Exercise for Everyone

When you wake up, spend a few moments lying in bed. Enjoy the exhiliration of the morning air, the shimmer of sunlight along the edges of the drawn shades, the familiar yelp of your neighbor's dachshund. Sense the life coursing through your body. Notice your breath, the pulsing of blood in your fingertips, the tug of gravity upon your arms, legs, and trunk.

Get out of bed slowly, observing the shift in your center of balance as you move into an upright position. Stand erect, without strain. Only human beings stand in such a way, their spines a vertical oblation to the divine. Feel your feet on the ground. Step attentively, aware of the pressure as your soles touch the earth. Expand this awareness in various ways as you go about your morning activities: notice the roundness of the toothbrush handle, the chalky sweetness of the toothpaste, the hard scrape of the comb against your scalp, the satisfying pinch as you tug your shoelaces tight. Each of these sensory experiences is part of waking up; each of them can be greeted with a grimace or a grin. This is where you begin to exercise your will, setting the course for the day. Will you react impatiently to whatever comes your way, or will you greet events with as much serenity as you can muster, containing yourself long enough to form an appropriate response? Will you let petty worries rule your day, or will you remember your higher aims? What comes our way each day is only partly under our control, but how we respond is entirely up to us.

Once you are up and about, it's time to spend a few minutes in a specific, concrete spiritual practice. For many people this takes the form of sitting meditation.

It is best to sit before the disruptions and disharmonies of the day have had a chance to intrude. We are in a sensitive state just after awakening. To some extent, we are still participating in the rhythms of the night, the silence and stillness that enveloped us until a few minutes ago. Our vulnerability is acute, which is why most heart attacks take place in the early morning. But this vulnerability can become our strength, for it means that we are malleable and thus in a position to welcome spiritual influences that will help us to reshape ourselves in a positive way.

Every religion offers its own variation on morning meditation, conforming not only to particular theological precepts but to varying cultural conditions (morning prayer in a southern Indian ashram may well differ from that in a northern Canadian ashram). Rather than present a dizzying array of alternatives, I've chosen to offer you a basic morning sitting, developed and tested over decades by thousands of practitioners from different traditions. Consider this sitting to be an open vessel, into which you may pour the understanding and methods of your own tradition. It may be used exactly as I present it, or you may adapt it as needed.

One caveat: it is advisable to avoid eating before the morning sitting, as the weight of the food, and the process of digestion that it unleashes, can interfere with the subtle energies involved.

Pick a quiet place, if possible a room with a door that you can close. You may sit in a chair, or on a *zafu* (sitting cushion) or a pile of pillows in a cross-legged or lotus position. Find a comfortable arrangement. Arms should be relaxed, one hand cupped lightly in the other, palms up. The spine should be erect. To achieve this, imagine that a string has been attached to the top of your head and is gently pulling you upward. This motion straightens and relaxes the spinal column. Not only will you find the position comfortable—it can be sustained for hours, if necessary, without undue muscular strain—but it carries spiritual significance as well, for only an erect posture befits our stature as beings of flesh and spirit—"children of God," in the lovely Christian phrase, or "God's vice-regents," as the Koran expresses it (we hear, in common speech, echoes of the spiritual symbolism of verticality in such terms as "rectitude" and "moral uprightness").

Once you have established a stable, upright position, a brief relaxation exercise will help prepare you for deeper levels of contemplation. Imagine that a warm, nourishing light is shining on the top of your head. The light softly massages your scalp, erasing all tensions and anxieties. Very slowly, the light moves down to your forehead, smoothing all the little muscles, melting away the tightness. The light caresses the skin with infinite gentleness. Slowly it glides down your face, washing the tension from eyes, lips, and jaw. Let the light bathe your neck and shoulders, let it take away the strain in arms, wrists, hands. The light floods your chest with warm radiance. It flows down to your solar plexus, where you might discover a tight knot of muscular and emotional tension. Never mind; the warm light washes this away as well. Let the light pass down your groin, your legs, and onto your feet.

Follow this procedure slowly and carefully. When you are finished, no muscular or nervous tension should remain.

After the initial relaxation exercise has been completed, return your attention to your chest. Turn inward and enter the temple of your heart. Sit in silence and stillness, remembering why you are here. Breathe slowly, in a natural, relaxed manner. Let your breath anchor your sitting. If in the midst of contemplation you suddenly find yourself miles away, remembering yesterday's dinner or anticipating tomorrow's flirtation, don't be concerned. Simply return to your breathing. Let its rhythm steady you and transport you inward, to begin again your silent vigil.

After thirty minutes, the contemplation ends. Leave the prayer as gently as you entered it. The transition back to ordinary consciousness can be a time of fertile discovery: how can I retain the balance, the tranquillity, the sense of wonder that I knew during contemplation? Learn the "taste" of this final moment, just before the world invades with all its pricks and proddings.[1]

Dr. Dean Ornish on How to Find Time to Meditate in the Morning

Dr. Dean Ornish, the bestselling author of *Dr. Dean Ornish's Program for Reversing Heart Disease,* has long studied the relationship between spirituality and health. When I asked him for tips on how to find time for a moment of quiet reflection, he offered the following advice:

"I try to meditate every day. But often I just don't have the time for it, no matter how early in the morning I get up. So I play a little trick on myself. I say, 'You have a minute, don't you?' It's hard to tell yourself that you don't have a minute to do something so important and so healthy. So I meditate for a minute. Sometimes after I've meditated for one minute, I keep on meditating. Other times, I really only have a minute. In any case, it's important to keep returning to that meditation throughout the day, to the peace and calm that it brought. So now and then in the day, I stop and remind myself of that morning meditation."

Morning praise, St. Martin's Abbey

Christine Knodt

CONTEMPLATIVE CLOSE-UP:
THE DIVINE OFFICE

Every day at 4:50 A.M., a brass bell rings in the living quarters of St. Mary's Monastery, a Catholic Benedictine community nestled in the forests of western Massachusetts. Slowly, the monks emerge from their cocoons of sleep. A minute later, each hears a knock on his door, along with a muffled voice whispering *"Benedicamus Domino"* ("Let us bless the Lord"). The monk replies, *"Deo Gratias"* ("Thanks be to God").

Bell, knock, and prayer bring the monastery to life. The bell represents heaven's call; the knock alludes to the saying of Jesus, "Knock, and it shall be opened unto you" (Matt. 7:7); bell and knock together remind the monk of who and where he is. The prayer signals the monk's joyful response to the divine summons, articulated by St. Benedict, the fifth-century founder of Western monasticism, in his *Rule:*

> Let us get up then, at long last, for the Scriptures rouse us when they say:
> *It is high time for us to arise from sleep* (Rom 13:11). Let us open our eyes to the
> light that comes from God, and our ears to the voice from heaven.[2]

At St. Mary's, both bell and knock resound at the hand of Father Bede Kierney, O.S.B. After twenty years in the monastery, reports Father Bede, "It's all routine. We go to sleep and wake up at the same time, in the same way, every day of the year"—a humble regimin that, as St. Benedict suggests, leads to "the cultivation of virtues" and, in time, to "the very heights of perfection."[3]

Within minutes, Father Bede and his brethren have left their sleeping quarters and made their way over a gravel path to the monastic church, where each finds his seat in the choir. The monks have entered another world: in winter, a world of darkness, for night reigns outside and the lamps remain extinguished until the time for formal prayer begins; in summer, a world of sunlight, pouring through the long windows that line the aisles or filtered in pastel shades through the rose window above the altar; year-round, a world of pew and choir, lectern and altar, silence and song.

Meanwhile, in a Scottish-style manor house a few hundred yards away—the home of St. Scholastica Priory, a community of Benedictine nuns—a similar process unfolds. By 5:05 A.M., black-robed sisters are seated in their choir stalls, directly across from the monks. Silence reigns. At 5:10, the lights snap on. Five minutes later, the church bursts into song. Monk and nun join in praise and thanksgiving, the great monastic chorus dipping and soaring, whispering and proclaiming, some voices as rarefied as heaven's air, others as solid as the earth, a choir linking heaven and earth in the ancient cycle of prayer known as the Divine Office.

The Office consists of seven periods (or "Hours") of prayer, reading, ritual, and silence, spaced throughout the day and night, by which Christian monks and nuns—and a vast number of ordinary folk around the world—offer their lives to God. Through this round, Christians sanctify their daily course, reorienting themselves at regular intervals to the points of their spiritual compass; the process has obvious parallels to the five-part Islamic *salat* described in the preceding chapter.

The two morning Hours, Vigils and Lauds, share this intention: to offer oneself in service to God at the beginning of the day. In this effort, silence plays a crucial role. Each Hour contains at least one stretch of silent prayer, during which one stands quietly before God. "When I first arrived at the monastery, I found this time to be a pain in the neck," says Father Bede. "But now it is the happiest time of the day." This period of interior recollection constitutes the fundamental contemplative exercise of the Christian tradition. During each Hour, this silence is mirrored by many smaller silences, as the choir passes from one section of the Office to the next. One doesn't rush from prayer to prayer, for this would be spiritual gluttony at its worst. Each portion of the Hour is preceded and followed by a moment of quiet repose, allowing one to knit one's whole being into a single offering. The Divine Office is built of silence and song, stillness and movement, outward recitation and inner prayer. From the first Hour of Vigils to the last Hour of Compline (see chapter 9, "Going to Sleep," for more on Compline), the Office unfolds with a rhythm at once mundane and sacred, bringing monks and nuns into an intimate relationship with the day and with the Creator of all days, allowing them to answer with all their being the biblical summons, "Awake, O sleeper, and arise from the dead, and Christ shall give you light" (Eph. 4:14, RSV).

Praying the Divine Office

Praying the Office demands a special disposition: As St. Benedict explains,

> We believe that the divine presence is everywhere. . . . But beyond the least doubt we should believe this to be especially true when we celebrate the divine office. . . . Let us consider, then, how we ought to behave in the presence of God and his angels, and let us stand to sing the psalms in such a way that our minds are in harmony with our voices.[4]

No easy task, this demand for harmony of mind and body; St. Benedict calls for nothing less than the reorientation of the entire being toward the sacred. We should bring to the Office the same tranquillity that comes to us in our morning sitting: a state of transparency through which the divine can shine unimpeded.

For those interested in sampling the morning office, here is an abbreviated version of the Hour of Lauds, a composite cobbled from various services throughout the week:

INTRODUCTORY PRAYER
Lord, open my lips, and my mouth will proclaim your praise.

(*Bow*) Glory be to the Father, and to the Son, and to the Holy Spirit. As it was in the beginning, is now, and ever shall be, world without end, Amen.

MORNING PSALM (PSALM 119:145—49)
I cried with my whole heart; hear me, O Lord: I will keep thy statutes.
I cried unto thee: Save me, and I shall keep thy testimonies.
I prevented [awoke before] the dawning of the morning, and cried: I hoped in thy word.
Mine eyes prevent [awaken before] the night watches, that I might meditate in thy word.

Hear my voice according unto thy lovingkindness; O Lord, quicken me according to thy judgment.

(*Bow*) Glory be . . .

OLD TESTAMENT CANTICLE (ISAIAH 45:15, 18–19)
Verily thou art a God that hides thyself, O God of Israel, the Savior.

For thus saith the Lord that created the heavens; God himself that formed the earth and made it; he hath established it, he created it not in vain, he formed it to be inhabited; I am the Lord; and there is none else.

I have not spoken in secret, in a dark place of the earth: I said not unto the seed of Jacob, Seek ye me in vain: I the Lord speak righteousness, I declare things that are right.

(*Bow*) Glory be . . .

PSALM OF PRAISE (PSALM 100)
Make a joyful noise unto the Lord, all ye lands.

Serve the Lord with gladness: come before his presence with singing.

Know ye that the Lord, he is God, it is he that hath made us, and not we ourselves; we are his people, and the sheep of his pasture.

Enter into his gates with thanksgiving, and into his courts with praise: be thankful unto him, and bless his name.

For the Lord is good; his mercy is everlasting; and his truth endureth to all generations.

(*Bow*) Glory be . . .

SCRIPTURE READING (ROMANS 12:14–15, 17–18, 21)
Bless them which persecute you: bless, and curse not.

Rejoice with them that do rejoice, and weep with them that weep.

Recompense to no man evil for evil. Provide things honest in the sight of all men.

If it be possible, as much as lieth in you, live peaceably with all men.

Be not overcome of evil, but overcome evil with good.

SILENT PRAYER
(a few minutes of silent contemplation)

Our Father who art in heaven,
hallowed be thy name.
Thy kingdom come, thy will be done,
on earth as it is in heaven.
Give us this day our daily bread,
and forgive us our trespasses,
as we forgive those who trespass against us.
And lead us not into temptation,
but deliver us from evil.

CONCLUDING PRAYER
We ask this through Jesus Christ, your Son, who lives and reigns with you
and the Holy Spirit, one God forever and ever, Amen.

BLESSING
May the Lord God bless us, guide us, guard us from evil, and lead us to life
everlasting, Amen.

WAKING UP: A CONTEMPLATIVE HARVEST

Morning Prayers

When my older son turned fifteen months or so, he began to wake up at the crack
of dawn. As Carol and I heard John stirring in his crib, we would glance at each
other, groan, and scoot under the covers for an extra minute of sleep before the
inevitable hunger cries commenced.

One day, however, something magical happened. John awakened much too
early, as usual—we heard the creaking of his crib bars as he hauled himself to his
feet—but the crying never came. At first there was silence, and then we heard the
most extraordinary sound. John was singing, in a voice that soared and swooped,
burbled and trilled, filling the air with a stream of words that made no sense—they
certainly weren't English—but seemed rich with meaning. Carol and I got out of
bed and padded to the doorway of the nursery. There was John, babbling away, a
beatific expression on his face. For a moment I thought of intruding, but I held
back, amazed by the transparent joy in my son's eyes. Was he serenading an angel?
Exploring a new inner world of delight? Talking it over later, Carol and I decided
that only one word seemed to catch the flavor of what John was doing that morning

(and, as it happened, nearly every morning for the next six months): John was praying.

If so—and I believe to this day that his joyful prattle was a rudimentary form of prayer—then he was in good company. For this is one of the few universals in world religions: when people wake up, they pray. The *salat* is one example, the Divine Office another. Here is a cornucopia of prayers and related practices from spiritual paths around the globe:

JEWISH MORNING PRAYERS

Like many other religions, Judaism prescribes for its members a cycle of daily prayers. The prayers said at dawn, known as the *Shaharith*, include a massive assortment of blessings, psalms, biblical quotations, and rabbinic texts. In addition, the *Shaharith* always include the Shema, the fundamental proclamation of faith. Drawn from various biblical books, the Shema declares God's glory in words of surpassing power and beauty. Small children learn the Shema as soon as they can speak; the elderly hope to die uttering its majestic phrases. Many Jews who don't attend morning synagogue begin the day by reciting the Shema at home as attentively and lovingly as possible. This great prayer begins:

> *Hear O Israel, the Lord our God is one Lord:*
> *Blessed be his glorious kingdom for ever and ever.*
> *And thou shalt love the Lord thy God with all thine heart, and with all*
>   *thine soul, and with all thine might.*
> *And these words, which I command thee today, shall be in thine heart:*
> *And thou shalt teach them diligently unto thy children, and shall talk of*
>   *them when thou sittest in thy house, and when thou walkest by the way,*
>   *and when thou liest down, and when thou risest up.*
> *And thou shalt bind them for a sign upon thy hand, and they shall be as*
>   *frontlets between thine eyes.*
> *And thou shalt write them upon the posts of thy house, and on thy gates.*

BLACK ELK'S PRAYER TO THE DAYBREAK STAR

Traditionally, Oglala Sioux greeted the new day by going outside to offer a prayer to the morning or daybreak star (*anpo wicahpi* in Lakota). In a 1931 interview, the famed Sioux spiritual teacher Black Elk described his practice:

> I usually get up about the time the morning star rises and my people were
> to have knowledge from this star and people seemed all to know this. They

were eager to see it come out and by the time the daybreak star came out the people would be saying, "Behold the star of wisdom."[5]

In this activity, we see the marriage of ritual and symbol that so often underlies the traditional approach to waking up. The morning star signified, according to Black Elk, "the desire for and the certainty of more light to those who desire."[6] By sighting the "star of wisdom" each morning, the Sioux asked the powers that govern the universe to help them in their quest for a more sacred way of life.

A ZOROASTRIAN PRAYER AT DAWN

The *Zend-Avesta*, the scripture of Zoroastrianism, includes the following fervent petition, to be said upon arising for the benefit of all creation:

> I pray for the entire creation . . . for the generation which is now alive, for that which is just coming into life, and for that which shall be hereafter. And I pray for that sanctity which leads to prosperity, and which has long afforded shelter, which goes on hand in hand with it, which joins it in its walk, and of itself becoming its close companion as it delivers forth its precepts, bearing every form of healing virtue which comes to us. . . . And so the greatest, and the best, and most beautiful benefits of sanctity fall likewise to our lot.[7]

THE MORNING PRAYER OF THE ABALUYIA

To the Abaluyia of Kenya, all goodness flows from God. Therefore, upon arising, an Abaluyia elder will kneel toward the rising sun and beseech God for health, happiness, and freedom from evil. These requests might be intended for the benefit of the one who prays ("Bring all fortunes to me today!" goes a line from one Abaluyia prayer), or for others ("mercy upon our children who are suffering").[8]

MORNING WORSHIP AT THE FAMILY ALTAR

In many religions, household altars provide a focus for morning prayers. One example is the *butsudan* ("Buddha altar") of Shin (Pure Land) Buddhism. In most Shin Buddhist households, the altar sits in a central location, and its presence can be felt at all times. To Taitetsu Unno, professor of religion and East Asian studies at Smith College, the *butsudan* is the sacred focus of family life: "I remember my father saying, 'If there is a fire, the first thing that we save is the altar.'"

Typically, the family gathers around the altar for worship before breakfast. One principal activity is the recitation of the *nembutsu* ("remembrance of the Buddha"), which consists in repeating *"Namu-amida-butsu"* ("I take refuge in Amida Buddha," the Buddha of Infinite Light and Life. Another is the chanting of Buddhist sutras—the sacred writings that house the living voice of the Buddha. One radiant passage from a frequently chanted sutra, the Sukhavativyuha Sutra, describes the characteristics of true spiritual attainment:

> Full of equanimity, of benevolent thought, of tender thought, of affectionate thought, of useful thought, of serene thought, of firm thought, of unbiased thought, of undisturbed thought, of unagitated thought, of thought (fixed on) the practice of discipline and transcendent wisdom, having entered on knowledge which is a firm support to all thoughts, equal to the ocean in wisdom, equal to the mountain Meru in knowledge, rich in many good qualities. . . . they attain perfect wisdom.[9]

The *butsudan* itself takes the form of a cabinet or other enclosure containing a scroll inscribed with the name of Amida Buddha, along with flowers, bells, incense, candles, rice offerings, and other ritual materials. Each of these items holds special significance. For example, the candles, customarily white, represent the Buddha's illuminative wisdom; they are never blown out, but extinguished with a candle snuffer or the hands. Together, the material goods in the altar represent the entire cosmos, gathered up and offered to Amida Buddha. By praying at their altars each morning, Buddhists offer themselves as well, consecrating their lives to the attainment of what Unno calls "the realization of freedom." In this quest, he says, daily prayer is indispensable: "As I grow older, ritual becomes more and more important. Doctrine matters, of course, for one must understand the teachings. But ritual is essential, for one must bring the body, the whole being, into practice."

The Morning Routine

It's difficult to find much spiritual significance in washing our ears, brushing our teeth, or sitting on the toilet bowl. Yet many religions see the need to bring these earthy activities under the auspices of the inner life. Indeed, since we usually wash and dress, shave or put on makeup, in a fog, mulling over today's chores or yesterday's romantic encounter, these morning procedures cry out for attention. Their very intimacy gives them a special value: for if I don't treat my own body and its daily functions with respect, how will I treat the body of other human beings (not to mention their souls) and the body of the world?

WASHING

Washing carries tremendous spiritual importance. The body is the mirror of the soul; a clean body signifies a clean soul, a being set upon the way of godliness, of enlightenment. Moreover, we wash with water, mother of life; washing thus connects us to the origin of all things.

Immediately upon awakening—as early as 3:30 A.M. in summer, 4:30 A.M. in winter—Zen monks wash their faces. Each monk is limited to three bamboo cups of water. He holds the cup in one hand, and with the other he scoops the water to his face "like a

Morning ritual—the Lopez boys, New Mexico

cat," as one text puts it.[10] This austerity fulfills the advice of Zen master Dogen, "Use two cups and save one for your descendants." A Zen bath also follows strict religious protocol. In some monasteries, the monk bows three times toward an altar outside the bathroom that contains a statue of Badarosatsu, who achieved freedom from rebirth while in the bath. Then the monk says, "I must cleanse my body and my heart." After his bath, the monk reaffirms his principal objective in life, proclaiming, "I have cleansed my body; I pray that I may cleanse my heart."[11]

In Islam, washing plays a critical role in waking up and preparing for morning prayer. An ablution (*wudu* in Arabic) restores a Muslim to a state of ritual purity before facing the day and facing God. *Wudu* begins with a consecration, in the form of the opening words of the Koran: "In the Name of Allah, the Beneficent, the Merciful." The washing follows a special sequence, ordained by the Koran:

> O believers, when you stand up to pray wash your faces, and your hands
> up to the elbows, and wipe your heads, and your feet up to the ankles.
>
> SURAH 5:5[12]

This order reveals a descending hierarchy of being, beginning with the face, home of the intellect and window of the soul, and ending with the feet, pedestals that mingle with dust and dirt. By such a simple act as washing, Muslims thus link heaven and earth and find their proper place in the sacred cosmos described by the Koran. An essential part of Islamic practice, morning washing is carried out with scrupulous care by nearly a billion Muslims around the world.

Devout Jews wash their hands soon after arising each morning. While washing, they utter the following blessing:

Blessed are you, O Lord our God! King of the universe, who has sanctified us through your commandments and has commanded us concerning the washing of hands.

GOING TO THE TOILET, TOOTH-BRUSHING, AND OTHER PREPARATIONS
We tend to be modest about urination and defecation, as much because of their intense intimacy as because of their association with filth. At the same time, however, we can acknowledge their tremendous importance. Without an efficient system of waste removal we would rapidly poison ourselves; moreover, as any gardener or farmer knows, the products of elimination nourish the earth. In keeping with this understanding, a Zen monk will pray before he goes to the bathroom, declaring his devotion to all Buddhas and asking for a successful visit to the toilet. In the same way, he will pray before and after brushing his teeth, declaring that he polishes for the benefit of all living beings and promising to "crush delusion as this toothbrush has been crushed in the mouth."[13]

Perhaps no people have explored more deeply the religious aspects of the morning routine, from the most mundane toilet functions to the most sublime prayers, than the "twice-born" Brahman males of India. Their approach exemplifies a conception of human life to which many of us pay lip service but that is, in truth, rare these days: the belief that every human gesture has meaning, that our least act affects the universe in ways beyond accounting.

A Brahman awakens two hours before sunrise to say his initial prayers, a blend of petition, thanksgiving, and adoration that varies from one region of India to another. These prayers are followed by a dazzling arabesque of sacramental movements. For instance, the Brahman makes sure that the first glance of the day falls upon something auspicious: a gold ring, silver coin, mother, maiden, or child. He then leaves his bed, but not before begging forgiveness from Prithivi (Mother Earth) for stepping on her. After rinsing his mouth with three sips of water, he drapes the sacred thread, symbol of his state as one "twice born" into spiritual life, over his right ear. Like everything else in the Brahmanic morning ritual, this gesture carries meaning, for a Brahman treasures his right ear as one of the most sacred organs of his body—it was in that ear that his parents first whispered to him the holy mantras that sustain his soul.

The Brahman then goes outside to urinate and defecate, making certain that he is at least one hundred yards from any dwelling. Hands and feet are scrubbed with clay a set number of times. Other cleanings follow: tooth-brushing with a milky twig, a bath—preferably in a river that flows into the sea—all enacted with sublime dignity and attention. Finally come the great morning devotions, which involve breathing exercises, mantras, invocations, circumambulations, and fire offerings, a sacred choreography too complex to be reproduced here. The process concludes with a wonderful prayer that runs in part:

> May all in this world be happy, may they be healthy, may they be comfortable and never miserable. May the rain come down in the proper time, may the earth yield plenty of corn, may the country be free from war, may the Brahmans be secure.[14]

Clearly, the specifics of traditional Brahmanic morning practices remain embedded in a particular cultural matrix. It's difficult to imagine, for example, living in New York City and going outside to urinate at least one hundred yards from any dwelling. The universal lesson to be drawn from a Brahman's morning is this: that our smallest gesture—petting the cat, hauling the garbage, even sitting on the toilet—can be an opportunity to hallow our lives, to offer thanks and praise.

Cooking is a sacred process—a nun praying in her kitchen, Ladakh, Northern India   Linda Connor

three

EATING

I gazed at the blood orange. It sat alone
on the china plate, its ruby rind a vivid contrast to the bone white porcelain.
That orange was the center of my life. I hadn't taken a bite of food for two
days, and over the past three weeks my intake wouldn't have fueled an average-
sized ant, much less a two-hundred-pound, six-foot human being. The reason
was illness, a mysterious invader that had ravaged my taste buds, so that the
smallest morsel of food set my mouth ablaze. Even water tasted like liquid fire.
My doctor patted me on the back and said, "It'll pass"; my wife patted me on
the head and served up a regime of soft foods—pudding, Jell-O, creamed
spinach, a feast for a toothless centenarian—all to no avail. In three weeks, I had
lost twenty pounds.

Then, as rapidly as it had attacked, the illness retreated. It was time to celebrate. But how to break my fast? By this time, I had grown accustomed to
hunger. It was a familiar friend, a mangy dog ever at my side. What bone would
I toss it as a first course? There were many ways to silence a growling stomach:
lobster, chocolate cake, pâté de foie gras, matzo ball soup, lamb curry, key lime
pie . . .

And then I remembered oranges. In a flash, the issue was settled. I rushed to
the gourmet deli down the street; five minutes later I was back home, my prize nestled inside a small brown bag. I took a plate from the cupboard, placed it on the
kitchen table, and then removed my fruit jewel from its paper dungeon. It glowed
on the table, a miniature red sun, its skin mottled here by delicate copper flaming,

there by the black sunspot of a bruise. I peeled the sun, setting free its crimson juice, its carmine pulp. I detached a wedge of the sun, raised it to my lips, and crushed it with my teeth.

The taste of blood orange flooded my mouth, and with it came a wave of gratefulness for all that had helped to produce this food and deliver it into my hands. Sun, soil, and rain; planters, harvesters, and retailers; apiculture and horticulture; evolution, whose slow-motion magic wand had transformed an inedible Jurassic fruit into the ambrosia of the gods; God, fount of all fruitfulness—I gave thanks to one and all. In that first bite after my three-week fast, I learned what all condemned prisoners, downed pilots, and exiles know: that food is life, and that eating is saying yes to life.

Eating is at once the most common and the most mysterious of acts. Most of us sit down to table at least three times a day, and we would shudder to learn how many acres of bread and oceans of milk and wine we consume in a lifetime. Yet for almost all of us, eating remains a nearly unconscious activity, something that we do willy-nilly between waking and working, or between innings at the ball game. We eat quickly, sloppily, distractedly, oblivious to the significance of what we consume, and scarcely aware of the process of eating itself. It can fairly be said, in a century in which physicists are plumbing the secrets of the atom and physicians are lifting the veil on the biochemistry of life, that the mysteries of the soup bowl, the hamburger, and the jug of milk—what these things really are, how we receive them, and how they help to shape the contours of our lives—remain terra incognita.

Eating is all things to all people. To a teenager, it's the means to fuel the body for more important activities, like strutting through the mall; to an infant, it's the milky cord that bonds him to his mother; to an artist, it can be the catalyst for a masterpiece, as Proust discovered when he transformed the memories unleashed by a mouthful of orange cake into *Remembrance of Things Past*.

Eating links us to all beings who now live and all beings who have ever lived. We eat only what is alive or has been alive: fried locusts, raw mushroom, hot dog, bun. When I eat a broccoli floret, the life of that plant enters into and becomes part of my own. Eating reveals our dependence on other living things and on the divine goodness that gives life to all things. Without food, we die. This truth finds beautiful expression in the following lines by the seventeenth-century English poet Alexander Pope:

> Look round our World; behold the chain of Love
> Combining all below and all above. . . .
> See dying vegetables life sustain,
> See life dissolving vegetate again;
> All forms that perish other forms supply,

(By turns we catch the vital breath, and die)
Like bubbles on the sea of Matter born.

No wonder that the Lakota Sioux offer thanks to the animals that they hunt and kill, believing that these creatures have willingly surrendered their lives for the sake of human survival. John Lame Deer remembers his uncle saying, "There's more to food than just passing through your body. There are spirits in the food, watching over it."[1] Food is spiritual nourishment, be it supernatural—Jewish manna, Christian eucharist, Greek ambrosia, Hindu soma—or merely the daily portion of meat and potatoes.

CONTEMPLATIVE CLOSE-UP: EATING IN A ZEN MONASTERY

All religions make much of eating. In Zen Buddhist monasteries, the monks pay special attention to every aspect of food, including its nature, provenance, preparation, consumption, and spiritual meaning. While discursive thought plays its part in this enterprise—after all, a cook needs to plan a menu—the Zen monk's understanding of food is determined above all by the practice of mindfulness. Shunryu Suzuki, the first master of San Francisco's Zen Center, describes mindfulness in this way:

> We have to think and to observe things without stagnation. We should accept things as they are without difficulty. Our mind should be soft and open enough to understand things as they are. When our thinking is soft, it is called imperturbable thinking. This kind of thinking is always stable. It is called mindfulness.[2]

Mindfulness, then, is a sure means to "understand things as they are"; it requires, Suzuki Roshi assures us, no special effort. During mindfulness practice, we simply register events as they occur. We don't analyze; we observe. When a reaction arises, whether intellectual, emotional, or physical, we see it as just another event in the stream of life, and we carry on with our mindful attention to things as they are.

For the Zen monk, mindful eating begins with the obtaining of food. Perhaps it will be bought from a vendor. How does a monk find the money to make his purchase? Traditionally, by begging. He walks along the street, head down, quietly chanting "Ho." In his hand, he carries the core symbol of Zen Buddhist monasticism, the begging bowl, or *jihatsu*. The bowl, an extension of the monk's hands, lies open to the cosmos, accepting whatever comes its way. The monk wears a broad-brimmed hat, so large that it cuts off his view of those who give him alms or food.

Nor can the donor see the monk's visage; the gift is thus given and received in a state of impartial generosity, free of the idle curiosity or personal involvement that may disrupt tranquillity. The monk bows with each donation, acknowledging his absolute dependence on the charity of others and his gratitude for their kindnesses.

Often the monastery's food supply is collected from local farms. Monks venture into the countryside, gathering whatever squash, beans, and other vegetables farmers deem unfit for market: the monks are happy with these lowly foods, which reflect the simplicity and humility to which they aspire. They also grow vegetables in small monastic gardens. Mindfulness is practiced assiduously in the cultivation of these foods, as it affects not only the state of the monk-farmer but also the state of his crop, and thus the state of all monks who will eat his produce—and, as such influences multiply endlessly, the state of all beings with whom these monks will interact. As this suggests, the cultivation and eating of food, even in an insignificant, wayside monastery, comes to affect the welfare of the world.

Once collected, the food must be cooked. To bend over a hot stove is an honor reserved for senior monks, who understand that cooking is a sacred process, an alchemy through which the living substance of the world is transformed into sustenance for human beings. This task requires experience, gravity, and insight. In *Instructions for the Zen Cook*, the Zen sage Dogen explains that the role of cook (*tenzo*) "is awarded only to those of excellence who exhibit faith in Buddhist teachings, have a wealth of experience and possess a righteous and benevolent heart. This is because tenzo duty involves the whole person."[3] Again, food is life, and the cook is the caretaker of life. One is reminded of G. I. Gurdjieff's remark, when asked if cooking was a branch of medicine, that "medicine is a branch of cooking."

The long process of obtaining and preparing food—really a single religious activity stretched over months—culminates, of course, in a meal. Zen monks eat three times a day. They try never to eat as you or I might eat, distractedly munching pretzels or chips in front of the television or gulping a cheeseburger on the run. At mealtime, mindfulness is observed with special care. Breakfast may be a simple affair of rice and pickles, but it is preceded and followed by chanting from holy scripture, as well as by the recitation of the ten names of Buddhas past and present who guide the monk in his spiritual efforts. At lunch—a more extensive repast consisting of rice mixed with barley, miso soup, vegetables, and pickles—the monks engage in five reflections (*Gokan no be*):

1. To think about our efforts and how they have brought us our food.
2. To think about our good and bad deeds, and whether we deserve this food.
3. To overcome gluttony and other vices.
4. To see food as a medicine that sustains our life.

5. To eat food to allow us to continue the search for enlightenment.

These reflections are followed by three vows: that the first bite be taken to destroy all evil; the second, to sustain all good; and the third, to save all sentient beings.

During the meal proper, absolute silence is maintained. In addition to obeying the ban on talking, the monks take care to make no noise with their mouths, stomachs, or bowls. Each monk eats as mindfully as possible, attending to the movements of his hands, lips, mouth, and throat, and the appearance, odor, and taste of the food. What a wonderful irony that the monk, devoted to a life of asceticism, may derive more gustatory experience from one mouthful of food than many of us do in a month of meals.

The clapping of wooden blocks marks the beginning and end of the meal. Leftover morsels are collected and offered first to buddhas and bodhisattvas, then to local fish or birds. Bowls are ceremonially washed and wiped, in a precise, highly ritualized manner. Even the water in which the bowls are scoured—that same dishwater for which we ordinarily have so much contempt—has meaning; the monk recites a prayer praising this liquid for its "taste of heavenly nectar" and then offers it to heavenly beings with the exclamation, "May you all be filled and satisfied!"[4]

EATING: A CONTEMPLATIVE HARVEST

Table Blessings

"Gratitude is the memory of the heart," wrote J. B. Massieu. Through table blessings, we

Mindful Eating: A Basic Exercise

As we can see in the practice of Zen monks, the essence of mindful eating is to bring attention to every step. Let us remember, as we sit down to eat, the holy nature of our meal: that when we eat, we take the substance of the cosmos into our bodies, we accept the sacrifice of other living beings as a necessary means for our sustenance. How can we repay this precious gift?

Start by letting go of concerns and activities that steal attention from the moment at hand. Make eating itself your immediate focus. Eat slowly, absorbing the impressions in each bite of food. Be attentive to every part of the process: how your fork spears the peas or shovels the carrots, how your muscles stretch and contract as hand and arm join forces to lift the food toward your mouth. Be aware of opening your lips to receive the morsel. Attend to the tastes and smells, the dance of tongue and teeth as you chew.

Let us remember that as animals we, too, are links in the great food chain; that our bodies will one day be fare for other creatures. This mindfulness practice is food as well, for it nourishes our souls; let us practice it whenever we can.

remember in our hearts and proclaim with our lips the divine source of all food, all nourishment. Gratitude for food thus becomes gratitude for creation, for life itself.

My family usually says a traditional Christian table grace, such as:

For what we are about to receive, may the Lord make us truly grateful.

Sometimes we ask our older son to extemporize. John is happy to oblige, usually in startling ways: he may thank God for the pepperoni on his pizza, or include heartfelt thanks for the presence of a beloved relative or friend, or add, as a sly coda, a wish that the Red Sox win the pennant. Although these forms of grace are peculiar to the Zaleski household, the practice of beginning a meal with a brief prayer of thanksgiving is found throughout the world. Here are some examples.

JEWISH BLESSINGS

We have already encountered, in the Introduction, the traditional Jewish practice of *berakot*, or blessings. Above all, the need to utter blessings is felt at mealtimes, lest our eating be spoiled by forgetfulness of God's mercy.

In Hebrew, the word for "universe" derives from a root that means "to conceal." According to Jewish mystical tradition, sparks of the divine, manifestations of God's presence, lie concealed within the physical world. Any blessing—indeed, any good deed—fans these sparks into greater flame and may release them. When we say a blessing over food, we thus help to reveal God's presence in the world.

A blessing over bread:

Blessed are you, O Lord our God! King of the universe, who brings bread out of the earth.

A blessing over wine:

Blessed are you, O Lord our God! King of the universe, who creates the fruit of the vine.

A blessing over vegetables:

Blessed are you, O Lord our God! King of the universe, who creates the fruit of the earth.

Jan Watson

A blessing before the meal

A blessing over fruit:

Blessed are you, O Lord our God! King of the universe, who creates the fruit of the tree.

HINDU BLESSINGS

A traditional Hindu blessing over food begins when the senior member of the household takes water in cupped hands and offers it to Brahma, Lord of all creatures. All the other diners then sprinkle water around their plates, each saying, "I sprinkle truth with knowledge." Rice (which accompanies every Indian meal) is pressed into three small balls, and each is dedicated to a particular deity. The three balls are then compressed into one. Finally, water is again cupped in the hand, while the following prayer is recited: "Food is Brahma, its essence is Vishnu, the eater is Shiva"—thus linking both food and eater to the infinite spirit that pervades and rules the Hindu cosmos.[5]

NATIVE AMERICAN BLESSINGS

Many Native American families begin a meal with the ancient saying "All our relations," thus honoring all relatives, near and far, present and absent. Sometimes special thanks are offered to "those who have gone before," our ancestors who gave us life. A plate may be heaped with food and set aside for the ancestors, alongside other plates on the main dining table or on its own table; occasionally, this ancestral offering will be taken outside.

To explore the relationship between mindfulness and the culinary arts, coauthor Paul Kaufman visits with Ed Brown—Zen priest, baker, cook, and author of several popular cookbooks.

IN THE KITCHEN WITH ED BROWN

Ed Brown is cooking lunch for us in the kitchen of his white stucco house in the sedately funky community of Fairfax, a short drive north of San Francisco. Ed has just moved in and the modest space is still unfamiliar territory. "Not a very professional kitchen," he sighs, adding onions and garlic to a sauté that he calls "leftovers." Each rhythmic flip of his spatula emancipates a heady wave of captivating odors. "Cooking is not just cooking," he observes. "Suzuki Roshi once said to me: 'You are working on yourself . . . you are working on other people.' His idea is that things are not just things and that food is not just food."

Ed was a student of Shunryu Suzuki Roshi, the Soto Zen master who founded the San Francisco Zen Center and the Zen Mountain Center at Tassajara Springs in Monterey County, California, America's first Zen monastery. When Ed came to Tassajara thirty years ago he began as a dishwasher and, a year later, became the head cook: the *tenzo*, as the monk responsible for preparing the community's meals is called. He became a Zen priest in 1971. At the moment, he is absorbed in the task of cutting corn from the cob.

As Ed cuts away with quick, sure strokes, the yellow kernels drop onto the cutting board in orderly platoons. "Most people stand the corn on the end and then the kernels bounce all over the place. It makes a lot more sense to set the corn down flat. In our particular school of Zen, we emphasize the idea of beginner's mind: finding out how to do things all the time. So I learned how to chop vegetables by just practicing and trying things out." Ed adds the corn to the leftovers, onions, and garlic.

Mindful cutting—in the kitchen of the Insight Meditation Society

Robert Bussewitz

My images of monastic asceticism were colliding with the sensual pleasures of Ed's approach to food preparation. He explained: "In the monastery, you have to eat very quickly. The whole meal takes forty-five or fifty minutes but you are chanting, putting out your bowls and utensils, and unfolding your cloths. You are served and then you chant. After that, you have five or six or seven minutes to eat your food. After that, you wash your bowls and put everything away. You are not encouraged particularly to savor or enjoy your food. On the other hand, there is a Zen tradition of hospitality. At Tassajara this has become a tradition of making really nice food for visitors."

The approach to food preparation as awareness has its roots in Buddhism's development in China, where monks were drawn to the native Chinese ethic that work itself could be a spiritual practice. With the further articulation of that philosophy in Japan, Zen took to aesthetic practices and traditions such as tea ceremony and theater, which became vehicles for mindfulness, concentration, and absorption. The outward doing reveals the inner life. "You can see the quality of a person's awareness reflected in what they are doing," says Ed.

Ed describes himself as having been a physically oriented child, cycling and playing a lot of basketball, often by himself. In Zen Buddhism, he found a meditative tradition that emphasizes the union of mind and body and a belief that true calmness is found in activity. And, in cooking, Ed found a physical and sensory experience that suffuses the body with attention, with presence of mind. His spiritual forebear is the thirteenth-century Zen master Dogen. Dogen's *Instructions* were written for his disciples living in medieval Japanese monasteries and "for followers of the Way in succeeding generations." Dogen writes:

> When you prepare food . . . maintain an attitude that tries to build great temples from ordinary greens, that expands the buddhadharma through the most trivial activity. . . . Handle even a single leaf of green in such a way that it manifests the body of the Buddha. This in turn allows the Buddha to manifest through the leaf. This is a power which you cannot grasp with your rational mind. It operates freely, according to the situation, in a most natural way. At the same time, this power functions in our lives to clarify and settle activities and is beneficial to all living things.[6]

In the monastic community, meals are managed by those who have awakened the bodhisattva spirit within themselves. This means putting one's full energy and attention into the act of meal preparation, putting the awakened mind to work in the kitchen. Dogen asks that we handle food carefully, with respect, as if the food itself were our own eyes.

Ed serves the lunch and pours us green tea. "One of the classic ideas of Zen," he says, "is to see into your nature. Seeing into your nature means you don't have anything to prove. You don't have to prove to anyone or yourself: 'I'm a good person.' 'I'm a spiritual person.' 'I'm a holy person.' You don't have to get any particular sorts of credits. 'Oh, I've had such and such a state.' 'Oh, I've attained such and such a level.' People have an idea that in order to be spiritual, you have to go sit on a dock or other place, and be quiet. That you have to empty your mind. But trying to empty your mind is really an obstruction. In Zen, colloquially, we say: 'Don't put another head over your head.' Don't set up a nest where you hide out. Don't keep your mind apart from things. To relate to anything is a kind of spiritual work. Give your head a rest. Let your mind go out into things. As Dogen suggests, the Way-seeking Mind is actualized by rolling up your sleeves." And, thank goodness, by eating.

Fasting: A Talk with Kabir Helminski

Fasting, like grace before meals, plays a part in every religious tradition. But nowhere does it dominate the spiritual landscape more than in Islam, with its cele-

Mindful Eating and Health: Advice from Dr. Dean Ornish

I asked Dr. Dean Ornish, director of the Preventive Medicine Institute in Sausalito, California, and author of several bestselling books on diet, stress, and heart disease, for his advice on mindful eating and its relationship to health. He responded:

"If you eat with awareness, it has a number of powerful benefits. I used to eat while watching TV or reading the newspaper. I could go through a whole meal and then look down at my plate, notice that it was empty, and think, *Gee, I wonder who ate that?* I didn't even taste it.

"As human beings, we need a certain amount of gratification, and if we don't get it in quality we tend to make up for it in quantity. I've noticed that when people pay attention to what they're eating, they enjoy it more fully, and as a result they don't eat as much.

"They also pay more attention to the subtle qualities of the food, and to its effects. For instance, people who eat food with a lot of fat may notice that they have a slow, groggy feeling afterward, while people who eat a lower-fat diet may feel more clear-headed and energetic. Experience itself becomes the teacher. You don't have to rely on an expert, a

brated fast of Ramadan, during which Muslims abstain from all food and drink (even water) from dawn to sunset throughout the ninth month of the year. This austere discipline, so different from the eat-when-I-feel-like-it policy that most of us pursue, finds its roots in the Koran:

> O ye who believe! fasting is prescribed for you, even as it was for those before you, that ye may ward off [evil].
>
> SURAH 2:183[7]

As this passage indicates, fasting in Islam means more than a chance to drop some pounds, wean oneself from a craving for chocolate, or feel light-headed from hunger by the time evening rolls around. Fasting is a moral action that helps the Muslim to live a holy life. But how does abstinence from food and drink accomplish this? To understand more fully the spiritual dimensions of this extraordinary practice, I turned to Dr. Kabir Helminski, an authority on Islamic practice and a sheikh of the Mevlevi order in the United States.

Helminski believes that the ritual denial of food and water runs against the grain, and that in this lies its benefit. "When you fast," he told me, "you give up something lawful, something natural, something that you have every right to have. You give it up for the sake of God." The sacrifice is not slight, as Helminski made clear, pointing out that the Ramadan fast proscribes not only food and drink, but also sex, smoking, and even gossip. "You learn to say no to certain impulses and to listen to something deeper. This is all too rare an experience in our culture. We may say no in order to achieve an egotistical end, but we rarely say no in order to reach something deeper."

What, then, is this "something deeper"? What is it that fasting brings to light? When I asked Helminski, he suggested that fasting leads to "purification of the heart." He explained that "through fasting, you become transparent to yourself, you move into a different state, one that is lighter and purer." This has, he added, far-reaching physiological effects. "You give your organs a complete rest and purification. Even a sip of water would activate your inner organs and end this period of rest. The process of cleansing is noticeable. For one thing, the breath changes. Usually it becomes unpleasant. But there is a saying that 'The breath of one who is fasting is the sweetest to Allah.'"

doctor, or a book to tell you what to eat or what not to eat."

To help increase awareness during a meal, Dr. Ornish offered this tip: "Look at the color. Look at the texture. Experience the smells. Take a bite and close your eyes. At that moment, you are focused completely on the food. Throughout the meal, you can repeat that moment. Close your eyes and bring yourself back to the food."

Fetid breath signals, one suspects, the departure of poisons from the body. The process is reminiscent of detox programs for alcoholics and drug users. Indeed, Helminski pointed out that "fasting is the opposite of addiction. All addiction numbs us, while fasting leaves us emotionally naked." This leads, of course, to considerable discomfort. "If an American comes to fast after thirty, forty, or fifty years of regular eating, an emotional response is inevitable. At first you get touchy and sensitive, for you reveal to yourself things that have been suppressed." Helminski hastened to add, however, that this irritability soon fades. In his experience, the fast becomes a little easier each year. You come to like it. Each night, the fast is broken by eating a date and taking a sip of water, followed by prayer and a meal. But you don't really want to eat. Food seems anticlimactic; you're no longer obsessed with it."

Fasting can take many forms. One may eat nothing for many days, as Christ did during his forty days in the wilderness. One may eat very little year round, as do Christian and Buddhist monks who are taught never to eat between meals and always to leave the dinner table before they feel satiated. One may eat only certain foods, as do Jews who observe kosher dietary laws. Whatever the regimen, fasting sharpens the mind, settles the body, and sweetens the heart.

I urge you to bring fasting into your life. You might begin by eliminating a certain kind of food (red meat, sweets), or by not eating more than you need. Try ending your meal when your belly is settled but not stuffed. In time you may graduate to more elaborate or extensive fasts, depending upon health and predilection. Experiments with fasting may be tiny or grand; if undertaken with prudence, all will bring you closer to your heart's desire.

Tea Mind—approaching each motion with attention and exactness.

The Way of Tea

The Japanese tea ceremony, a ritual serving of a cup of tea and a special meal, is as much about one's state of mind as it is about drinking and eating. The tea ceremony originated in Zen monasteries, where monks sipped green tea to stay awake during long hours of meditation. It evolved as a discipline when Sen Rikyu, the great sixteenth-century tea master, blended the mindfulness of Zen with a rich aesthetic sense that imbues the act of serving, drinking, and eating with larger meaning.

Tara Bennett-Goleman, who has been a student of the Japanese tea ceremony for two decades, observes: "'Tea Mind' refers to the qualities of awareness inspired by the art of tea—tranquillity, simplicity, naturalness, harmony. As my tea practice deepens, I experience Tea Mind spilling over more often from the tea room into my daily life."

The Japanese use the term *mitate,* or "reseeing," for the way in which the tea ceremony brings new awareness to familiar acts. During the ceremony, attention is directed to the present moment. Talk during tea, for example, deals only with matters pertaining to the here and now. As Tara puts it, "This makes it easier to savor the subtle details of the occasion: the taste of the tea, the aroma of the incense, the sound of the whisk as the host mixes the green tea powder into a frothy brew."

When guests come into Tara's tea house, she greets them in silence. The guests concentrate on her movements as she prepares the tea, approaching each motion with attention and exactness: wiping the tea container, ladling boiling water from kettle to tea bowl, whisking the tea; every movement is precise, done just so.

The mindfulness of tea can transform life beyond the tea room. "Bringing Tea Mind into the world includes having a deep peace in oneself that is undisturbed by small annoyances," Tara says. "Sometimes I'll be rushing through Manhattan in order to be on time for my tea lesson. I get to the tea school, frazzled from the rush. I take off my shoes and put on my white socks and black robe, silently walking past the stillness of the tea rooms, pausing to see the tea garden, then going to prepare the utensils to serve tea. I find that cleansing the utensils has a purifying effect on my mind. Suddenly there is a quiet island in the midst of Manhattan. No sound except for an occasional chirping cricket from the tea garden.

"During the tea, we slow down to meet the gracefulness of each movement, the silent rapport, the simplicity of the room, the beauty of each tea object. The mind empties, each movement becoming more full, nestled in timelessness; attention wraps itself intimately around each moment.

"Then the tea lesson is over. Two hours could have been two weeks or two minutes. As I leave the tea school, the light of the late afternoon glows. Sounds, sights, smells, sensations are no longer distractions pulling the mind in all directions at once. They simply engage the senses one after the other, while Tea Mind sees each thing as it comes and goes, delighting in all."

Tomales Bay

Richard Blair

WORKING

I once had a friend whom I'll call Marvin. When I first clapped eyes on him, I was just out of college and Marvin was pushing eighty. We met in the stairwell of a three-decker house in Cambridge, Massachusetts, on the day I moved in. I was struggling up the winding stairs with a box of books when I heard a clatter from above. Someone was rushing down from the third floor. A second later, a white-haired leprechaun burst into view. "I spied you outside," said Marvin. "Thought you'd need some help." He then wrestled the box out of my arms—it must have weighed close to fifty pounds—and heaved it into my apartment.

As I soon learned, this was Marvin in a subdued mood. Marvin loved to work. He loved to think about work, talk about work, even dream about work. He relished describing his checkered career, which stretched back three-quarters of a century and always involved physical labor: he had served as a baker, farmer, ice-cream maker, soldier, and street sweeper. ("That was back when horses ruled the roads," he said. "We had a lot to sweep up, and I don't mean litter.") Marvin spent his retirement planting a vegetable garden, repairing the neighborhood cars, and building model ships. I never saw him without a tool in his hands or a blueprint in his mind. When I asked him why he worked so hard, he looked at me as if I were daft and said, in his high-pitched voice with its dash of a Scottish accent—I learned later that it was a quote from Thomas Carlyle that his father had taught him—"Blessed is he who has found his work; let him ask no other blessedness."

Marvin, I now realize, was a bit of a sage. He had discovered one of life's secrets: the holy meaning of work. He would have agreed heartily with the observation of the French portraitist Eugène Delacroix that "we work not only to produce but to give value to time." Work, as Marvin knew, gives direction to our hours. It turns us from spinning tops into arrows, creatures with an aim. Work bestows dignity, for it leads to the discovery of truth, the creation of beauty, the cultivation of goodness.

At the same time, it is easy to paint a darker picture of human toil. "Work!" shrieks Maynard G. Krebs, the prototype of all slackers, on the old *Dobie Gillis* television show. How many of us groan inwardly on Monday morning and greet Friday with a "TGIF"? Work is penance, suffering, trial. Even language confirms this common experience: the Greek word for work, *ponos*, has the same root as the Latin *poena*, meaning pain and punishment. Technology, if anything, has only increased our sense of work as prison, by its steady attrition of those forms of labor—handicraft, farming, and the like—that are tied to the natural rhythms of the day or the common needs of ordinary life.

We find both views of work—as divine and demonic—expressed in the first chapters of Genesis. Adam and Eve, bowered in Eden, enjoy a variety of work both mental and physical (naming the animals, tilling the earth) that adds meaning and purpose to existence. Then comes the Fall, and with it work becomes a curse instead of a blessing ("In the sweat of thy face shalt thou eat bread. . . . thorns also and thistles shall it bring forth to thee"). If this myth is true—and authentic myths are always true on the deepest level—then work is both gift and punishment. Work marks our separation from the divine, and at the same time offers a path to the divine.

Here is a puzzle, then, and one we can't avoid. The answer, I believe, is this: that all depends upon how one works, and this in turn depends upon one's understanding of work. That is to say: work is a physical problem with a spiritual solution. As A.K. Coomaraswamy put it, "Man's activity consists in either a making or a doing. Both of these aspects of the active life depend for their correction on the contemplative life." If we bring contemplation to our making and doing, we may move, even in the midst of activity, from the hustle and bustle of illusion to the great silence of reality. We may discover the true nature of making and doing, and learn how and why these actions bring us to God. Simone Weil found that even the most grueling sort of menial labor possessed this miraculous ability to introduce us to reality:

Physical work is a specific contact with the beauty of the world. . . . The artist, the scholar, the philosopher, the contemplative should really admire the world and pierce through the film of unreality that veils it and makes of it . . . a dream or stage set. They ought to do this but more often than not they cannot manage it. He who is aching in every limb, worn out by the effort of a day of work, that is to say a day when he has been subject to matter, bears the reality of the universe in his flesh like a thorn. The difficulty for him is to look and to love. If he succeeds, he loves the Real.[1]

Work not only brings us from illusion to reality; it also, according to several traditions, allows us to participate in God's own labor. Pope John Paul II, who has written extensively on the subject, observes that the human being, "created in the image of God, shares by his work in the activity of the Creator." Moreover, adds the Pope, the human being "continues to develop that activity, and perfects it."[2] According to Genesis, God has been a worker from

Participating in God's own labor—Brother Anthony's fire, St. Martin's Abbey

Christine Knodt

the very beginning of the cosmos, creating for six days and "resting" on the seventh. Human beings, through their own labors, not only parallel this primordial work but help the Creator to unfold his divine plan for the good of all creation. This same exalted vision can be discerned in Jewish folklore about the forty-nine wise men whose prayers and good deeds sustain the world; it emerges also in the Koran, where Adam's work in naming the animals earns him—and, by extension, all human beings—the title of God's vice-regent on earth.

Every religion teaches that work, if approached correctly, leads to wisdom. For one thing, work is a superb ascetic discipline, a tonic that nourishes just those qualities—endurance, courage, concentration—that support the inner life. As the old saw goes: work builds character. Simone Weil offers a surprising perspective on this in an essay with the delightfully odd title of "Reflections on the Right Use of School Studies with a View to the Love of God." Weil says that "every school exercise . . . is like a sacrament" and that,

> paradoxical as it seems, a Latin prose or a geometry problem, even though they are done wrong . . . can one day make us better able to give someone in affliction exactly the help required to save him, at the supreme moment of his need.[3]

But how can a problem in Euclidean geometry teach us how to help someone in need? As Weil sees it, schoolwork constitutes an exercise in attention. The memorization of grammar charts, the unraveling of geometry problems, the deciphering of an obscure Latin ode: each of these mundane assignments demands attention. Each obliges the student to face reality—the first step, suggests Weil, in learning how to love. Attention is the essence of love, for it allows us to see our neighbor with empathy. Attention is the essence of prayer, for to pray is to attend with all our being to God. Weil's observations on schoolwork can easily be extended to any work carried out with loving attention, for all such work enlarges heart and soul; thus the famous Benedictine monastic saying, *laborare est orare* ("to work is to pray").

Tradition offers two ways by which we can encounter the sacred while at work: through the people that we meet and through the work itself.

These days, when so many of us toil in the service economy, spending our days helping other people, the first avenue has grown increasingly important. Speaking generally, in working with or for others, our task is *to see people as they really are*: posssessing "divine nature, whose form is existence, intelligence, and bliss," as the Vedas put it; "children of God," as the Gospels declare. It's a formidable task, no doubt, to discern God in that beetle-browed man with the raspy voice who screams at you across the counter, but it can be done. Witness Mother Teresa, radiating love as she bathes the befouled bodies of the Calcutta untouchables. The secret of his fortitude, as she never tires of explaining, is simply this: that she sees the dying and decrepit in her charge as icons of Christ (see chapter 6, "Being with Others," for more on this practice).

The second way to discover the sacred in the workplace is *to understand work as craft*. Craftspeople, despite their lowly economic status, hold a very high rank in traditional cultures. Consider this curious exchange between a gate-crasher and a guard from a fourteenth-century British bardic manuscript:

"Open the door!"
"I will not open the door."
"Wherefore not?"
"The knife is in the meat and the drink is in
the horn and there is revelry in Arthur's
hall and none may enter therein but the son
of a king of a privileged country, or a
craftsman bringing his craft."[4]

At the time of revelry, when noble deeds are acknowledged and honors bestowed, craftspeople rank with the highest of royalty—above king's counselors, bishops, and abbots. So it is in all traditions: crafts workers may be poor, perhaps unable to discourse with eloquence, but nonetheless they carry the life of the nation in their hands. The apocryphal Book of Ecclesiasticus thus describes the lot of craftspeople in ancient Jerusalem:

> They shall not sit on the seat of the judge, and they shall not understand the covenant of judgment: neither shall they declare instruction and judgment; and where parables are they shall not be found.
> But they will maintain the fabric of the world; and in the handywork of their craft is their prayer.[5]

Craft, this passage tells us, has a twofold glory: it sustains the cosmos and it is a way of prayer. These are high claims, but I believe that they are warranted. Through craft, we can discover the harmonious interaction of body, mind, and spirit and participate in the larger harmonies of the cosmos. "If any man will be a saint, let him dig or make," writes W. R. Lethaby.

Craft brings one closer to the rhythms of life, to the spirit that animates all creation. This is evident in the following letter by a young, anonymous correspondent, published many years ago by Mohandas Gandhi in his newspaper, *Young India:*

> I went from the streets of a great Western City, full of towering houses, terrific and deafening noises, into the quiet halls of an ethnographical museum . . . and came into the rooms where there were many objects from the East, representing the arts and crafts of Asia and the Pacific. . . . I could almost smell sandalwood and *champak* flower. Life itself came from the things in the room which Eastern hands had held so close and fashioned so carefully and tenderly. Life had been put into fabrics and carvings of wood,

and life emanated subtly out of them, again like a perfume, a soft glow, warm and strangely thrilling after the iron streets of the Western City.[6]

The essence of craft is to make or to do something with attention and love. As the anonymous author above indicates, this gives to one's work "a soft glow, warm and strangely thrilling." It may be a useful pot, a hearty stew, or an interoffice memo—what matters is to understand one's work as prayer, and to enact this understanding. Nor does it matter whether the surrounding culture is tribal or technological. The understanding is universal. It rests, for instance, at the heart of an entirely Western craft, that of the Shakers, to whom we now turn.

CONTEMPLATIVE CLOSE-UP: THE SHAKERS

Less than thirty miles from my hometown in western Massachusetts, I discovered the outskirts of heaven. You can do the same. Just drive up Route 7 past the smokestacks of Pittsfield, turn left onto Route 20, crest a hill or two, and you'll discover a scene as lovely as any on earth: a scattering of elegant nineteenth-century structures on a mint-green meadow, sprinkled with sugar maples and elms, that laps the foothills of the Berkshire mountains.

Quintessential New England, you think to yourself. Then you notice something unusual about the buildings. Neither colonial nor Victorian, they stand outside the normal architectural canon of the region. Yet there's nothing eccentric about them: they seem drenched in calm, clarity, and common sense. In the middle of the complex stands a massive four-story central house, like a squared-off boulder, its only ornamentation dozens of finely latticed windows. Nearby, a dairy painted pollen yellow stands out in a sea of white clapboard and ruddy brick. In the distance, a round gray-stone barn topped by a two-tiered white steeple rises up like a wedding cake atop a stoneware platter.

The composition, as a whole, is lovely and serene beyond measure. No wonder, for every element—from the horse barn to the laundry shop, from the icehouse to the schoolhouse—serves both as a place of work and as a place of prayer. This complex of buildings is Hancock Shaker Village, founded in 1790, the most perfectly preserved of the many Shaker communities that once dotted the Eastern seaboard. The buildings, sturdy yet elegant, immaculate yet practical, represent Shaker architecture at its best (and Shaker architecture is always at its best), and in the inevitable use of "perfect" to describe their lines, forms, and volumes, we have the essence of Shaker spirituality.

One needn't visit Hancock Shaker Village to encounter the brilliance of

Shaker craft. Shaker design is everywhere: in shopping malls, mail-order catalogs, even the cheesiest television shopping programs. Stroll into any furniture store, and you will find Shaker (or neo-Shaker) forms. Chairs, tables, desks, brooms, baskets, all exhibit the unmistakable Shaker marriage of organic simplicity and austere practicality. What is the source of this style, which appeals intensely to our innate sense of balance, harmony, and peace? Not a design studio, not even a craftsperson's atelier—for these are the channels but not the source. Shaker style is born in Shaker religion.

The Shaker faith arrived in America in 1744 under the leadership of Mother Ann Lee, a charismatic Christian leader who taught the virtues of simple living, hard work, and fervent worship. According to Mother Ann, the purpose of life was to glorify God by living the lessons of the Gospels. All the hallmarks of classical Shaker life—pacifism, celibacy, common property, absolute honesty in all business dealings—spring from this fundamental allegiance to New Testament ideas. America was hungry for such a teaching, and for a while Shaker communities sprouted up and down the East Coast. But the severe strains of the Shaker life—especially the demand of celibacy—led to heavy attrition. Today only a few Shakers remain, consisting almost entirely of nonagenarian women who remember wistfully the splendid days of Shaker music, Shaker schooling, and Shaker prayer.

Despite the relegation of Shaker religion to near-extinction, everyone who comes in contact with Shaker life bears witness to its purity and beauty. Listen to this nineteenth-century description of a Shaker village:

> The streets are quiet; for here you have no grog shop, no beer house, no lock up, no pound . . . every building, whatever may be its use, has something of the air of a chapel. The paint is all fresh; the planks are clean bright; the windows are all clean. A sheen is on everything; a happy quiet reigns.[7]

In this peaceful atmosphere, the Shakers developed an approach to work that, I believe, retains immense value for us today. Its core lies in Mother Ann's famous motto, "Hands to Work and Hearts to God." In this saying, the Shakers fulfill the second precept of Ecclesiasticus, quoted above, that "in the handywork of their craft is their prayer." To the Shakers, work *is* prayer. Work is worship and worship work. It's no accident that Shakers use "laboring" as their term for worship. The elevation of work to the status of prayer is hardly new in Christian history, of course. But to bring such a saying into frontier America, with its sweatshops and slavery, was radical indeed, for until Mother Ann arrived on the scene, Americans had understood work as necessary suffering, a mark of servility. As one outsider wrote to a Shaker friend:

> None of your community think work is degrading while, in society at large, many men are ashamed of work, and, of course, ashamed of men (and women) who work, and make them ashamed of themselves. Now, the Shakers have completely done away with that evil. . . . that is one of their great merits, and it is a very great one.[8]

The Shakers excelled in all manner of work, from stitching dresses to tanning hides, from weaving cloth to churning applesauce, from making baskets, buttons, and buckles to growing medicinal herbs. They considered inventiveness a special gift granted them by God for his greater glory, and they introduced many innovations to the world, among them the clothespin, the circular saw, and the screw propeller. In addition, Shakers notably improved a number of existing products, from fire engines to sundials to hydraulic water systems. What boggles the mind is that this furious activity unfolded in a handful of communities whose combined membership, including children, added up to less than the population of a small New England town. Shakers, it seems, took very seriously the claim of Ecclesiasticus that work, first and foremost, must "maintain the fabric of the world."

For Shakers, work was a sacred duty that elevated the soul, strengthened the body, curbed the appetites, and brought order out of chaos. These achievements were not sought haphazardly; rather, the Shakers had a fully developed spiritual methodology for work-as-prayer. Five rules governed their daily lives:

1. *Work must be practical.* The Shakers eschewed all fluff and filigree. Consider the Shaker chair: light, plain, and strong—light enough to lift aside or hang on a peg when floor space is needed, plain enough to fit comfortably in any setting, strong enough through clever buttressing to support with ease the person for whom it was designed.
2. *Work must conform to objective laws of craft and nature.* This follows from the first rule. If work is to be practical, the worker must know and obey the laws of craft and the laws of nature in regard to issues of strength, balance, harmony, and so on. To know and obey these

Shaker designs—work as spiritual craft

laws, which Shakers understood to be the physical expression of the spiritual order of God, the worker must know his or her material as intimately as possible. If these laws are obeyed, then the product will possess its own innate beauty.

3. *Work cannot be rushed.* This follows from the second rule. If wood set aside for a chair needs another month or year of seasoning, so be it. If a worker needs extra time to lay a brick, so be it. Shakers could afford to take their time; they planned on their material goods lasting for centuries, and their souls lasting forever.

4. *The worker strives for perfection.* This follows from the third rule. Shakers believed that if they labored long enough and carefully enough, they would achieve perfection. This quest finds its roots in Jesus' call for us to "be perfect, even as my Father in heaven is perfect." For Shakers, perfection served as both goad and goal, an impulse to great effort and a destination worth enormous sacrifice.

5. *The worker never spares or promotes himself.* This follows from all the preceding rules. Life is short; one must make use of every moment; hard work is demanded. At the same time, the very ability to work is itself a gift from God. This awareness led directly to the Shaker dislike of self-aggrandizement. Shakers never signed their creations. All belonged to God. When Carol and I visited the Shaker community at Sabbathday Lake in Maine a few years ago, we wandered into the cemetery, where we discovered the ultimate expression of this passion for anonymity: the burial ground contains a multiplicity of graves but only one marker. It reads, simply, "Shaker."

WORKING: A CONTEMPLATIVE HARVEST

Work as Detachment

Recently, I found myself in Union Square in New York City. Like most urban parks, this particular patch of scrubby brown-green grass shelters a daily parade of children playing, lovers snuggling, office workers catching a snooze, drug dealers flashing their wares, and homeless people trundling their shopping carts filled with cardboard and rags. Everyone seemed to be having a good time—and no one was working. All well and good, I thought, at least until I looked up at the park's most famous statue, a life-size representation of perhaps the most revered religious figure of the twentieth century, Mohandas Gandhi. The Mahatma, swathed in robes and leaning on his staff, peered intently at the crowd. I thought I saw displeasure on his face. In fact, I was sure of it. Perhaps it was just an accident of light, but the Mahatma was definitely frowning.

At first, I was taken aback. But after a moment of reflection, I realized the rightness of it. For Gandhi wasn't one for snoozing or smooching or drugs. Gandhi didn't approve of idleness in any form. He wrote, read, taught, and turned his spinning wheel both day and night. He liked to point out that "God created man to work for his food and said that those who ate without working were thieves." In saying this, Gandhi paraphrased the *Bhagavad Gita*, which proclaims, "He who eats without performing this sacrifice, eats stolen bread."⁹ For Gandhi— and for the Hindu tradition of which he remains the most famous, if heterodox, example—work is the very essence of life:

> I cannot live without work. I crave to die with my hand at the spinning-wheel. If one has to establish communion with God through some means, why not through the spinning-wheel?¹⁰

Through the spinning wheel—that is, through the simple tasks of everyday work—one may establish communion with God. It doesn't matter whether one is a typist in a law office or a sailor on Arctic seas: work is a gateway to God. And how, exactly, does one achieve this communion? Here the *Gita*, so beloved by Gandhi, serves as our guide.

The *Bhagavad Gita*, "The Lord's Song," is the most widely read of all Indian sacred texts. It unfolds as a dialogue between Krishna, the incarnation of divine power, and Arjuna, a warrior and aristocrat. Arjuna is about to plunge into battle against his blood relatives, an act that he considers reprehensible and wishes to avoid. Krishna states the case for Arjuna to go to war.

Nothing will be gained, Krishna insists, by avoiding the battle, or any given work:

> A man does not attain to freedom from action by not engaging in action merely, nor is the goal gained by simple abandonment of action.¹¹

The solution, suggests Krishna, lies in the twin practices of *detachment* and *sacrifice*. Arjuna—and all of us—should make of work a holy gift to the divine, offered in a state of tranquil detachment. Thus Krishna counsels Arjuna:

> All actions performed, other than those for God's sake, make the actor bound by action. Perform action for His sake, O son of Kunti, devoid of attachment. . . .

> Giving up all actions to [God], and with heart fixed on the mysterious link between man and the Deity, do battle without expectation, free from the feeling of [myself] and free from anguish.[12]

The man or woman who can follow Krishna's advice finds liberation in work. The key lies in the phrase "perform action for His sake." The *Gita* suggests that we work not for ourselves, nor even for the world, except insofar as the world is a manifestation of God. We work, simply, for God. On a practical level, this means that we work diligently at our appointed task without personal investment in the outcome; we work for the sake of the work, which we offer to God. If my job is to cook hamburgers over a sizzling hot stove—as it was for several years during my youth—I make the burgers as perfectly as possible. I slice the bread, melt the cheese, flip the patties with the utmost attention, because these humdrum acts, if performed, as the *Gita* asks, with "heart fixed on the mysterious link between man and the Deity," can become a holy choreography of sacrifice and praise, a gift that sets me "free from the feeling of myself" and points me toward a greater freedom, that of working in the service of the divine.

Right Livelihood

One of the cornerstones of Buddhism, the Noble Eightfold Path, enunciates eight ways to enlightenment: right understanding, right thought, right speech, right action, right livelihood, right effort, right mindfulness, and right concentration. Of these eight, "right livelihood" deals with the spiritual meaning of work. Traditional Buddhism insists that certain occupations—in broad terms, those that cause harm to ourselves or others—constitute "wrong livelihood" and must be shunned. Examples might include butcher, arms merchant, hunter, liquor store owner, and shoemaker (forbidden because shoes come from the skin of slaughtered animals). All other occupations are acceptable forms of "right livelihood," providing conditions in which Buddhist practice can flourish.

Some Buddhist masters have been adamant about the importance of right livelihood. Among the most notable was Suzuki Shosan (1579–1655), a Japanese warrior, teacher, writer, and monk who practiced in both Zen and Shin traditions. Shosan believed in the sanctity of all labor and urged workers to recite the *nembutsu* on the job. Speaking of farming, he advised:

> Farming is itself a Buddhist activity. There is no need to seek practice elsewhere.... If you cultivate the land, reciting Namu Amida Butsu with

every movement of the hoe, you will surely reach Buddhahood. Just leave everything to Providence, be honest, and do not arouse personal desires. If you follow this advice, you will enjoy the blessings of heaven and enjoy a good life now and in the next world.[13]

Working with Others

"How can I work better with other people?" Nowadays, we hear this question everywhere: in labor negotiations, in political debates, in the boardroom and the lunchroom. People seem uncertain of how to treat co-workers, of how to create an atmosphere of cooperation and trust. Experts are hired, at a mind-boggling cost, to teach the basics of ethics and etiquette to CEOs; meanwhile, social critics shake their heads over the pervasive decline of manners between employer and employee, teacher and student, parent and child.

In traditional societies these problems rarely arise. Almost without exception, such societies are communal; being with others is the order of the day. A few years ago, I visited the home of my maternal ancestors in Birkirkara on the island of Malta, that limestone chip floating in the Mediterranean halfway between Sicily and Libya. There my great-aunt Nena escorted me to the site, now abandoned, where the communal ovens once stood. For countless generations, my ancestors hauled uncooked loaves to this central gathering place several times a week, where they would gossip with neighbors while the raw dough baked. The warmth generated by these communal ovens, and the magical transformation that they wrought in flour and yeast, perfectly symbolizes the power of community. In old Malta, the rare thing, the condition that required interpretation, advice, and maybe even spiritual intervention, was that of being alone.

Now everything has changed. In Malta, the old ovens are gone, and vanished, too, is the sense of a closely bound community with common aims. There, as elsewhere, many people live by themselves or in atrophied nuclear families. The very concept of communal work seems atavistic: who bakes bread in common these days? At the same time, the question resounds: "How can I work better with others?" The answer may not lie in communal cooking, but I believe that much can be learned by studying traditional examples of group work, especially those whose roots run into deep spiritual waters. There can be no better place to begin than the barn-raising "bee" of the Amish and other radical Christian fellowships.

The choice of the word *bee* for this curious one-day explosion of work, food, and mutual support couldn't be more apt, for the event resembles nothing so much as the furious motion of a large and prosperous hive. Before the day of the barn raising, teams of forty to fifty men lay the barn foundations, collect timber, and tackle other heavy jobs. Meanwhile, the women handle the domestic duties, cooking breads and pies, sausages and hams, vegetables and stews. On the great day itself, a workforce of staggering proportions—upwards of 800 men and women, all volunteers—gathers at the site. The great mass plunges into action, women bustling about the food, men raising the bents, pike poles, rafters, walls, and roofs. The result is a minor miracle, as one witness reports:

> I was invited to a barn raising near Wooster, Ohio. A tornado had leveled four barns and acres of prime Amish timber. In just three weeks the downed trees were sawn into girders, posts, and beams and the four barns rebuilt and filled with livestock donated by neighbors to replace those killed in the storm. I watched the raising of the last barn in open-mouthed awe. Some 400 Amish men and boys, acting and reacting like a hive of bees in absolute harmony of cooperation, started at sunrise with only a foundation and floor and by noon, *by noon,* had the huge edifice far enough along that you could put hay in it.[14]

The point here isn't the precise methodology of Amish barn raising, but rather the "absolute harmony of cooperation" that takes hold at the event, a harmony born of a life regulated and blessed by religious laws and practices. As any Amish will attest, the effort expended on a "bee" finds its source in the effort expended on prayer, scripture study, and a culture designed to enhance, rather than thwart, a person's spiritual needs. While few of us are Amish, and few of us raise barns, we may all benefit from this example. We can awaken in ourselves the spirit of barn raising, by renewing our efforts at contemplative practice and building, in union with co-workers, neighbors, friends, and relatives, a vast work-barn of the spirit, a place where labor may be pursued with forbearance, generosity, and love.

Paul talks with Kazuaki Tanahashi, an artist and author-editor of Brush Mind, Moon in a Dewdrop: Writings of Zen Master Dogen, Penetrating Laughter: Hakuin's Zen and Art, *and* Essential Zen.

The Spirituality of Repetition

In the converted garage that is his west Berkeley studio, Kazuaki Tanahashi is preparing for an exhibit in Germany. He has completed several of the large paint-

Kazuaki Tanahashi at work

ings for the show: great, bold, open circles, done in a single stroke of brush and ink, that suggest a quiet expanse of interior life edged with the danger of chaos.

"Kaz," as he is known to his friends, learned calligraphy as a primary-school student in Japan. "The first thing our teacher told us was to keep our minds quiet and to start concentrating while we were grinding ink. He then said that the bottom of the ink stick should be kept exactly horizontal so that the ink stick is always straight up." Kaz was told that if his ink stick was leaning, his mind would be leaning; that if his posture was bad, his calligraphy could not be good.

Calligraphy developed in China thousands of years ago. Over the centuries, the recognition of outstanding artists and their distinctive styles evolved into a sense of "art." And as people studied this art, they discovered that the personality of the artist appeared in the work.

"Even though each calligrapher did the same characters as every other calligrapher," says Kaz, "it was clear that some drawings had greater depth, were more profound and moving than others. Naturally, contemplation was a part of what the great artists did, bringing to the work greater concentration, relaxation, understanding, and depth of the personality. Some calligraphers were skillful but didn't have a profound poetry within themselves. And so their art didn't last."

"The heart of spirituality is the repetition," says Kaz. "You repeat with awareness. You repeat the same thing over and over again." And because your energy isn't going into trying to create something 'new' or 'better,' it gets directed to your Self in a more subtle way. The brush is soft. It has a life of its own. You can never produce exactly the same stroke. So you learn about your inner state. Calligraphy is a direct representation of your personality."

Ancient ideogram for "Mindfulness." This ideogram was created over 3,000 years ago and has been used commonly throughout east Asia. The ideogram is composed of two characters or words: "present moment," represented by the top four strokes, and "mind/heart," represented by the bottom four strokes. It is presented here in four different styles: (1) Earliest, or Seal Script, (2) Formal, (3) Semicursive, and (4) Cursive. Calligrapher: Kazuaki Tanahashi.

Working: A Set of Everyday Exercises

Paul points out that this is the only chapter in the book that deals at length with activities outside the home. Beyond the front porch, strangers abound, rules change, the unknown lurks at every turn. We can make the workplace as much like home as possible, decorating it with pictures of our kids or flowers from our garden, but home it will never be.

This means that special demands exist for anyone trying to bring spiritual values into the workplace. One's job may be monotonous, fruitless, or destructive, one's co-worker may be a back-stabber, one's boss a dragon. How, in these circumstances, can we even think of sacred values and contemplative practices?

The *Bhagavad Gita* suggests that all work to which our role in life calls us is acceptable, if done in the right spirit. The *Gita* speaks of consecration and sacrifice, of offering up one's work to God. One way to achieve this is through awareness: keeping alive the realization, in some deep well within the heart if not always in conscious thought, that I work in service to the divine, not in service to my own egotistical needs and desires. Alternatively, I may engage in a simple, repetitive spiritual practice while I work. Suzuki Shosan speaks of reciting the *nembutsu;* such approaches can be found throughout the world, wherever traditional people "tell their beads" while at work, fingering a knotted or beaded cord as they farm or spin or beg. (See chapter 7, "Words," for more about these disciplines.)

Yet another possibility is to pause during work to remind oneself of one's spiritual role and responsibilities. This was the discipline of Brother Lawrence of the Resurrection, the seventeenth-century Catholic monk and cook who developed the Practice of the Presence of God. Throughout the day, Brother Lawrence would break his labors and turn his mind to God. "By this short and sure means," he reported, "I arrived at a state in which it would have been just as impossible not to think about God as it was difficult to get used to doing so in the beginning."[15]

From these diverse practices, we can distill three exercises to help beginners bring about the marriage of outer and inner work.

THE PRACTICE OF BARE ATTENTION

Try at all times to be aware of your work. If you swing a hammer, sense the weight of the tool, the tension in your forearm as you lift the shaft, the momentum of the head as it sails toward the wood, the force of the impact. If you sit before a word processor, sense the life in your arms, legs, and feet. Feel the pressure of the keys against your fingers. Efforts like these, practiced throughout the day, return us to the open attention and serene fullness of being that we enjoyed during the morning sitting. They embrace reality in all its sensory glory and thus bring us closer to the truth about ourselves and the world. As Josef Pieper said, "A man is wise when all things taste to him as they really are."

THE PRACTICE OF PUTTING ONESELF IN ANOTHER'S SHOES

How can I learn to work well with others? By becoming the other. When Sally snaps my head off, I struggle to remember her home life: her shabby furniture, her delinquent children, her unloving husband. There but for the grace of God go I— a truism that remains ever true. If I were in Sally's shoes, perhaps I would find myself paralyzed with despair, unable to work at all. Truly, I can learn from her courage. If I know nothing about Sally's background, nothing to explain or excuse her rude behavior, I can see myself in her failings, for surely I have faults at least the equal of hers. Discovering Sally in myself and myself in Sally reminds me that we are joined in a common enterprise.

THE PRACTICE OF OFFERING ONE'S WORK TO GOD

No matter what my work may be, I am free to offer it in service to God, or for the salvation of other human beings, or even for my own spiritual edification. All these intentions will help to expunge egoism from my work and give my labors a deeper meaning. Here the advice of Krishna reigns supreme: "Perform action for His sake ... devoid of attachment." Experiment with this practice: if you hate your boss, do the best work that you possibly can *for his benefit;* such an effort, which cuts across the grain of many habits and prejudices, may prove to be a blessing for both of you. Work with detachment: if you are a waitress clearing a table after a rude patron has left the restaurant, leaving three pennies as a tip, be the best waitress that you can be. Every sweep of the sponge as you clean up his mess is your response, not only to his rudeness, but to the cosmos of which he is a part. Our work is our signature upon the world; let us write with care and love.

These, then, are the three levels of work in the world: work by oneself, work with others, work for the sacred. If we inhabit these levels with detachment and devotion, we may discover that they merge into one, that our daily labor serves at the same time ourselves, our neighbors, and God; and that through this sacramental understanding of work, the toil of exile may yet become the tilling of Eden.

SIMPLE PLEASURES

*E*very clear night, I bathe in starlight. An hour or two after nightfall, when the kids are in bed and the dishes are washed, I scoot outside, turn my face to the sky, and let the ancient photons from Betelgeuse, Arcturus, and Sirius—particles of light a million years old, according to the astronomers—sprinkle down upon my forehead, wash over my cheeks, and splash across my lips.

During this starry ablution, I like to visit old friends as they wheel across the sky: Virgo with her swirling skirt of galaxies, Orion brandishing his nebular sword, Ursa Major lumbering in the icy polar regions. Sometimes I search out the planets; Jupiter or Saturn is almost always visible, each staring solemnly at the earth with a yellow, untwinkling eye. Most often, however, I merely look upward in silent wonder. Since I was a child, I have loved astronomy for its infinite vistas, endless variety, and moments of deep reflection. Stargazing is, I believe, an ideal contemplative pastime, an exquisite simple pleasure.

What do I mean by a simple pleasure? Quite simply, those activities that we turn to as respite from the daily grind. While I prefer stargazing, others turn to reading, knitting, or baking; studying classical guitar or modern Greek; hoeing a garden or rowing a boat. We need our simple pleasures as surely as we need oxygen to breathe. "To do great work, a man must be very idle as well as very industrious," observed Samuel Butler. Simple pleasures release us from the stressful bonds that hobble our energies and offer instead freedom and fun. Indeed, thinking about simple pleasures is itself a simple pleasure, a foretaste of the joy that these pastimes deliver.

Simple pleasures fall outside the normal round. Most people seek them during a lunch break, in the evening, on the weekend, on vacation. We could easily use another term, "vacation activities." This is a happy choice of words, as it happens, for it contains a subtle truth: that the aim of simple pleasures is to vacate oneself. Through simple pleasures we empty out the dust that clouds our minds and the cobwebs that clutter our hearts. A defense attorney, weary from a day of combat in the legal battlefield, comes home and picks up her violin; a high-school teacher takes a stroll in the woods as soon as classes end. Each seeks renewal through temporary escape from the daily grind. We need to understand that this escape is normal and healthy, that it helps rather than hinders spiritual work. To seek out simple pleasures is to accept the universal law of tension and relaxation, in-breath and out-breath, systole and diastole. Simple pleasures constitute, in effect, miniature retreats, abbreviated versions of a sojourn into mountains or desert. Every time a carpenter takes a coffee break, he becomes for a moment Moses on Mt. Sinai; whenever a nurse feeds the carp in her backyard pond, she joins hands with Basho on the road to the deep north. Each knows that in order to work in the mud, one must play among the stars.

The sacred traditions, both East and West, understand full well the importance of simple pleasures. We see this in tales of Zen monks and Franciscan friars, in their shared love of gardens, pools, and mountain paths, of painting and music, of jokes played on themselves and others. We see it, too, in the customs of the Navajo, who relish a holiday gathering of the extended clan or a solitary horseback ride through the buttes. Such pastimes are never production-oriented, never for gain. This makes for an ironic contrast with modern tastes: the stitching of an Amish-style quilt may well constitute a simple pleasure for a harried housewife from Chicago, but to an Amish housewife it is work, pure and simple. The Amish seek refreshment elsewhere, perhaps through a buggy ride to a neighbor's house for an hour of cooking.

Along with vacating us, enjoying a simple pleasure also replenishes us. What can bring us greater nourishment than playing or listening to music? If we are jangled or jumpy, nothing restores us faster than the sublime harmonics of a Bach fugue, where beauty chases beauty in an endless circle of delight. Beauty always brings vitality, for it is none other than the sensible manifestation of the good and the true. All simple pleasures work in this way, by bringing us face-to-face with a beauty that renews, whether it be the moors wreathed in mist on a weekend hike, or a child's wondering eyes as we read out loud from Andersen or Grimm.

Wu-Wei: *The Taoist Heart of Simple Pleasures*

Of all religions, perhaps Taoism understands best the appeal of simple pleasures and their dual role as sweeper of cobwebs and bringer of enchantment. According to the *Tao Tê Ching*, the key to human happiness lies in *wu-wei*, or "actionless action"—a paradoxical expression that closely echoes the "passive activity" we seek in our morning sitting. To practice *wu-wei* is to live in harmony with the ebb and flow of reality, to be one with the Tao, the fathomless, transcendent, immanent, eternal, undefinable heart of all being. And how does one practice *wu-wei?* In part, through simple pleasures.

Picture a young ballerina dancing with consummate poise or an old man shuffling serenely down a country road. Each one flows with natural life, conforming without strain to the twists and turns of macadam or music, moving quietly from one moment to the next. They flow like water. In traditional Chinese texts, water, celebrated for its purity, simplicity, and ease of motion, is the most common symbol of the Tao. Listen to these lines from the *Tao Tê Ching*:

> The softest thing in the world [i.e., water] dashes against and overcomes the hardest; that which has no substantial existence enters where there is no crevice.
> I know hereby what advantage belongs to doing nothing with a purpose.[1]

Fishing, painting, singing, walking, knitting, baking, gardening, boating: these simple pleasures, if done in the proper spirit, become "actionless actions," *wu-wei*, imbued with quiet, peace, and beauty. The following tale about the Taoist sage Chuang Tzu underscores the close bond between Taoism and simple pleasures:

> One day, while Master Chuang Tzu fished at a local stream, the prince of Ch'u approached him with a startling offer. He wished Chuang Tzu to put down his pole and take up the reins of government as prime minister. Rather than answer the prince directly, Chuang Tzu began to talk of a famous sacred tortoise, now thousands of years old, that lay bejeweled in a splendidly carved box on the prince's regal altar. "Would this tortoise," asked Chuang Tzu, "rather lie in elegant death on your altar or be scampering alive through the mud?" "Alive in the mud, of course," answered the prince. "And I, too," said Chuang Tzu, "would rather scamper through the mud than be boxed in by the job of prime minister."

In all that we have described so far, simple pleasures offer a sanitarium for the soul, a resting place for refreshment and renewal. Sometimes, though, simple pleasures involve more formal contemplative practice. For example, while a Buddhist might take up gardening because he finds mucking around in the mud to be a wonderfully sloppy escape from the precise discipline of the *zendo*, he might also discover seeding and weeding to be a golden opportunity for engaging in mindfulness practice. Someone else may strap on ice skates to erase the tensions of the workplace, only to find the rink to be an ideal place for reciting sacred mantras. Some activities lend themselves especially well to this dual potential for informal revitalization and formal practice. Perhaps the most popular example of all is that simple pleasure known as walking, which we will now explore in depth.

CONTEMPLATIVE CLOSE-UP: WALKING

A good friend of mine sums up his passion for walking like this: "When I'm angry and need to let off steam, I walk. When I'm blue and need some cheering up, I walk. When I'm churned up and need to calm down, I walk. When I want to think, or dream, or taste the world as it is, I walk." My friend, who has worn

Lawrence Hudetz

A path in the woods—walking is a universal mode of contemplation

out several pairs of shoes on his diurnal and nocturnal hikes, likes to quote this line from George Macauley Trevelyan: "I have two doctors, my left leg and my right."

Walking is a universal medicine and mode of contemplation. The quintessential simple pleasure, it requires no equipment, not even shoes, as countless walkers from warmer climes attest. One simply puts one foot in front of another. There need be no destination, no aim at all; the joy lies in the walk itself, in the delight of movement, the beauty of the landscape, the faces of the fleeting crowd. For Walt Whitman, walking meant liberty, well-being, and robust self-confidence:

> Alone and light-hearted I take to the open road,
> Healthy, free, the world before me,
> The long brown path before me leading wherever I choose.
> Henceforth I ask not good-fortune, I am myself good fortune,
> Henceforth I whimper no more, postpone no more, need nothing,
> Done with indoor complaints, libraries, querulous criticisms,
> Strong and content I travel the open road.

Whitman captures the exhilaration of this simple pleasure, its twin gift of releasing us from the chains of habit and of endowing us with the autonomy of the open road. To walk is to sense freedom in every swing of arm and leg. To sense freedom is to refresh one's soul, to know oneself to be a creature of infinite possibility and immeasurable destiny.

But Whitman never offers a method for others to follow; his own exuberance is sui generis, born of a self-confidence so exceptional that it skirts the edges of self-adoration. Happily, other writers do explain more concretely the ins and outs of walking as spiritual practice. One example is the eighteenth-century English essayist William Hazlitt, for whom walking brings an invitation to contemplation:

> The soul of a journey is liberty, perfect liberty, to think, feel, do just as one pleases. We go on a journey chiefly to be free of all impediments and of all inconveniences; to leave ourselves behind, much more to be rid of others. It is because I want a little breathing-space to muse on indifferent matters, where Contemplation
>
> May plume her feathers and let grow her wings. . . .

Give me the blue sky over my head, and the green turf beneath my feet, a winding road before me, and a three hours' march to dinner. . . . I laugh, I run, I leap, I sing for joy. From the point of yonder rolling cloud, I plunge into my past being, and revel there, as the sun-burnt Indian plunges headlong into the wave that wafts him to his native shore. Then long-forgotten things, like "sunken wrack and sumless treasuries," burst upon my eager sight, and I begin to feel, think, and be myself again. . . . mine is that undisturbed silence of the heart which alone is perfect eloquence.

We've all experienced the happiness that walking brings, especially when we enjoy the right conditions of blue sky, green turf, winding road, and ample time. As Hazlitt explains, this happiness heals body, mind, and heart. The body delights in motion, in suppleness and balance; the mind delights in memories; the heart delights in "that undisturbed silence . . . which alone is perfect eloquence." Here we meet the paradox at the heart of walking (and of all simple pleasures): walking brings stillness, "singing for joy" brings silence, outward adventuring becomes inward discovery.

Sometimes, it happens that a walk leads to a revelation not only about ourselves, but about the world. As we become sensitive to our surroundings—as we listen to the rustling of hedge mice, the swish of grass underfoot, the yelp of distant dogs; as we feel a breeze lift the fine hairs on our forearms; as we smell the moisture of an approaching storm; as we see the essential dignity and beauty of the faces that flicker by—we may be given a glimpse of eternal truth. Such was the experience of Bede Griffiths, Catholic monk and priest, while still a schoolboy in England between the wars:

One day during my last term at school I walked out alone in the evening and heard the birds singing in that full chorus of song, which can only be heard at that time of the year at dawn or at sunset. . . . Everything then grew still as the sunset faded and the veil of dusk began to cover the earth. I remember now the feeling of awe which came over me. I felt inclined to kneel on the ground, as though I had been standing in the presence of an angel; and I hardly dared to look on the face of the sky, because it seemed as though it was but a veil before the face of God.[2]

This revelation led Griffiths into an English Benedictine monastery and then to India, where he established several ashrams, contributed greatly to Christian-Hindu ecumenism, and became a well-known exponent of the contemplative life. It is astonishing but true that this abundant output can be traced back to the results of an adolescent walk!

The Simple Pleasures of Nature: A Conversation with Norman Boucher

For Norman Boucher, author of *A Bird Lover's Life List and Journal*, a hike in the New England woods is the ultimate simple pleasure. The season doesn't matter: in summer, he laces up running shoes and pads silently under the great green canopy; in winter, he straps on snowshoes and duckwalks through the drifts. The woods beckon

Nature is meditative

Boucher like movie theaters or gambling casinos beckon others; they provide a release, both physical and mental, from the pettiness of human life. "When I escape to the woods," Boucher tells me, fixing me with his wry, birdlike eyes, "I escape to an idea: the idea of a wild place, the place beyond the end of the road, where things are better, where I can get away from human complications for another world, equally complicated, in which the human role is diminished."

I mention to Boucher that when I was a boy, I feared the woods and their lack of human warmth. He counters by suggesting a different perspective. "I seek a sense of proportion. If you take away the support of things made by human hands, you have to relate to the world in a more humbling way. If you fall and break a leg in the Everglades, an alligator will get to you long before the rescue team. Nature short-circuits your hubris." Nature's otherworldliness, then, is what most appeals to Boucher, whether on a jaunt to the local park or on a canoe expedition into the wilderness. "The more I learn about nature," he says, "the stranger it seems. When you start going into the wilds, it is easy to anthropomorphize. But when you watch more closely, these connections seem thinner and thinner. Something *other* seems to be happening. As a boy, I would go to church every Friday to pray the stations of the cross. I was the only one in this big, cavernous building. I find in the natural world the same sense of stillness and enclosure that I found in church."

In the mysterious natural realm where human beings no longer dominate the landscape, Boucher discovers the possibility of contemplation. "Nature is meditative, in that it focuses you. It takes you out of yourself and deeper into yourself at the same time. You feel in a sharper way; you see yourself better. When I was a serious Zen student, I found that sitting had a similar effect. At first lots of things would come up that I had brought with me, but in time that quieted down. I learned to see more freshly."

This discipline of seeing lies near the heart of Boucher's love of nature. As a result, when he goes into the woods he rarely carries a field guide. "I usually go walking with, at most, a pair of binoculars. Sometimes I remember to put a hand lens in my pocket to look at insects and small flowers. But I seldom take a field guide, because I am out there to observe. A guide inhibits my observations. I see only the features that it emphasizes. I prefer to look closely, jot down or remember everything I can, and then look into the guide later. I see more this way. Mostly I rely on opening my senses as much as possible. Nature is a real treat for the senses." A recent visit to the Everglades provides a vivid example. "The Everglades is amazingly rich in wildlife, from the algae breeding in the water to the eagles, storks, and alligators that seem to be all over the place. I have canoed in mangrove swamps on sunny days when rain nevertheless appears to be falling on the water just before the bow of the canoe. But what I am seeing is hundreds of thousands of fry—newly hatched fish—moving out of the way of the canoe. The water is like the primordial soup. You can't go to the Everglades without thinking about origins, the origin of life, of our life, of our world."

Boucher emphasizes, however, that one needn't be in an extraordinary landscape for the simple pleasure of entering the woods to work its magic; a pocket park in a city or town will do the trick. "I have been doing some lunchtime birding," he says, "to see what migrant species are around. I head for a wooded place a few blocks from my office. The birds are making incredible journeys of hundreds, even thousands of miles, and most people are oblivious to it. People pass bushes in which there are white-throated sparrows, and they have no idea that these birds are on their way to South America and have spent the summer nesting in the high peaks of New England or the trees of Canada." He shakes his head, marveling simultaneously at the blindness of people and the beauties of nature. He adds, however, that this blindness can be cured. "It is miraculous, this thing called creation. Looking at nature is a way of seeing and hearing and sensing the miraculous."

Walking as Formal Practice:

Walking, like other simple pleasures, offers not only informal discoveries and delights, but also opportunities for formal spiritual practice. The best-known example is walking meditation, or *kinhin*, as it is known in Japanese Zen monasteries. *Kinhin* frequently accompanies *zazen*, the classic Zen sitting meditation whose aim is to still the mind and free it of illusions in order to reach a state of nondual awareness. We may define *kinhin* as *zazen* in motion.

To practice *kinhin* in Rinzai Zen monasteries, the monk stands erect, left fist cupped in right hand and pressed against the chest, elbows at right angles, gazing at a point two yards in front of his feet. Maintaining this posture, he walks briskly around the meditation room, or *zendo*, counting in-breaths and out-breaths as he moves. Each step lasts one full breath of inhalation plus exhalation. The monk walks attentively, aware of where and how his foot touches the floor. If he encounters a wall or other obstacle, he turn to the right and continues to walk. In Soto Zen monasteries, the walking usually goes on at a much slower pace with much smaller steps, usually no more than six inches or so; in addition, the right fist is cupped in the left palm. No matter what the style, the intention remains the same: to focus attention on the breath while in motion in order to clarify the mind.

In Vipassana or insight practice, walking meditation (*cankamana* in Pali) assumes a different form and intent. Many Vipassana monasteries in Southeast Asia contain a "meditation terrace," a flat, straight walkway of perhaps thirty feet, on which monks stride back and forth practicing *cankamana*. The aim of this walking meditation is to be aware of the fluctuations of one's body as one walks, as an expression of the transitory nature of all phenomena. Most Vipassana practitioners pay special attention to the movement of the feet in *cankamana*, often dividing every step into five component parts: lifting the foot, moving the foot forward, lowering the foot, placing the foot on the ground, and letting one's weight settle on the foot.

Walking Meditation:
An Exercise for Everyday Life

Formal Buddhist walking meditation can be adapted to meet the needs of ordinary daily life. You might, for example, decide to practice modified walking meditation on the way to work in the morning.

I suggest that, at least at first, you adopt the Soto method of walking slowly and deliberately—but not so much so that others notice what you are doing.

Try to attend to every motion, from the moment that you lift up your foot until the moment that it settles back to earth. Sense the tug of gravity on your soles, the swish of skirt or pants against your legs. Notice the way your center of balance changes as one foot falls and the other rises. Once you have studied these basic elements of walking, you may encompass more peripheral movements, like the swing of your arms or the nearly imperceptible bob of your head. In time, your attention should expand to include the world around you: the chirping of birds, the stink of car exhaust, the faces of the people that you pass. Here you might want to add a practice of blessing or prayer, such as *metta* practice or the practice of seeing others as Christ, both described in the next chapter, "Being with Others."

SIMPLE PLEASURES:
A CONTEMPLATIVE HARVEST

Coauthor Paul Kaufman writes of a visit to his friend Rohana, her garden, and mindfulness.

Rohana's Garden

Rohana's house sits behind a high wooden fence on a quiet urban street. The inside of the fence is thickly lined with vines and shrubs, suggesting an embrace by nature that is at once affectionate and slightly possessive. Indeed, the house's ship-gray color, with blue and white trim on the bay window, lends it the air of a permanently landlocked storybook vessel.

Rohana stands on a red brick path lined with oyster shells and rounded stones that winds through the garden and nearly circumnavigates the house.

"I've been gardening for about thirty years," she says, as we pause in front of a russet-colored blossom. "Wherever I've lived, I've had some

Walking meditation in the garden

kind of garden. It encompasses a lot of things for me, including creativity and hard physical work. The garden is a living thing and I have to be aware of it every day."

The garden is part of Rohana's morning practice. Her routine is to sit for half an hour upon awakening. She alternates her morning sitting with walking meditation. She follows this with chanting and prostrations, turns on the soaker hoses in the garden, and goes for a walk up a nearby hill. Afterward, she does some more watering and then goes to work as a psychotherapist.

"Buddhism talks about cultivating the mindfulness factor of enlightenment," she observes. "When I am literally cultivating my garden, I have to be aware of whatever I'm working with, because when I'm not mindful in the garden there are immediate consequences. The garden lets me know. If I'm not mindful when I'm weeding I can pull out something that I really want to keep, and it's gone."

Rohana and I walk under a redwood arbor covered with the leaves of a Concord grape. "I have fond memories of my children picking grapes," she says. "My dad was very tall and he would thrill the kids, getting the ones that were up so high that nobody else could reach them. So this is my small remembrance of that." She tells me that the grapes are trellised so that the raccoons can't reach all of them. "Raccoons have grape parties," she says with a smile. "Other animals come, too." Rohana sees this as part of the gift of creating an environment in which all beings take interest, a gift that gives her an opportunity to perceive the complex life around her in the garden.

I watch her carefully pick a few mildew- and rust-laden leaves from a rose bush. "Taking infected leaves off the rose bush," she says, "and putting them aside so that the rust or mildew doesn't spread to other plants is a meditative activity. It's also a very loving activity; caring for the garden requires my mind to stay relatively focused. I can be in the garden all afternoon and into the evening until it's so dark that I can't see anymore, and it doesn't feel like time has passed in the usual way. I can concentrate for extended periods. And that is very helpful."

She observes that the garden harbors not only abundant life but also decay and death. This knowledge keeps her from becoming too attached to anything in particular. She is learning to take whatever comes in a balanced way. Rohana associates this with equanimity. "I've always kept a compost pile in the garden. When I'm gardening I know that although I may have killed this sprout, it will become part of the garden again, and so that cycle of life is there. The awareness of impermanence is there. It's always present."

At the gate, we turn to look back at the garden. "One of the wonderful things about a garden," she says, "is that it has a life of its own. And that life will go on when I'm gone. I can see something that will not only exist after I'm gone but will grow over time. I have a kind of a vision of what it is going to be. I love the long view, the lifetime view, and even beyond the lifetime view!"

Paul describes the simple pleasures of playing the piano while his partner Libby Colman sits near him and weaves.

The Well-Tempered Weaver

When she returns home at the end of a workday, Libby is happy to get away from words. At work, she counsels single parents with young children who are struggling to live together in transitional housing. All day she listens to troubles, bolsters morale, defuses anger, and negotiates disputes. Libby's preferred form of meditative surrender to wordlessness is weaving. Her loom is in our living room, right next to my piano.

In spiritual rhythm

Libby started knitting when she was eight years old. "It was very soothing," she says, "the yarn passing through my fingers like worry beads." Knitting went well with raising three children. "I could pick up the work or put it down at a moment's notice. The worst the kids could do was tangle the yarn."

After her children were grown, Libby went to Arizona and stayed with a family of Navajo weavers at Arizona's Canyon de Chelly to learn their craft. She pitched her tent on the rim of the canyon, meditated each morning, and, for two weeks, spent eight to ten hours each day weaving.

Navajo weaving is done on a loom that displays the work as it progresses. "I liked watching my work grow," she says. Learning to weave also corresponded to a change in Libby's life: the end of active mothering and the beginning of deeper reflection on the pattern of her life.

After dinner, or just before we go to bed, or on a Sunday morning, Libby goes to her loom and I go to my piano. Loom and piano, Libby and I, sit side by side, like copilots of a preindustrial, time-travel rig. I play a Duke Ellington song called "Lost in Meditation," in which a lover dreamily enters the old feeling of being with the beloved, who, alas, is no longer present. As I play this music, I am taken in by it,

I feel liberated. Why should this be? The notes printed on the page are formed and fixed, unchanged and unchangeable. How can there be such freedom in fixedness?

Similarly, warp and woof impose constraints on design. The patterns evolve from abstract, almost mathematical forms in Libby's mind, to a sketch on graph paper, to the colorful visual field that becomes her total reality as she weaves. The rug she is working on now is a wedding gift for her son, Jonah, and daughter-in-law, Rupam. The design incorporates yarn that belonged to Rupam's deceased grandmother.

As she weaves, thoughts float through Libby's mind, thoughts of the past and of the future, of Rupam's grandmother and the unborn grandchildren, and thoughts of us.

I may have played the first Prelude in Johann Sebastian Bach's "Well-Tempered Clavier" a hundred times before. On each new occasion, the Prelude demands that I pay homage to it, that I faithfully recommit to its hidden intentions and bring it to life in the here and now of my own sound and subjectivity. Its phrases become a sturdy, perfect prayer. Beethoven said: "It takes spiritual rhythm to grasp music in its essence. Music gives the mind a relation to the total harmony . . . which is Unity."

Libby says that the music I play guides the rhythm of her movements as she weaves. Without dividing my attention, I become aware of her presence beside me. Unconscious of time, we meditate in spiritual rhythm, with pattern and song, doubleness and union.

The Three Spiritual Principles of Simple Pleasures

In a sense, no one needs tips on the practice of simple pleasures. Barring the cartoon tycoon who, while sprawled on the beach with a mint julep in hand, still scours his *Wall Street Journal* and barks out business deals, we all know the value of periodic breaks from our ordinary work. There are, however, three principles that will help us to reap the spiritual rewards of our favorite pastimes.

CHOOSE A SIMPLE PLEASURE THAT MEETS YOUR NEEDS

Simple pleasures should enhance the inner life; needlepoint or fly-fishing has obvious advantages over gambling or small-arms training. But it's not only a matter of avoiding vice. Each of us tips the scales to one side or the other in terms of inner development, and simple pleasures are a way of finding balance. The majority of us work in service jobs that entail frequent contact—and often friction—with others. If you find yourself overdosing on people, all the more reason for you to seek a simple pleasure that brings a measure of silence and solitude. A friend of mine spends his days teaching physics to crowds of prank-playing, hormone-charged teenagers; no wonder he spends his nights in a nearby meadow watching birds of prey on the prowl. When a great horned owl floats across the field of his binoculars, my friend enjoys a frisson of wonder, calm but intense. He has entered the same world of absolute "otherness" that Norman Boucher discovers in the mangrove swamps; he finds a rare measure of peace while watching this mysterious creature, ancient symbol of wisdom and death, in the midst of its own daily round.

NO SIMPLE PLEASURE REMAINS SIMPLE WITHOUT CONSCIOUS EFFORT
My owl-watching friend remembers when, a few years back, he transformed his simple pleasure into a complex pain by going overboard with optical devices, guidebooks, observing stools, and the like. Before long he was spending so much time assembling his equipment that he had no time to look through it. Fortunately, a serendipitous dip into the pages of *Walden* set him straight. He read Thoreau's advice to "simplify, simplify, simplify," trimmed his supplies down to an inexpensive pair of binoculars, and now revels every night in the owl's dark beauty. On the other hand, there's much to be said for preparing oneself properly. Rohanna's garden flourishes because she has learned about blossoms, bugs, fertilizers, and the like. Norman Boucher takes a dim view of naturalists who go into the woods with no idea of what to look for. Their dream is to see with pristine eyes; the reality is that they see with unprepared eyes and as a result see almost nothing. Even the simplest of pleasures is a craft, a discipline that demands time and effort.

EVERY SIMPLE PLEASURE IS AN OPPORTUNITY FOR MINDFULNESS
AND PRAYER
In this respect, simple pleasures differ not at all from other activities: all can be a doorway to contemplation. This hardly means that you must turn your pastimes into deliberate exercises in mindfulness training, with a special focus on breath or some other physiological event; it can simply mean bringing your attention to bear more fully on the activity in which you are engaged. When you knit, enjoy the flash of the needle, the scratch of the yarn, the transformation of fabric from chaos into pattern. When you ice-skate, enjoy the cold breeze on your cheek, the glint of the ice, the giddiness of gliding without restraint. Savor simple pleasures, drink them to the full. As Norman Boucher says of walking in the woods, these pastimes lead us out of ourselves and into ourselves simultaneously: out of hubris and into humbleness, out of ruts and into freedom, out of fantasy and into reality.

Inverness porch   Marty Knapp

six

BEING WITH OTHERS

*T*he annals of exploration contain more than their share of peculiar stories: green valleys glimpsed in the depths of Antarctica, abominable snowmen encountered in Himalayan blizzards—the sort of thing that, if it weren't recounted by reputable people, would be relegated to the supermarket tabloids. But of exploration's strange stories, perhaps none is as fascinating, or as spiritually provocative, as that of the "invisible companion."

The phenomenon has been reported on every continent: an alpinist or polar explorer, tramping alone under desperate conditions, suddenly senses the presence of another person, someone whose mere presence offers succor and hope. Perhaps the most famous account comes from Francis Sydney Smythe, who describes the being that accompanied him during the most difficult stretch of his 1933 ascent of Mt. Everest:

> In its company I could not feel lonely, nor could I come to any harm. It was always there to sustain me on my solitary climb up the snow-covered slabs. Now, as I halted and extracted some mint cake from my pocket, it was so near and so strong that instinctively I divided the mint into two halves and turned around with one-half in my hand to offer it to my "companion."[1]

To bestselling author Sophy Burnham, such presences are most likely angels; to psychiatrists, they may be projections of the unconscious. Whatever the explanation—and it may differ from one case to the next—all accounts of invisible companions teach the same lesson: that the need to be with others is as fierce a longing as hunger, thirst, or sexual desire. A man or woman too long alone grows stunted and gnarled, like a lone tree on a wind-swept plain. When Daniel Defoe's fictional hero Robinson Crusoe clapped eyes on Friday, after a dozen years of solitude broken only by the poor companionship of tortoises and goats, his happiness knew no bounds; he writes that "a secret Joy [ran] through every Part of my Soul." Robinson speaks for us all. We rejoice in parents, siblings, children, that constellation of shared blood and belief that we call family. We rejoice in friends: in their kindnesses, their enthusiasms, even their excesses. We rejoice in our lover, in the very friction of human flesh. We rejoice in our communal existence, and we gather in churches, synagogues, mosques, temples, *zendos*, ashrams, to celebrate together the mysteries of life.

Nothing brings us greater joy than other human beings. "What a piece of work is a man!" exalts Shakespeare in *Hamlet*. "How noble in reason, how infinite in faculties, in form and moving how express and admirable, in action how like an angel, in apprehension how like a god." We love only what is human. We respect animals that project an alien otherness (scaly snake, eight-limbed octopus), but we adore those creatures that resemble us (cuddly puppy, courageous lion). Even the divine dons human form to attract our attention: thus wisdom becomes Sophia, a dazzling woman, and God a luminous man.

But this is only half the story.

We must also admit that nothing brings us greater despair than other human beings. "Hell," grumbles Jean-Paul Sartre, "is other people." What an image: the human being as the depths of despond, the stygian darkness. It's impossible not to see a grain of truth in this bleak assessment.

Even saints have trouble being with others; how much harder it is for us ordinary folk! How many times do we perceive other people as nuisances, ants at a picnic? It's easy enough to be calm and collected while on solitary retreat. One thinks fondly of one's friends, even longs for their companionship. But it's another matter entirely to face them in the trouble-and-strife of ordinary life; too often, the demigod of memory turns into the demon of reality.

Well, then, what is a human being: a glimpse of heaven or a glimmer of hell? The truth, no doubt, lies somewhere in between. Human beings have been aptly described as creatures with their feet in the gutter and their eyes on the stars. According to C. S. Lewis, "humans are amphibians—half spirit and half animal."

It is precisely people's twofold aspect that makes them so important to our inner lives. When we encounter another person, we never know what will ensue. We may stike up a conversation with the woman sitting next to us on the bus and secure a lifelong friend. A high-school acquaintance may call up at midnight to confess his greatest sin. Faced with the incalculable behavior of others—faced, that is, with the imponderable mystery of this "half-spirit, half-animal"—we need to keep on our spiritual toes. The enormity of the task before us can be gauged by the old Christian maxim:

The will of God is other people.

How to fathom the depths of this extraordinary saying? It suggests, at a bare minimum, that other people serve as a gateway to the divine, that God speaks to us through every personal encounter.

Here are three of the blessings that come from being with others:

1. *Being with others reveals new ways of thinking and feeling.* No matter how well read, highly educated, or widely traveled we may be, our life remains terribly limited in scope. Other people give perspective; an hour of conversation with the right person at the right moment can overcome decades of ignorance. I am reminded of the tale, commonplace in fairy literature, of the man who for years searches fruitlessly for a buried treasure, or a holy scroll, or a lost lover. Finally, at the end of his rope, he prepares for suicide by giving away his money to the first wayfarer he meets—and that chance acquaintance turns out to be his salvation, who through a few choice words leads the protagonist to his heart's desire.

2. *Being with others reveals the truth about ourselves.* When I spend ten minutes with a man or woman of genuine sanctity, my own unsettled state becomes only too obvious. If I spend ten minutes with a troubled friend, my inability to help becomes equally apparent. Being with others teaches us our limits, shattering the illusions painted by self-love.

By the same token, of course, being with others reveals our strengths. You may notice that you sit more calmly, think more clearly, work more efficiently than your neighbor. This knowledge is invaluable, because it tells you what gifts you possess that can be put at the service of other human beings, and because it offers a temptation to pride. All such temptations are useful. The weight lifter builds muscle by overcoming the force of gravity; we build an inner life by overcoming the force of temptation.

3. *Being with others teaches us that we find love by loving.* This is the Great Rule of the spirit. The more the sower plants, the more he reaps; the more we give, the more we receive. Love can't be defined; dictionaries flail about helplessly when faced with

this task, relying upon second-cousin synonyms like "affection," "attachment," "brotherhood," and "goodwill." These are all grand things, to be sure, but none of them is love. Love, like life, is an absolute, beyond definition. The Gospel of John declares simply that "God is love." Each of us, whatever our religious beliefs, can grasp the meaning of this graceful equation. Without love, we have no life; and love is the life we have when we are "being with others."

CONTEMPLATIVE CLOSE-UP: HOSPITALITY

Nearly all great children's stories have this in common: they celebrate hospitality. In *Homeward Bound,* a reclusive naturalist discovers a cat named Sassy besotted and sick after a tumble down a waterfall; true to the children's book ethic, he bundles her into his cloak, carries her to his cabin, feeds her his milk and bread, warms her under his blankets, and nurses her back to health. In *The Lion, the Witch, and the Wardrobe,* the faun Tumnus, at great personal peril, welcomes Lucy to his Narnian burrow, a "little, dry, clean cave of reddish stone with a carpet on the floor and two little chairs ('one for me and one for a friend,' said Mr. Tumnus)."[2] In *The Hobbit,* Bilbo Baggins, although pining for quiet and solitude, entertains a score of dwarves with raspberry jam and apple tart, mince pie and cheese, ale and coffee.

The reason for this universal largesse seems clear enough. Children's books deal in first and final things: in courage, love, and sacrifice; in the crowning of kings and the destruction of dragons; in the triumph of virtue in all its forms. And no virtuous action matters more than hospitality. Of this truth, anyone who has been stranded can easily attest. We've all been guests in need of a host. We've all been homeless for a day—because of poverty, or a missed train connection, or because we hitchhiked in the rain and no one picked us up. I once passed a night tramping the streets of Poughkeepsie, New York, after my Vassar College girlfriend had failed to find me a place to stay. This was a few decades ago, when Vassar was an all-women's school and hawk-faced matrons roamed the dormitories, rousting any males foolish enough to linger past the ringing of the 9:00 P.M. parietal bell. Downtown Poughkeepsie was wet, cold, and hostile, and I still remember the flush of joy that rushed up my spine when I discovered an unlocked coin laundry. The rest of the night was spent in relative comfort snuggled between two clothes dryers whose rumble and heat, renewed by a handful of quarters, instilled in me the lifelong conviction that even machines can practice hospitality.

How much greater, then, the hospitality of human beings. The Hasidic sage Rabbi Nachman of Bratzlav insisted that "hospitality is even greater than arriving early at the house of Torah study." When human beings open their homes to another, they open their hearts as well. Boundaries are erased, hostilities put aside, friendships sealed. Hospitality makes brothers and sisters of us all. Its magical power to smooth out differences and unite opposites stands revealed in its Indo-European root, *ghosti*, which means both "guest" and "host," as well as "stranger." Hospitality draws the stranger into the home and transforms him into a guest, a person spiritually equal to the host.

The Welcome of the Desert

For the great Western faiths of Judaism, Christianity, and Islam, a single image—it appears in both Bible and Koran—symbolizes hospitality and reveals its religious roots: the great patriarch Abraham dashing from his tent beneath the oaks of Mamre to greet three strangers approaching from the desert. Abraham prostrates himself before the men and offers them water, bread, and shade. He orders a lamb slaughtered and roasted, asks his wife, Sarah, to bake some cakes, and then waits hand and foot on the strangers' every need. In response, these mysterious beings proclaim that Sarah, heretofore barren, will bear a son.

The Bedouins of the Arabian desert, long celebrated for their commitment to hospitality (*diyafah*), make much of the story of Abraham. As they point out, it recurs several times in the Koran, in tales that emphasize the reciprocal courtesy of the patriarch and his guests. Indeed, in one version of the tale (Surah 11:73), the visitors refuse to accept the roasted calf that Abraham offers, a rejection that fills him with fear and confusion. "Hospitality," says Muhammed, "is a right"—and to spurn it is to tear at the very fabric of religion and society.

Bedouin tales of hospitality abound. Popular folk heroes include the warrior poet Hatim al-Ta'i, who sacrificed his herd of camels to feed a crowd of strangers, and the man who bragged that even his dog practiced hospitality and pointed to its many fleas as proof. Often, these tales—and reports by travelers of Bedouin hospitality—underscore the intimate relationship between guest and host. W. Thesiger writes in *Arabian Sands:*

> I pondered on this desert hospitality and compared it with our own. I remembered other encampments where I had slept, tents on which I had happened in the Syrian desert and where I had spent the night. Gaunt men in rags, hungry looking children had greeted me, and bade me welcome with the sonorous phrases of the desert. Later they had set a great dish before me, rice heaped around the sheep which they had slaughtered, over which my host poured liquid golden butter until it had flowed down onto

the sand; and when I had protested, saying "Enough, enough," had answered that I was a hundred times welcome. Their lavish hospitality always made me uncomfortable, for I had known that as a result of it they would go hungry for days. Yet when I left them they had almost convinced me that I had done them a kindness staying with them.[3]

Competition is fierce among Bedouins to serve as hosts. When a stranger approaches, men rush from their tents exclaiming, "May I lose my right hand if thou wilt not dismount at my tent."[4] H. R. P. Dickson, an Englishman who was cared for by a Bedouin wet-nurse as an infant and thus enjoyed "blood affinity" with all Bedouins, reports another greeting:

> O Guest of ours, though you have come, though you have visited us, and though you have honored our dwellings: We verily are the real guests, and you are the Lord of this house.[5]

A third, very popular greeting is "You are among your family." Indeed, once together in the tent, host and guest become like kin. As a result of this extraordinary understanding, to welcome a stranger is to guarantee his safety, even if he turns out to be a deadly enemy. During the stay, a precise code of etiquette reigns. The host is obliged to hover over his guest, offer him the finest food and drink, and answer his every beck and call, without asking his name or the purpose of his travels.

What lies behind the Bedouin's devotion to the open door? What lessons can we draw from it?

- *Hospitality is divine.* To Bedouins, this means first and foremost that hospitality affirms their relationship to God. When Bedouins accept Islam, they become *djar*, meaning "protected neighbor." They come under God's protection and accept God's hospitality. All earthly hospitality is understood as an extension of this divine hospitality, a reflection of God's goodness.
- *Hospitality offers solidarity in the face of adversity.* Bedouins inhabit a harsh landscape of sand, sun, and wind, where hospitality can mean the difference between life and death. Their beneficence is thus an exact expression of the

In sandy earth
or deep
in valley soil
I grow,
a wildflower
thriving
on your love.

Song of Songs 2:1

We find love by loving

Shendl Diamond /Translation by Marcia Falk

golden rule, to "do unto others as you would have them do unto you."

- *Hospitality teaches the joy of self-emptying.* The Bedouin spare neither themselves nor their possessions in their efforts to be hospitable. Real sacrifice is involved; there's nothing easy about offering your last morsel of food or the shelter of your home to someone you've never set eyes on before. Yet through this practice of humbly serving the needs of others, Bedouins find life. Witness the tale told by Theodore Lascaris, an emissary of Napoleon Bonaparte who found hospitality in the tent of a Bedouin widow. Although destitute, the woman killed and roasted her last sheep to feed her guest. When asked why she made this extraordinary gesture, she replied, "If you entered the dwelling of a living person and did not find hospitality there, it would be as though you had paid a visit to the dead."[6]

Here we discern a great law of the spiritual life: that denying oneself to serve the needs of others brings peace and happiness in its wake. "Only the lowly," said Rabbi Simhah Bunam of Psyshcha, "are able to comprehend the highness of God." Rabbi Nachman of Bratzlav, savoring the paradox, wrote that humility "causes a person to advance and keeps him from falling from his high level. . . . we must pray and plead with God to make us worthy of true humility and lowliness."[7]

Bedouins live every day on this paradoxical ladder of humbleness, on which those who descend find themselves raised up, while those who ascend wind up at the bottom. Self-emptying brings self-fulfillment; this is palpably evident in Thesinger's final comment on his stay among the Bedouins: "they had almost convinced me that I had done them a kindness staying with them."

Seeing the Other as God

I described briefly in chapter 4 the charitable work of Mother Teresa, who plucks maggots from the ulcerated flesh of the Calcutta poor and then, with supernal tenderness and solicitude, escorts these suffering souls into her home where they find food, shelter, clothing, and love. How can she do this? we ask in wonder. How can she bear the ugliness, the stench, the violence, the suffering? In part it is because Mother Teresa has learned the same lessons in humility as have the Bedouin. "I am God's pencil," she has said, "A tiny bit of pencil with which he writes what he likes."[8]

But there is something else at work here, something possibly even more profound. When most people look at the beggars of Calcutta, they see nothing but filth, disease, and pain. They mutter a prayer or toss a coin, avert their heads, and hasten on their way. But when Mother Teresa looks at this human detritus, she sees the face of God:

> In the slums I see Christ in the distressing disguise of the poor. . . . Those lepers, those dying, those hungry, those naked: they are Jesus! . . . It is a privilege for us to serve them, because in serving them we are really serving Christ himself who said, "I was hungry, I was naked, I was homeless, I was sick. . . . You did it to me."[9]

To see God in other people is to share in their misery as well as their glory. There's nothing pleasant about washing lepers or feeding the dying. But in these activities Mother Teresa finds "something beautiful for God." Obviously, by beauty she means here something more than pleasing ornamentation or a lovely sheen. She speaks of the beauty to be discovered through that self-emptying hospitality in which—as the Bedouin know—guest becomes host, and host servant. Listen to this excerpt from her speech accepting the Nobel Peace Prize:

> [We] must give to each other until it hurts. It is not enough for us to say: I love God, but I do not love my neighbor. St. John says you are a liar if you love God and you don't love your neighbor. How can you love God whom you do not see, if you do not love your neighbor whom you see, whom you touch, with whom you live. And so this is very important for us to realize that love, to be real, has to hurt.[10]

The Rules of Hospitality

We may summarize the lessons of the Bedouin and Mother Teresa, of Bilbo Baggins and Tumnus the Faun, in two golden rules of hospitality:

- *Remember the other.* Your guest needs your help. Rush forward with assistance, with food, shelter, warmth, and good tidings. In so doing you are imitating the ways of God, who answers our needs without hesitation or skimping.
- *Forget yourself.* You are here to serve, not to be served. The hearth, the kitchen, the bed are yours; your needs have been met—at least, your physical needs. As for your spiritual needs, see to them by helping others with open arms and open hearts.

BEING WITH OTHERS:
A CONTEMPLATIVE HARVEST

Generosity

A few years ago, I was seated in one of our local ice-cream shops, sharing a cup of chocolate frozen yogurt with my son John, when I heard someone cough just behind me. I swiveled around and found myself facing a bone-thin young man, poorly shaved and dressed in army fatigues. A small girl clung to his side. I'm sorry to admit it, but I felt irritated, for this specter and his waif had interrupted a pleasant conversation. I waited impatiently for him to speak.

"Excuse me," he said. "I—my wife and my kids and I—our car has broken down." He gestured vaguely out the window. "We need twenty dollars to get it repaired. We want to go home to Ludlow."

Twenty dollars? Immediately, annoyance prickled across my chest and into my solar plexus. *You've got to be kidding,* I thought. *This is another scam, like that con artist in New York City who wheedled fifty dollars out of me with a made-up story about a missed bus and an ill mother.* So I looked him in the eye and lied through my teeth.

"Sorry, I don't have any change."

I turned back to my son—and several things happened at once. It dawned on me that I had lied, and that my son had heard me lie (although I was certain that he didn't understand how to count money). And an instant later, I realized with rock-hard certainty that the beggar had been telling the truth. I turned around, ready to offer him what he needed, just in time to see the front door of the yogurt shop swinging shut.

This story has a coda: an hour later, walking my son around town, I spotted the young man accosting another passerby, obviously asking for money. This time, he had his wife in tow. I crossed the street to avoid meeting his eyes.

What interests me most about this memory is the shame I felt at my failure to help. I knew that I had dropped the ball in a crucial human interaction; that I had behaved poorly toward this stranded family, my son, and myself; that I had lost an opportunity to open my heart to a fellow traveler on our common journey. In the glare of my remorse, I saw clearly for one precious moment the divine nature of giving alms, lending a hand, responding to the pleas of others—in a word, of *generosity.*

All religions celebrate generosity. They value it so highly that one's motive in giving becomes secondary to the charitable act itself. The Baal Shem Tov said:

If you do a good deed but have an ulterior motive, it is better not to do it at all. The only exception is charity. Even though there may be an ulterior motive, it is still a good deed, since you sustain the poor, no matter what your motive is.[11]

In Buddhism, the virtue of giving is known as *dana*, and it holds the place of honor among personal spiritual practices. To Theravada Buddhists, *dana* comes first in the litany of ways to acquire merit; to Mahayana Buddhists, *dana* begins the ten perfections on the path of the bodhisattva (the heroic figure who stands on the threshold of Buddhahood, seeking awakening for the sake of all sentient beings). Indeed, the bodhisattva is the very embodiment of *dana*, as he or she gives of himself or herself without stinting—even to the point of postponing enjoyment of the fruits of enlightenment—to work for the salvation of all beings. *Dana* may take the form of giving Buddhist teachings, money, or food. Whatever its mode, it always involves sacrifice; a celebrated Jataka tale (a story of the Buddha in a previous incarnation) includes an account of how, during one lifetime as a rabbit, the Buddha offered himself as food for a starving wayfarer.

Perhaps the most impressive religious manifestation of generosity occurs among the Jains of India. Following a teaching of great antiquity, Jains organize their lives around the doctrine of *ahimsa*, or nonviolence. All organic structures—stones, rivers, fires, winds, trees, spiders, elephants, human beings—are understood as alive and deserving of tender care, in order to help their struggle toward salvation. Some Jains cover their mouths with a small white cloth to avoid inhaling insects, and most prefer not to eat after dark, for fear of consuming unseen bugs. For the same reason, water is always strained before drinking. Most Jains avoid working in agriculture, which entails the cutting of plants, digging of soil, squashing of bugs, and other unacceptable events. This extreme solicitude toward tiny animals has impressive repercussions in contemplative practice. Jains ordinarily walk with great mindfulness, eyes downcast, to avoid treading on insects or worms; similarly, sitting meditation is highly regarded because when stationary one is less likely to do harm to other beings.

Lovingkindness with Sharon Salzberg

Sharon Salzberg, cofounder of the Insight Meditation Center in Barre, Massachusetts, pours me a cup of tea as we sit in her dining room overlooking the barren winter hills of central Massachusetts. Through the window I see men and women strolling around the grounds of the center, some practicing walking meditation, others running errands. They shiver against the cold—the temperature is pushing zero—underscoring the warmth of Salzberg's dining room, of her hospitality, and of her words. She is telling me about a Buddhist practice that she has engaged in for over a decade: *metta,* or lovingkindness.

"*Metta* practice teaches us our own capacity for love," says Salzberg. "We are capable of much more love than we imagine. The Buddha said that the mind is naturally radiant and pure. Through *metta* practice, we discover the heart's capacity. We discover that the heart is large enough to include everybody."

This practice, Salzberg says, can be undertaken in any circumstance: while doing sitting meditation or walking down the street, while washing dishes or driving the car. If you do *metta* practice during sitting meditation, she explains, the first step is to look for the good in yourself. Simply think about yourself, your way of being and doing, and recognize whatever seems good or right. If you can't find anything good, then you simply honor your wish to be happy. "The urge to happiness is universal and good, a mark of life," she says, adding that "All beings want to be happy, but very few know how."

The practice is then extended by looking for the good in others. "*Metta,*" says Salzberg, "literally means friendship." If you can find nothing good in another, then you simply reflect on the other's wish to be happy—itself a reflection of your own wish. Salzberg recommends that in this preliminary exercise, you choose a person with whom you have no emotional entanglements—like a bank teller or store clerk.

Another form of *metta* practice comes into play when you are out in the world, perhaps simply by strolling down the street. As strangers come your way, you offer each of them one of four classical phrases, which Salzberg calls "expressions of the heart":

May you be free from danger.
May you have mental happiness.
May you have physical happiness.
May you have ease of well-being.

Salzberg suggests that you make these offerings silently to whomever you encounter—a police officer, a child, a robin, an alley cat. Then, she says, "You see what happens. You might make a connection with that being, or you might simply feel less fear, or you might have a greater sense of being grounded in yourself." She cautions, however, that results are unpredictable: "Once a friend of mine started sending *metta* to a small angry dog on a path, and it bit him."

Metta practice, warns Salzberg, has its dangers. Used improperly, it can lead to complacency or, conversely, to a devastating feeling of self-deficiency. But under the guidance of a skilled teacher, Salzberg says, *metta* practice can profoundly affect one's life. She recalls one student who had a terrible year, filled with pain and suffering. What sustained her through her agony? "The thought," says Salzberg, "that somewhere in the world, someone was directing lovingkindness her way. To know that this energy existed, and that she was receiving it—what an extraordinary support that was."

Friendship

Surely one of the principal ways of "being with others" is through friendship. Strangely enough, the great religions have little to say on the subject. The reason, one suspects, is the very ordinariness of the theme. We learn about friendship in early childhood, from parents and peers. What need is there of contemplative counsel? Happily, poets and philosophers have stepped into the breach. In *De Amicitia*, Cicero rejoices in the splendor of friendship, explains its moral basis, and describes the virtues that it requires:

> Friendship is just this and nothing else: complete sympathy in all matters of importance, plus goodwill and affection, and I am inclined to think that with the exception of wisdom, the gods have given nothing finer to men than this. . . . Those who say that virtue is man's highest good, are of course very inspiring; but it is to this very virtue that friendship owes its beginning and its identity; without virtue friendship cannot exist at all.[12]

To go by Cicero's definition, true friendship is rarer than platinum, for who can steer a steady course of "complete sympathy in all matters of importance"? The truth, however, is that while virtue may make a friendship, friendship makes for virtue. We make friends because we wish to be open and affectionate toward others; our friends in turn offer a field for the free exercise of these virtues, and thus help us to better ourselves. Listen to this passage from Ralph Waldo Emerson:

> O friend, my bosom said,
> Through thee alone the sky is arched,
> Through thee the rose is red;
> All things through thee take nobler form,

And look beyond the earth;
The mill-round of our fate appears
A sun-path in thy worth.
Me, too, thy nobleness has taught
To master my despair;
The fountains of my hidden life
Are through thy friendship fair.

Friendship, says Emerson, clarifies one's seeing, vivifies thinking, glorifies feeling. Friendship masters despair, brings the nobility of all things to the fore, sets the heart free of care. The result of these gifts is the purification of the soul: "The fountains of my hidden life / Are through thy friendship fair."

A contemporary of Emerson's, Thomas Carlyle, pinpoints the exact method by which friendship strengthens the inner life:

How were friendship possible? In mutual devotedness to the Good and the True; otherwise impossible; except as Armed Neutrality, or hollow Commercial League. . . . Infinite is the help man can yield to man.

True friendship exists when human beings share a love of goodness and truth. Two friends alone, like two legs on a table, offer a wobbly situation at best. But two friends anchored to a third, spiritual center form a rock-solid foundation to support everything that comes: hardship, suffering, exaltation, love. True friend-

Without virtue, friendship cannot exist

ship between two human beings exists only when there is a third friend present: call this third friend God, or dharma, or simply the sacred.

While discussions of friendship are scarce in traditional religion, symbols of friendship abound. One remarkable example is the sacred pipe of the Lakota Sioux. In 1947, a young scholar of Native American religions named Joseph Epes Brown tracked down Black Elk—the remarkable visionary whom we have already encountered—in Nebraska, where the old Lakota was working as a seasonal potato-picker. "During that first encounter," writes Brown, "we simply sat side-by-side on a sheepskin and silently smoked the red stone pipe I had brought with me as an offering in the traditional manner."[13] Through this humble gesture, Brown began to gain Black Elk's acceptance and, eventually, access to the spiritual lore of this great sage.

This pipe, often called a "peace pipe," is the central unifying symbol of the Lakota, employed in medicine, vision quests, gatherings among friends, and on countless other occasions. According to Brown, every aspect of the pipe carries meaning:

> The pipes . . . are understood to be an axis joining and defining a path between heaven and earth. Microcosmically the pipe is identified with human beings, the stem being the breath passage leading to the bowl, which is the spiritual center or heart. In solemn prayer, as each grain of carefully prepared tobacco is placed in the pipe, mention is made of some aspect of creation, so that when the bowl is full it contains the totality of time, space, and all of creation including humankind.[14]

Brown adds that

> The filled pipe is thus Totality, so that when the fire of the Great Spirit is added, a divine sacrifice is enacted in which the Universe and humankind are reabsorbed within the Principle, and become what in reality they are.[15]

All who smoke the pipe unite under the guidance and protection of Wakan Tanka (the Great Spirit). Often the smoking of the pipe will conclude with the declaration, "We are all related," a clear affirmation that the pipe symbolizes spiritual friendship.

A Note on Practice

When it comes to being with others, nothing beats courtesy, kindness, and common sense. There's nothing esoteric about hospitality, lovingkindness, generosity, and friendship, the four topics covered in this chapter. Most of us learned at our mother's knee the basic rules that govern being with others. At the same time, there exist a number of specific practices, from Buddhist *dana* to Jain *ahimsa*, that shed light on a particular aspect of being with others. Some of these practices, such as the *metta* exercises taught by Sharon Salzberg, can be used by anyone; others, such as the smoking of the sacred pipe among the Lakota, belong within a specific cultural-spiritual context. All these practices help to relieve suffering, inspire love, and bring lasting joy.

And yet: something more is called for. For my hospitality may be shabby, my generosity pinched, my lovingkindness timid, my friendship violent. How many times have I tossed a coin at a beggar while refusing to look him in the eye? Something dies in me in that moment of cowardice, and perhaps something dies in the beggar as well. How can I give my food, my money, my time, my roof, in a spirit of genuine kinship, ready to greet the one who receives my gift as brother or sister?

Here, I believe, the teachings of Mother Teresa come to our aid. We need, above all, to see others *as they really are.* Ordinarily, we cover people with masks, and see this one as a preening peacock, that one as a chattering monkey. We can begin by not imposing our likes and dislikes on other people. What an extraordinary act of friendship, to free people from our judgments and biases!

To see others as they are, we must bear witness to their essential beauty. To approach a beggar without illusions is to see him cloaked in rags (and emphatically not to deny the reality of those rags), but also to see him as cloaked in the dignity of a child of God—to see him, in Mother Teresa's simple formulation, as Christ. A Buddhist might say that we must see the beggar as a potential bodhisattva; indeed, the teaching can be found in one form or another in all religions. Cyril Connolly quipped that "in every fat man, a thin one is wildly signaling to be let out." I believe that in every person, a spark of the divine is wildly signaling to be acknowledged and loved. Let us greet other people as beings of infinite mystery and inviolable dignity, deserving by their very nature our love and respect. Then we will see hospitality, generosity, lovingkindness, and friendship flow effortlessly from us to them and from them to us, and being with others will be, as it should, a blessing without end.

Scribe   Bill Aron

seven

WORDS

*I*t was in 1987, on a rainy morning in downtown Tokyo, that I lost the power of words.

It happened like this:

I had arrived in Japan the night before on a flight from Vancouver that featured bad food, wailing kids, and patches of turbulence that rattled my teeth. I didn't sleep a wink. In a daze, I stumbled off the plane, into a taxi driven by a white-gloved young man who crooned old Elvis Presley tunes as we careened toward downtown Tokyo, and finally, at 4:00 A.M., into a Western-style bed at a luxury hotel renowned for its ankle-deep carpets and enormous bathrooms (the latter a rarity in space-pinched Japan).

The next morning, I gulped down some *kohi* and made for the streets. Tokyo at last! My head swam with images culled from textbooks, novels, and Kurosawa films: Admiral Peary laying siege to the shogun; geisha girls hobbling around in clumpy wooden shoes; cherry blossoms falling onto tranquil Zen ponds. This was my first visit to Japan, and I was eager to see it all. Leaving the hotel, I snapped open my umbrella, checked my tourist map, and turned left toward the subway stop. My destination was central Tokyo.

Instantly the noise of the city—inconceivable to one who has not been in Japan—assailed me. Horns bleated, trucks rumbled, sirens wailed, loudspeakers blared from buses, crosswalks, storefronts, and *pachinko* parlors, all against the general background roar of twenty million voices. The voices, I noticed, sounded hectic, urgent—but what were they urging? All at once, it dawned on me that I had no idea what they were saying. Even the Indo-European roots that I ordinarily leaned upon in foreign lands had vanished. *No matter*, I thought, *I'll look for signs.*

I found the signs, millions of them. Tokyo is so plastered with messages that it makes Times Square look like a Shaker meeting room. But all the writing was in kanji, that extraordinary script that looks, to the untrained eye, like the jagged spikes of an electrocardiogram.

I whirled around. No voice made sense. No sign made sense. The word, source of all sense, had vanished without a trace. I had no linguistic handholds; I was teetering on a verbal abyss. The final blow came when I arrived, by sheer chance, at the subway entrance. For a while I glared at the colorful panel of slots, dials, and levers, all carefully marked in undecipherable code, ready to dispense tickets to various longed-for destinations. Although I was fifteen minutes by subway from downtown Tokyo, I might as well have been on the moon. I turned around and headed back to bed.

In time I learned enough Japanese phrases to ride the bullet trains and order octopus on a stick. And throughout this episode I retained, of course, my knowledge of English, more precious to me than my money belt. I still had words to spend. But that first morning in Tokyo I caught a glimpse of somthing literally unspeakable: the possibility of a life without words.

Imagine a world stripped of words and you arrive at Hell: a world without communication, without exchange, without love. Words make us human, as Walker Percy explains:

> As soon as one . . . comes face to face with the nature of language, one also finds himself face to face with the nature of man. What took place when the first man uttered a mouthy little sound and the second man understood it, not as a sign to be responded to, but as "meaning" something they beheld in common? The first creature who did this is almost by minimal definition the first man.[1]

Words are intimately connected to thought, to the very flow of consciousness. "How can I tell what I think till I see what I say?" asked E. M. Forster. At first glance, this quip may be no more than a gloss on the old saw, "think before you speak," but I think that Forster is driving at something more profound. He is suggesting that thought and speech are one and the same; that our thoughts lead at best a shadow existence until they are married to words. As another old saw has it: "Speech is the mother, not the handmaid of thought."

Monks debate, Dharamsala, India

Approaching this level of being—the very act that makes us human—we immediately enter the religious realm. Words, no less than silence, escort us to the spirit. Listen to Whitman exult in the inner life of words:

All words are spiritual—nothing is more spiritual than words.—Whence are they? along how many thousands and tens of thousands of years have they come? those eluding, fluid, beautiful, fleshless, realities, Mother, Father, Water, Earth, Me, This, Soul, Tongue, House, Fire.

Whitman, a sublime artist but a slipshod analyst, never explains just why words are so spiritual. Emerson gives the answer: "Words and deeds," he says, "are . . . modes of the divine energy." To turn an inchoate thought into words is a divinely inspired act, like turning water into wine. Words ground us in the sacred, as all religions affirm. The Gospel of John begins with the remarkable declaration that "in the beginning was the Word and the Word was with God, and the Word was God," thereby equating Christ and Logos (the ultimate reality of the cosmos, from the Greek for "word"). Islam proclaims the Koran as the literal word of God. The Buddhist koan, a paradox constructed from words ("What is the sound of one hand clapping?"), is intended to point directly toward ultimate Reality.

How we use words, and how words use us, greatly determines the quality of our everyday lives. "We are all made of words," writes the Kiowa author N. Scott Momaday. "Our most essential being consists in language. It is the element in which we think and dream and act, in which we live our daily lives. There is no way in which we can exist apart from the morality of a verbal dimension."[2] Our life requires words as surely as it requires air; it's no accident that we breathe and speak through the same bodily channel. In the Amassalik Eskimo language, the word for "to breathe" also means "to make poetry." A Netsalik Eskimo named Orpingalik presents a similar idea:

> How many songs I have I cannot tell you. I keep no count of such things.
> There are so many occasions in one's life when a joy or a sorrow is felt in
> such a way that the desire comes to sing; and so I only know that I have
> many songs. All my being is song, and I sing as I draw breath. . . . It is just
> as necessary for me to sing as it is to breathe.[3]

In ordinary life, we encounter words in four fundamental ways: through speech, reading, writing, and silence. We'll explore each of these modes in turn, beginning with the most fundamental of all, the world of speech.

CONTEMPLATIVE CLOSE-UP: SPEECH

You can find more than eggs and milk in the neighborhood grocery store: you can find wisdom as well. A while back, I took John, who was five at the time, to our local gourmet market. Soon enough he grew antsy and began drumming on some large bins of brine-soaked pickles, to the vexation of the proprietor. I decided to lure John from his musical debut by showing him some of the odd foods on display. The chocolate-covered ants wowed him; the shaggy mushrooms with six-inch caps amazed him; but what really sent him over the top were the cows' tongues—long, flabby slabs of gray-brown meat wrapped in plastic. They looked dead, very dead. My son stuck out his own tongue. "Ugh!"

"Your tongue is different," I said, admiring its healthy pink coating.

"I know, Dad," he said in an exasperated voice. "My tongue talks."

Indeed. This "little member," as the Bible calls it, is a most peculiar organ. For as John said, it talks. It sets us apart from the animals, and at times it sets us apart from one another. For the tongue declares war, destroys reputations, topples empires. But it also woos lovers, declaims poetry, praises God. The tongue unites us as well.

Ambivalence toward the tongue and its deeds runs throughout sacred writings. "A wholesome tongue is a tree of life," reads the Book of Proverbs (15:4), but the same text immediately warns that "death and life are in the power of the tongue" (18:21). Jesus advises that "by thy words thou shalt be justified, and by thy words thou shalt be condemned" (Matt. 12:37). These statements suggest that everyday speech carries great potential for good or evil and imposes on us an equally great responsibility. How many times have I blurted out something and then wished I could retract it? How many times have I remained silent and later reviled myself for not saying what was needed? Conversely, in a moment of inspiration I may say something at just the right moment and staunch a terrible wound, or I may keep silent when attacked and as a result prevent a skirmish from becoming an all-out war.

As in the case of simple pleasures, there exist very few religious practices dealing with ordinary, workaday speech. However, the traditions do emphasize three important points:

1. *Few words serve better than many.* In many cases, taciturnity is a mark of spiritual maturity. We've all had the experience of joining in a group conversation dominated by one or two voices. When a third voice suddenly breaks in, the heavy talkers stop, and everyone takes notice. Words, like gems, are more precious when they are rare.

2. *Beauty of expression matters, but the truth matters more.* The Hasidim tell the following story:

> A learned man who partook of the Sabbath meal at the home of Rabbi Baruch Medzibozer, the grandson of the Baal Shem Tov, said to his host: "Let us now hear you talk of your doctrine; you speak so beautifully!"
>
> "May I be struck dumb ere I speak beautifully!" was Rabbi Baruch's reply; and he said nothing more.[4]

Reb Baruch isn't condemning beauty per se; indeed, the same Hasidim who tell this tale grow rapturous over the beauties of Torah. The point is that the truth comes garbed in sackcloth as well as silk, and we must beware of mistaking the silk for what it wraps.

3. *All words connect us to the sacred.* Another Hasidic saying, from the Baal Shem Tov, reminds us that

> thy profane words are composed of the same letters of the alphabet as thy sacred words. Therefore, in the former, too, there is holiness. Bring them to their Source.[5]

Even cursing, by the very fact of being speech, shares mysteriously in the divine nature. This observation is not meant to excuse letting your tongue run riot the next time that you stub your toe; rather, the Baal Shem Tov's remark recognizes the preciousness of all words, and thus the need to guard the tongue as if it were a temple gate—which it is.

The World of Prayer

Although the great religions remain terse when it comes to ordinary words, they speak eloquently and at great length on the subject of sacred words—that is, words of prayer. Every tradition has its own beloved prayers; we have encountered some already, such as the Buddhist sutras chanted at the home altar before breakfast. Here I'd like to focus on a particular kind of prayer: the short, repetitive prayer—sometimes no more than a single word or phrase—that lies at the center of contemplative practice around the world. Let us consider examples from three different traditions: mantra, *dhikr*, and Jesus prayer. Each involves the repetition of a brief phrase that is understood to contain the condensed wisdom of the whole tradition; each can be said in any circumstance—sitting on a cushion in the morning sitting, driving a car, typing correspondence, eating dinner.

MANTRA

Ever since the Beatles sat at the feet of the Maharishi Mahesh Yogi in the 1960s, the word *mantra* (Sanskrit for "sacred utterance") has been part of the Western spiritual vocabulary. Most of us know that it refers to a sacred word or set of words repeated at great length. But perhaps the primordial power of the mantra is not clearly understood. According to Indian tradition, a mantra is eternal and uncreated, divine power itself in the form of sound. To utter a mantra is therefore to put oneself into an intimate relationship with God or the Absolute. While some mantras serve special purposes—to cast a spell, for example—most often they work to still the mind and inspire the heart through simple, repetitive prayer.

Perhaps the most famous of all mantras is the single syllable OM, understood to be the sound and symbol of ultimate reality, the divine word in its purest form; it is perhaps the oldest mantra known, dating back nearly 3,000 years. Another mantra, familiar to anyone who spends much time on the streets of major Western cities, celebrates various names and incarnations of Vishnu, the all-pervading godhead:

Hare Krishna
Hare Krishna
Krishna Krishna
Hare Hare
Hare Rama Hare Rama
Rama Rama Hare Hare

While we associate mantras most often with Hinduism, they are an important part of daily religious practice in other religions as well. A celebrated Buddhist mantra, *Om Mani Padme Hum* ("Hail to the jewel in the lotus"), is repeated countless times each day by millions of Buddhists; in addition, it flutters on prayer flags, revolves within prayer wheels, and is carved on walls and floors throughout Tibet and northern India. According to one Buddhist text, this mantra is "the essence of all happiness, prosperity and knowledge and the source of the great liberation."[6]

In traditional Hinduism, a mantra will be recited only within a ritual context and under the direction of a guru. Nowadays, however, the use of mantras has become democratized, and they may be recited in any and all circumstances. Some of my Buddhist friends recite their mantras silently, some murmur in a low tone, and others speak their mantras aloud. All insist on the value of reflecting upon the mantra's meaning while reciting it; as they point out, the etymological root of "mantra" is *man*, Sanskrit for "to think," and to say a mantra thus implies conscious pondering rather than a mindless trancelike bliss. Nonetheless, a mantra's real power lies in the miraculous nature of the sound itself, a chord in the song of the absolute, uncreated cosmos.

DHIKR

The most common prayer practice of Islamic mystics, or Sufis, is the *dhikr*, the recollection of God. *Dhikr* brings one into a state of purity and tranquillity, as the Koran proclaims: "In the remembrance of Allah do hearts find rest" (13:28).[7]

Through the centuries, Sufis practicing *dhikr* have developed a rich technology of brief vocal prayer. The most basic form entails simply repeating "Allah." This act, it is said, brings the one who prays directly into the divine presence. In some Sufi circles, "Allah" is repeated rapidly and eventually shortened until only the final syllable, pronounced "Hu," remains. Eventually even the "Hu" is dropped and only breathing remains, the ground of life itself, the essence of Allah. Alternatively, a Muslim might repeat "La ilah illa Allah," rejoicing in the liquid alliteration of this first part of the Muslim profession of faith, "There is no god but God."

Unlike the five daily periods of ritual prayer, *dhikr* can be practiced anywhere and anytime. It may be said aloud or silently, although it should be noted that the Koran counsels a middle course: "Be not loud voiced in thy worship nor yet silent therein, but follow a way between" (Surah 17:110).[8] Traditionally, a Sufi doing *dhikr* will sit cross-legged, right leg on top of left leg, right hand on top of left hand. The prayer may be said in rhythm with the breath, "Allah" being recited on every out-breath.

With practice, Sufis say, *dhikr* passes from the tongue into the heart and becomes part of the innermost being; some speak of the prayer passing into every limb of the body, so that, as Anne-Marie Shimmel puts it, "the seeker becomes, eventually, completely heart; every limb of his is a heart recollecting God." Finally silence reigns, as the seeker's ego is extinguished and only God remains. "True *dhikr* is that you forget your *dhikr*," goes the saying.

JESUS PRAYER

In 1961 a young woman named Franny Glass, down from college to visit her boyfriend Lane, plucked from her pocketbook "a little clothbound book" and introduced millions of readers to one of the great religious classics. The scene unfolds in J. D. Salinger's bestselling novel *Franny and Zooey*, and the book that Franny made famous is *The Way of a Pilgrim*, a nineteenth-century Russian memoir that talks, as Franny put it, about "this really incredible method of praying"—a method known commonly as the Jesus prayer.

The Jesus prayer entails the ceaseless repetition of the phrase "Lord Jesus Christ, Son of God, have mercy on me, a sinner." Often the prayer is compressed to "Lord Jesus Christ have mercy on me" or even to the bare bones of the one word "Jesus," endlessly repeated. Although the prayer has been in use for nearly 2,000 years, our best source of information about it remains *The Way of a Pilgrim*. Of the author of this extraordinary text we know next to nothing: only that he was a young Russian with a withered arm, and that one fine autumn day in the 1850s he set out, carrying only bread husks, salt, and a tattered Bible, in search of the secret of continuous prayer. With the help of a *staretz*—a holy man of the Orthodox church—he discovered the answer in the methodical repetition of the Jesus prayer. Here he reports some of his results:

> Sometimes my heart would feel as though it were bubbling with joy, such lightness, freedom, and consolation were in it. Sometimes I felt a burning love for Jesus Christ and for all God's creatures. Sometimes my eyes brimmed over with tears of thankfulness to God, who was so merciful to me, a wretched sinner.... Sometimes by calling upon the name of Jesus I was overwhelmed with bliss, and now I knew the meaning of the words, "The Kingdom of God is within you."[9]

The Pilgrim recommends endless repetitions of the prayer; he himself says it up to 6,000 times a day! A prayer rope may be used to keep track of repetitions. Some people synchronize the prayer with the breath; in my experience, this is especially fruitful in conjunction with an abridged version of the prayer. You say

"Lord Jesus Christ" on the in-breath, during which you invite God's sanctifying presence, and "have mercy on me" on the out-breath, during which you expel your sins. At the end of the out-breath, of course, you are momentarily out of air—that is, helpless and thus dependent upon the divine mercy.

As with the other brief contemplative prayers discussed here, the Jesus prayer can be said under any circumstances; I turn to it often while cradling my infant son Andy in the middle of the night. In time, the Pilgrim tells us, the Jesus prayer becomes "self-activating": it moves from the mind into the heart—the same route followed, as you will recall, by the Islamic *dhikr*—where it sounds of its own accord, whether we attend to it or not; it even continues during sleep.

Brother David Steindl-Rast, O.S.B., author of The Music of Silence *and other works, discusses the Jesus prayer and other Christian contemplative prayers.*[10]

How I Pray

BY DAVID STEINDL-RAST

My earliest recollection of formal prayer is this: Resting on her bed after our noonday meal, my grandmother, rosary in hand, would let the beads glide through her fingers, silently moving her lips. When I remember how large her bed loomed from my perspective, I realize that I must have still been small. Yet when I asked her to teach me this mysterious game, she did. The stories behind the fifteen mysteries as my grandmother told them to me stayed in my mind and grew in my heart. Like seedlings taking root in good soil, they kept on growing and sending out runners. To this day, like an old strawberry patch, they keep bearing fruit.

Some thirty years later, on a different continent, my grandmother was again resting on her bed and I was kneeling next to her; this time, she was dying. My mother also knelt by her mother's deathbed, and together the two of us were reciting from the English breviary the prayers for the dying. Grandmother was in a coma, but she seemed restless. She would raise her left hand a little and let it fall back on the bed, again and again. We could hear the tinkling of the silver rosary that was wrapped around her wrist. Finally we caught on. We stopped the psalms and started the Sorrowful Rosary. At its familiar phrases Grandmother relaxed, and when we came to the mystery of Christ's death on the cross, she peacefully gave her life-breath back to God.

Another childhood memory of mine is connected with the Angelus prayer. All over my native Austria the chorus of Angelus bells rises from every church steeple at dawn, at high noon, and again before dark in the evening. At school one day—I was a first-grader then—I happened to stand by an open window on the top floor looking down on "the campus" you might call it, for ours was a big, beautiful school built by the Christian Brothers. It was noon. Classes had just finished, and everywhere children and teachers came streaming out onto the courts and walkways. From so high up, the sight reminded me of an anthill on a hot summer day. Just then, the Angelus bell rang out from the church and at once all those busy feet down there stood still. "The angel of the Lord brought the message to Mary . . ." We had been taught to recite this prayer in silence. Then, the ringing slowed down; one last stroke of a bell and the anthill was swarming again.

Now, so many years later, I still keep that moment of silence at noon. Bells or no bells, I pray the Angelus. I let the silence drop like a pebble right into the middle of my day and send its ripples out over its surface in ever-widening circles. That is the Angelus for me: the Now of eternity rippling through time.

I'd like to recount one more memory here, the memory of my first encounter with the Jesus prayer, the Prayer of the Heart, as it is also called. By then, I was older but still a child, twelve maybe. I was sitting with my mother in our doctor's waiting room, resting my right hand first on one knee, then on the other, then on the armrest of my chair, then on the windowsill of a window from which I could see only a high hedge and some spiderwebs. My hand was heavily bandaged, and I had come here to have the doctor change those bandages. After I had examined for some time a jarful of live leeches, which country doctors at that time still kept for bloodletting, there wasn't anything else in this bare room to keep me entertained, and I was growing fidgety.

Then my mother said something that surprised me: "Russian people know the secret of never getting bored." The Olympic Games were my only association with Russians, but if there was a secret method for overcoming boredom I needed to learn it as soon as possible. Only years later, when I came across *The Way of a Pilgrim,* did I understand my mother's mysterious reference, for that book was a translation from the Russian. It did tell me at length about that secret of never getting bored, but my mother had managed to summarize it so simply that it made sense to a boy of twelve: "You need only repeat the name of Jesus over and over with every breath. That's all. The name of Jesus will remind you of so many good stories that you will never find the time long." I tried it and it worked.

Boredom, as it turned out, would

never be a problem in my life anyway; rather the contrary. Later, in fact, when the Jesus prayer became my steady form of praying, I came to think of it more as an anchor that keeps me grounded when life is anything but boring. To borrow a phrase from the Roman Missal, the Jesus prayer keeps my heart "anchored in lasting joy."

After I read *The Way of a Pilgrim*, I made myself a ring of wooden beads that I move, one bead at a time, as I repeat the Jesus prayer. This movement of my fingers has become so linked with that prayer that I can keep it going with the help of my prayer ring, even while I am reading or talking with someone. It goes on like background music, not in the foreground of my awareness and yet heard at all times.

The wording I've come to find most helpful is "Lord Jesus, mercy!" The Russian pilgrim used a longer form, and I have experimented with various versions, but this one suits me best. Most of the time it expresses my gratefulness: as I face a situation and take it all in, I see this given reality as one facet of God's ultimate gift, which is summed up in the name of Jesus. Then, breathing out, I say the second half of the prayer, and the sense is: "Oh, with what mercy you are showering me, moment by moment!" Sometimes, of course, "Mercy!" can also be my cry for

help, say, when I am dead tired and have to go on to meet a deadline, or when I am reading about the destruction of the rain forests or the tens of thousands of children that starve to death every twenty-four hours on this planet of plenty. "Mercy!" I sigh, "Mercy!" The Jesus prayer has become so connected with my breathing in and breathing out that it flows spontaneously much of the time. Sometimes, while I am falling asleep, the prayer goes on until it melds into the deep breathing of sleep.

The Rosary, the Angelus, the Jesus prayer, these are some of the formal prayers I find most nourishing. They are by no means the only ones, merely the ones most easily described. How could I even begin to tell you what the monastic Hours of prayer mean to me? I have recently written a small book about them, *The Music of Silence*, in which I try to show how not only monks, but anyone in any walk of life can enter into those times of day at which time itself prays. Or the Lord's Prayer, or the Creed. I find them inexhaustible; I'd have to write a whole book about each of them. Yet, here we are still in the realm of formal prayer, and formal prayer is only like a little bucket in which a toddler scoops up and pours out, scoops up and pours out, time and again, water from the ocean of prayer.

WORDS:
A CONTEMPLATIVE HARVEST

Storytelling: A Conversation with Joseph Bruchac

According to sociologist David Riesman, storytellers "are indispensable agents of socialization. They picture the world for the child and thus give both form and limits to his memory and imagination."[11] Nowhere are storytellers and their craft more important than in Native America. Until Sequoya constructed his syllabary in 1821, all Native American knowledge was transmitted by word of mouth. As a result, every aspect of Native American oral culture, including songs, prayers, and stories, became a finely tuned instrument capable of conveying information of great complexity and depth. N. Scott Momaday, discussing the power of story in Kiowa and other native cultures, remarks that

> Storytelling is imaginative and creative in nature. It is an act by which man strives to realize his capacity for wonder, meaning, and delight. It is also an act in which man invests and preserves himself in the context of ideas. Man tells stories in order to understand his experience, whatever it may be. The possibilities of storytelling are precisely those of understanding the human experience.[12]

In traditional native culture, stories exist only when spoken; they possess an immediacy, vigor, and presence denied the printed word. Oral stories live in a way that printed stories never can. It may be that our culture's very surfeit of printed words, with over 10,000 books published each year in America alone, is directly responsible for the modern degradation of words in general. We saw earlier that when a person of few words speaks, his words count; in the same way, a culture of few words means a culture that values its words (consider, for example, the gemlike nature of medieval manuscripts before the invention of moveable type). In Native America, words have power, and stories bring life.

To learn more about Native American storytelling and its place in everyday spiritual practice, I talked with Joseph Bruchac, an Abenaki storyteller and author of a number of books about Native America, many of them anthologies of traditional stories. Bruchac, a lean man with a friendly face and an exceptionally melodic voice, began by underscoring the importance of story: "Storytelling is one of our most effective means of communication." he said. "If you simply tell something to someone, they may listen or they may not. But if you tell a story, people always listen. Stories go right to the heart."

Stories have always been part of Bruchac's life. As a child, he lingered around the potbelly stove at the local general store, listening to grown-ups tell of ordinary life and extraordinary adventures. He also slipped into the woods whenever possible, an activity that he associates with his love of stories. "Storytelling links us to the earth. As a child, I loved the forest. If you don't go into nature, then it remains an abstraction, and you can't appreciate it or speak about it. A lot of what I do now, with my storytelling, is to take people into nature."

As a first audience for his own storytelling efforts, Bruchac chose children, in part because of his keen sense of story as a teaching device. "You have to tell stories to kids," he said. "Terrible things happen to kids if they are not told stories. When I work with prisoners, I find that they almost never had a chance to listen to stories as children. As a result, their economic poverty is matched by intellectual and spiritual poverty. Storytelling is a way of giving someone great and lasting wealth." Bruchac also considers storytelling to be a refined tool for inculcating moral behavior. "Native Americans tell stories to children instead of hitting them. A story encourages the child to listen and to look within."

But surely, I pointed out, the child needs more than self-contemplation. Sometimes he needs to be told what to do, if only for safety's safe. Bruchac agreed. "Native American stories present strategies for survival. They teach us about a variety of paths that we may follow. The things that occur to a character in a story may be about to occur to you, so if you listen to the story, you will learn about your possibilities. Most Native American stories are lesson stories. You might learn how to make fire, or which berries are good to eat—or learn about larger moral issues."

Bruchac then brought up a second reason for bringing stories into everyday life, one intimately linked to child-rearing: the need for community. He spoke glowingly of communities, large and small, and several times veered our discussion toward the exploits of his children. "It's very important to me to be part of a family—and not the most important part. The next generation is more important than the last." Bruchac sees the storyteller as a key figure in any communal culture: "Storytelling holds the community together. Without storytelling, without community, we are—quite literally—mentally unbalanced. Within community, stories always appear. They come as a gift. In my culture, the storyteller is the glue that holds it all together. In West Africa, where I lived for three years, I discovered an old tradition of the storyteller traveling from longhouse to longhouse, telling stories. That storyteller was the glue."

But what of those of us with no training in Native American, African, or other traditional forms of storytelling? How does Bruchac recommend that we bring this art into our everyday lives? "Trust the story," he said. "Don't try to retell it word for word. When you tell a story, it comes to life inside you, and you live within the story. Trust that life." As the first step in learning to tell stories, he recommends the following: "If you want to be a storyteller, learn how to listen. It is a Native American tradition to begin a story with 'Listen!' Listening is a lost art; instead of listening, people wait for an opportunity to break in. There's a four-part mantra in my family: listen, observe, remember, share. If you learn how to listen, you will learn how to share."

Reading

THE LESSONS OF CHU HSI

Reading is the art of welcoming other minds into one's own, of making room for new ideas, foreign landscapes, unknown creatures, exotic dreams. Reading, in other words, is the art of mental hospitality.

Sacred text, Ethiopian church, Jerusalem

Linda Connor

One of the soundest guides to reading as an inner discipline is the twelfth-century Chinese educator, metaphysician, government official, and conversationalist Chu Hsi. Although little known in the West, Chu Hsi ranked—at least until the Maoist revolution—as perhaps the most influential Chinese thinker of the past millennium; by the fourteenth century, his version of Confucianism had become state orthodoxy and was carefully committed to memory by all who wished to navigate the labyrinthine corridors of the Chinese civil service.

Chu Hsi wrote at great length about reading, an activity that he believed set the foundation for a sound moral and religious life. Reading for pleasure or for the gathering of facts repelled him; he saw reading as an exercise that sharpened intellect, deepened insight, and strengthened moral muscles.

Among Chu Hsi's prescriptions for reading are:

• *Read with attention.* To Chu Hsi, this means reading with body and mind alert but tranquil; only then will the text's inner meaning become clear. If attention flags, he recommends that the reader take a break and then restart:

> There is a method to book learning. Simply scrub clean the mind, then read. If you don't understand the text, put it down for the moment, wait until your thoughts have cleared, then pick it up and read it again.[13]

- *Savor the text.* Chu Hsi talks about reading a good book the way others talk about drinking a fine whiskey: "You must frequently take the words of the sages and pass them before your eyes, roll them around and around in your mouth, and turn them over and over in your mind."[14] He advises reading the same passage repeatedly, until its essence is absorbed. You must read, he says, until the author's words and thoughts have become your own, for "only then can there be real understanding."[15] You needn't fear that this will lead to boredom, for "our tenth reading . . . is different from our first reading, and our hundredth reading, likewise, is naturally different from our tenth."[16]

- *Read little, but read with care.* Chu Hsi scoffs at those people who try to read massive quantities of text; far better, he says, to read little with care than to read much carelessly. "If today you are able to read a page," he says, "read half a page; read that half page over and over with all your strength."[17]

- *Read out loud.* This practice is common in many traditions; the spoken word has a palpable presence that mental reading, even if subvocalized, can never have. Chu Hsi says:

  > In reading a text, we must recite it aloud. We can't just think about it. If our mouths recite it, our minds will feel calm, and its meaning will naturally become apparent.[18]

- *Be open to the text.* Don't impose your own ideas. Accept the vision of the writer, be it clumsy or eloquent, agreeable or off-putting. That which is of value will remain with you. Chu Hsi adds that you would do well to read without any ulterior motive; read for the sake of the text itself.

- *Begin with material that you can understand.* Readers sometimes find themselves bewildered by strange terminology or impenetrable ideas. If this is your experience, Chu Hsi recommends that you look for a clear, simple passage and start there; like a cave mouth leading into a vast underground network, this will provide entry into the complex inner meaning of the text.

LECTIO DIVINA

Over the last two millennia, the Christian tradition has cultivated a spiritual approach to reading known as *lectio divina* (Latin for "divine reading"). To understand *lectio*, it is useful to know that in many religious cultures reading is held to be closely akin to eating. Through reading, we receive the richest food imaginable. St. Augustine in his *Confessions* recalls his youthful astonishment upon discovering that his teacher, Ambrose, could read without moving his lips; in fourth-century Africa (as in Chu Hsi's twelfth-century China, and indeed in all eras and cultures that valued the sacred), reading was rumination; one chewed one's words, as a cow chewed its cud, to extract the maximum nutrition. Benedictine scholar Jean Le Clerq explains:

> In the Middle Ages, as in antiquity, they read usually, not as today principally with the eyes, but with the lips, pronouncing what they saw, and with the ears, listening to the words pronounced, hearing what is called "the voice of the pages." It is a real acoustical reading . . . one understands only what one hears, as we still say: "entendre le latin," which means to "comprehend" it.[19]

In this chewing, this rumination, this pondering and puzzling over one's dinner of words, lie the beginnings of *lectio divina.*

Lectio's method couldn't be simpler: Rather than gloss over the text, one ponders it. St. Benedict, who might be called the patron saint of *lectio divina,* advises his monks to read each book "carefully cover to cover,"[20] and prescribes two hours of *lectio* in the summer and up to four hours in the winter (when, happily, most of us like to curl up and read in any case). In its classical form, *lectio* includes four stages: reading, memorization, meditation, and prayer. One begins by reading a text— usually scripture—and memorizing key passages. Memorization locks the precious words within the safe of one's heart, where they remain available for conscious meditation and at the same time work in subliminal ways. Meditation on the text extracts its essence. Often this process will lead naturally into deeper levels of prayer; ideally, *lectio* becomes a dialogue between reader and writer—in the case of scripture, between reader and God. Guigo the Carthusian describes the sequence:

> It is as the Lord says: "Seek and you shall find, knock and it shall be opened to you" (Mt. 7:7). Seek in reading, and you will find in meditating; knock in praying, and you shall enter through contemplation.[21]

Although primarily applied to scripture or writings of the church fathers, the method of *lectio divina* may be adapted to other texts. Poetry, essays, memoirs, and the like may all contain passages worthy of memorization, meditation, and prayer. If we read these texts with care and love, we will discover what a splendid tool *lectio divina* can be for unveiling the luminosity of words.

TORAH STUDY: THE COUNSEL OF RABBI JONATHAN OMER-MAN

The first ritual wish uttered on behalf of a Jewish boy at his *bris* (circumcision) is "May he enter the realm of Torah!" To outsiders, this world may seem circumscribed, for the Torah, in its strictest definition, consists solely of the first five books of the Hebrew Bible. But Judaism teaches that the Torah is in fact an endless ocean stretching between the present moment and eternity. To study Torah is to assimilate into one's being the whole of the scriptures, indeed all the works of law, lore, and spiritual instruction in which Jews have heard the voice of God. As Rabbi Jonathan Omer-Man writes:

> The Torah is the repository of all wisdom. Within its stories, its laws, embedded even within the structure of the Hebrew language in which it is written, can be found all that a person needs to know on his or her path on this earth. . . . At deeper levels of understanding, the Torah is revealed to be a detailed map of the cosmos, of the Divine plan, of every facet of creation, even of the personality of the Creator.[22]

In a recent conversation, Rabbi Omer-Man, who directs Metivta, a center for contemplative Judaism in Los Angeles, offered three concrete suggestions for those people interested in learning how to read Torah and incorporate it into daily life:

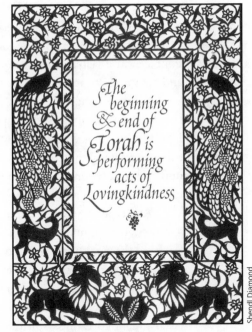

The beginning & end of Torah is performing acts of Lovingkindness

Shendl Diamond

- *Surrender to the text.* "I see scripture as a series of poems," Omer-Man said. "Poems don't have to be consistent with one another. Each has its own insight, and together they make an opus. We are too concerned with philology, with history. My aim is to get people to surrender to the text instead of mastering the text. This is a playful method, in the deepest sense of the word. It is creatively playful; it dares people to go in unexpected directions."
- *Hone your questions.* "The answers are all in the text," insists Omer-Man, "but the questions need to be refined. Working with a group, I find that over a year or two, questions become more refined, more appropriate to who and where the questioners are."
- *Expand your definitions.* "Talmud and mystical texts are all part of our Torah study. We see it as a seamless whole, from the first word of Genesis to the last word written on the subject. All study of Jewish texts reveals preexisting meaning. The Torah isn't just the five books of Moses; it is the five books

of Moses and everything since then. The totality of it is Torah. This is the justification for this kind of study. It requires ethical and personal work on oneself."

Writing

In 1577 a frail, small-boned, thirty-five-year-old barefoot friar found himself thrown into prison on trumped-up charges in Toledo, Spain. His cell, a window-less closet six feet wide by ten feet long, an oven in summer and an icebox in winter, became his home for nearly a year. During that time, he lived on moldy bread, water, and scraps of sardines. Three times a week he was stripped and scourged.

How might you or I deal with such torment? The little prisoner—whose name was Juan de Yepes y Alvarez, better known as St. John of the Cross—knew what to do. He paced, he prayed—and he wrote. With ink and paper supplied by a sympathetic warden, he penned lyrics of incomparable sensitivity and beauty. Four centuries later, these poems have been translated into a hundred languages and are valued as among the greatest of all religious poetry.

Similar stories of prison heroics abound; many is the literary masterpiece that has been composed to the jangle of cell keys, in the shadow of the iron grille. I tell the story of John of the Cross to point out that as long as one has some-thing to write with, the art of writing is always available, that it can be practiced under almost inconceivable duress, and that it can be for us, as it was for John, a lifeline to wisdom and hope.

Any type of writing can be a spiritual discipline. Dante wrote an epic; Basho, a travelogue; Donne, sermons and verse; Coleridge, essays; C. S. Lewis, novels. Each of these authors chose to work in a complex form, bending their wills and submitting their talents to the strict rules of the craft. For everyday purposes, however, another set of writers comes to mind: Dorothy Wordsworth, Fyodor Dostoyevsky, Pope John XXIII. What does this rather odd trio have in common? Each sought to express spiritual truths through the simplest, most homely of all literary forms—the diary or journal.

Journal writing, as anyone who visits a bookstore can testify, has become a very popular mode for spiritual expression. There's good reason for this. Journals are—or at least should be—spontaneous, revealing, and honest. Being utterly pri-vate, they can dispense with the disguises we wear in ordinary life. Journals can cut to the quick, unveil the heart. Journals reflect the immediacy of the moment and yet accrue day after day until they express a lifetime. Journals can be as eclectic as you wish; they can contain almost every other writing form: bits of poetry, scraps of song, rough drafts of novels. Journal-keeping is as easy as sharpening your pencil and bearing down.

The important thing is to bear down. Write whatever comes to your mind, no matter how pixilated or paltry. After all, every pencil has an eraser. But rarely will you need it, for you will discover, in rereading old diaries, that the embarrassing passages are as precious as the sober. Imagine the page as a painter's canvas; take a gob of red or yellow words and slap it down. Drench the paper in words. Let everything pour onto the page: ideas, memos, inspirations. In time you'll find your voice, and you'll begin to write with flair. Very rapidly, you'll discover that your journal—or poetry or novel or letters or song lyrics—becomes a means to greater self-understanding. Our thoughts remain embryonic while in the mind; they come to full term only upon delivery in words. In this sense, writing *is* thinking; and that is why so many traditions consider writing to be, at least potentially, an act of prayer.

Silence

My first experience of absolute silence came as a gift from a wayward squirrel. This squirrel, who has no name but who deserves a chapter of his own in the history of spirituality, for his actions changed many lives for the better and proved the reality of brotherly love, gnawed through a transformer wire near Buffalo, New York, on February 4, 1966. As anyone living on the East Coast of the United States at the time will remember, the result was the Great Blackout.

As the squirrel nibbled its way into history, I, along with millions of other bored teenagers, was watching Soupy Sales's afternoon television show—in my case, in the living room of my parents' house on Long Island. Just as Soupy reached for his chalk to write one of his famous double-entendre jokes on the blackboard, the screen crackled, shrank to a glaring white dot, and went blank. Had the television broken down? Curious, I switched to another channel. Nothing but frost. I tried another. More frost. Every channel was dead. Mystified and a bit worried—this was the 1960s, the Soviet Union still clawed at the throat of the West, and my thoughts immediately turned to nuclear war—I rushed to the radio. The airwaves emitted only a faint electronic hum. What in the world was going on?

I scooted outdoors and faced in the direction of New York City, fifteen miles to the east, half expecting to see a mushroom cloud. Instead, I saw nothing—not even the sky-glow of city lights that normally filled the horizon at this twilight hour. I didn't know what to make of all this, but I was beginning to enjoy the novelty of the experience. I headed back into the house. Inside, all was silent and still. I could hear no radio, no television, no record player, none of the omnipresent electronic gabble-and-gobble of my teenage years. There was no sound at all, other than the beating of my heart. Darkness reigned as well; the realm of light and the realm of sound had both been overthrown. There was nothing left to do but surrender to the new order of things. I shrugged my shoulders, snuggled down on the couch, and for the first time in my life, enjoyed the silence.

Later I learned that throughout the Northeast, the Great Blackout had brought great illumination into the lives of thousands of people; that stranger had rescued stranger, and neighbor had helped out neighbor; that people had fallen in love while trapped in elevators or on subway cars—nine months later, a mini baby boom rocked the region; that the churches had filled and the jails stayed empty (there was nearly no violence during the first Great Blackout). For a good chunk of the world's population, silence had finally arrived, and it had brought peace in its path.

Silence is the other side of words, their inner lining, their soul. The philosopher George Steiner observes that "language can only deal meaningfully with a special, restricted segment of reality. The rest, and it is presumably the much larger part, is silence."[23] Mother Teresa offers a more overtly religious view of the value of silence:

> We need to find God, and he cannot be found in noise and restlessness.
> God is the friend of silence. See how nature—trees, flowers, grass—
> grows in silence; see the stars, the moon and the sun, how they move in
> silence. . . . We need silence to be able to touch souls.[24]

In silence, we can hear the world, unhindered by the clamor of our own restless monkey minds. In silence, we hear ourselves, unhindered by the clamor of the world. In silence, we encounter the realities that shimmer behind the veil of appearances, of coming and going, of birth and death. That is why, to cite just one example from a vast range of world religious practices, a Lakota crying for a vision will enter a realm of absolute silence, broken only by the sound of prayers, burning tobacco, and wild beasts.

All religions make room for silence. Silence is the sound of eternity. "We learn speech from men, silence from the gods," wrote Plutarch. Early Buddhist texts describe the Buddha as beyond "the paths of speech," and his response to useless questions—those that "tend not to edification"—was often silence. John Climacus, the seventh-century Christian theologian, enumerates in one (rather long) sentence the spiritual treasures that silence guards:

Intelligent silence is the mother of prayer, freedom from bondage, custodian of zeal, a guard on our thoughts, a watch on our enemies, a prison of mourning, a friend of tears, a sure recollection of death, a painter of punishment, a concern with judgment, servant of anguish, foe of license, a companion of stillness, the opponent of dogmatism, a growth of knowledge, a hand to shape contemplation, hidden progress, the secret journey upwards.[25]

Among some religious groups, such as the Quakers—especially during the heyday of quietism—silence was considered the only adequate element in which to encounter God. Some Quaker meetings met regularly for years without a single voice breaking the silence. In our century, perhaps the most radical example of silence as a religious practice comes in the life of Meher Baba (1894–1969), the beloved Hindu teacher who abandoned speech in 1925, using first alphabet boards and then only gestures to communicate to the world, turning his energy away from the ego gratification of speech toward work with the poor and disabled, a sort of mute Mother Teresa.

Silence is a difficult discipline. Ambrose, the teacher of Augustine, asks rhetorically, "What ought we to learn before anything else, but to be silent, that we may be able to speak?" and adds that "it is more difficult to know how to be silent than how to speak."[26] John Climacus seconds this thought, remarking that "it is hard to keep water in without a dike. But it is harder still to hold in one's tongue."[27] In many religions, monks and nuns, who endure long periods of silence, describe it as the most trying of all spiritual practices (for more on this, see the conversation with Mother Mary Clare Vincent in chapter 9, "Going to Sleep").

Even more difficult, it has been said, is to find the proper balance between speech and silence. With the best of intentions, we find that we speak too much on one occasion and too little on the next. Even more difficult, perhaps, is to maintain inner silence in the midst of outer clamor. While we urge our kids to hurry up, or struggle with co-workers over a crucial business decision, can we keep at least a toehold in some silent, still chamber of the heart?

In Buddhist and Christian monasteries, sound and silence replace each other at set intervals, a rhythm that brings balance and serenity in its wake. In a Zen community, for example, the sounds of chanting, ringing bells, flowing water, and tramping feet alternate with the silence of *zazen*, of bathtime, and of mealtime. In a Catholic monastery, the ring of the Angelus or the sound of the Divine Office alternates with the silence of manual labor, private prayer, and *lectio divina*. We need this balance in our own lives as well. Not being monks or nuns, we lack the support of a fixed regimen and must find our own way. How to begin? Two exercises suggest themselves:

Holy book

1. Pick a day during which you'll maintain silence from the moment of awakening. Don't create needless difficulties: be sure to choose a day on which you won't be plagued by house-guests or repairmen. Unplug the phone, the television, the computer, and the radio. Let silence reign. If you can't manage a full day, an hour will do.

2. Pick a day during which you'll speak only when necessary. You'll find this to be a far more daunting task than keeping a strict silence. When you absolutely forbid speech, the rule is simple: no talking. As soon as you break the rule, you know it instantly. But if you decide to speak only when necessary, you're faced with the over-whelming complications of ordinary life, to which you are now applying a new ordering principle. If your child asks for a cookie, you can point to the cookie jar. But what if she asks you for assistance with her homework? What if a friend stops by to ask a favor or enjoy a cozy chat? How does one balance silence against hospitality?

This conundrum, at least, is dealt with at length by the desert fathers of the early church, who agree unanimously that hospitality always wins out. But other issues will surely arise. These two exercises run against the grain of habit and thus offer much in the way of self-struggle. Be sure to keep careful watch over yourself and your reactions; silence is a looking glass that discloses the self as well as a window that discloses the divine.

e i g h t

MOVEMENT

$\mathcal{T}$he terror struck without warning. I had been climbing easily, my eleven-year-old fingers agile enough to grip the tiny granite protrusions that afforded a handhold. On the forest floor far below, I could see my brother Jeff waving me on, and above me, silhouetted against the sky, the receding back of my friend Mike. It was Mike who had suggested this clamber up the precipitous mud-and-stone cliff behind his house, a proposal just pointless and reckless enough to catch a young boy's fancy.

Taking a deep breath, I reached for the next handhold. My fingers grabbed the rock, I began to heave myself up—and then I slipped.

I didn't fall. Within a nanosecond, I had regained my grip. But something dropped away nonetheless—my foolhardiness, or willpower, or courage. Sweat poured down my face, stinging my eyes and tickling my cheeks. My arms trembled; my stomach heaved. I was glued to the rock, unable to move.

"What's the matter?" came the cry from below.

I couldn't answer. I was too embarrassed, too frightened, and too furious at myself and the world to respond. Misgivings and self-recriminations flooded my mind. Why had I accepted this ridiculous dare? What if I tumbled to my death? I had heard about people falling off mountains and seeing their entire life flash before their eyes. Would this happen to me? *I was such a fool.* . . . Looking up, I could see my friend growing smaller as he ascended. Then he winked out of sight as he reached the top. I knew that I had to calm down. I couldn't go up and I couldn't go down. But something told me that I could go inward.

At that time in my life I had no experience of meditation or mindfulness, but I knew how to pray, however, thanks to my parents' insistence on a devout Catholic upbringing. In a panic, I began to beg God to deliver me; words rushed out of me helter-skelter, in a torrent propelled by self-pity and fear. And then something—to this day, I don't know what—told me that this was the wrong way to proceed. I stopped whining and began, in silence, to say the Lord's Prayer. A great stillness entered my body. I finished the prayer and began to ascend.

But I climbed in a new way. I wasn't studying the terrain carefully anymore, at least not in the conscious way that I had done before. Instead, I was coasting over it, some sixth sense telling me where to put my hands and feet. In the years since, I have read about similar swift ascents, by mountain climbers seized with inspiration and by monks trained in esoteric schools. All I knew was that I was going up rapidly, guided by some new intelligence inside myself. Within a few moments I had reached the summit, where I looked at my companions, shrugged, and said, "Quite a climb."

I tell this story not to illustrate the efficacy of prayer—that theme runs throughout this book—but to give an example, however insignificant, of the wisdom of the body. We are embodied beings, and much that we value comes to us through the flesh. Indeed, all civilization, according to Emerson in his essay "Society and Solitude," is an extension of the body:

> The human body is the magazine of inventions, the patent office, where are the models from which every hint is taken. All the tools and engines in earth are only extensions of its limbs and senses.

Movement vibrant with life, West Oakland, California

Lewis Watts

How we approach our body, then, is of uppermost importance. Certainly, it's more than a matter of health. Physical well-being is desirable, to be sure, and maintaining health, especially as one grows older, requires knowledge of our organism's needs and capacities. But haleness isn't the sine qua non of existence; many saints coughed their way through life, and more than a few spiritual exercises sap one's strength. What matters most is learning how the body can be the helpmate of the spirit, how muscle and sinew, blood and bones can contribute to the inner life.

So far, we have made much of bodily stillness: of sitting still in morning meditation, of pausing in our workaday whirl to pray the Divine Office or prostrate toward Mecca, of listening quietly to the voice of nature. But the story of the cliff points, I believe, toward a new possibility for contemplative practice, that of stillness in the midst of movement. As I lay pinned to the granite, something awoke in me, for just a moment; I had enough sense to remain still and let that something do my moving. What was that "something"? I can do no better than to call it the intelligence of the body, the language of the flesh, which expresses itself in motion.

Learning to speak that language is one of the most important goals of inner work and has given rise to a number of specialized activities, from yoga to ritual dance to pilgrimage. Let us look at some of the oldest and most widespread of these disciplines, the Asian martial arts.

CONTEMPLATIVE CLOSE-UP: THE MARTIAL ARTS

Practice Mind, Practice Body

Anyone exploring the backroads of my hometown eventually passes by an old brick factory building, originally a mill where millions of silkworms spun out the raw material of women's fashions under the watchful gaze of Yankee pioneers. Nowadays the worms are gone, the silence of their spinning replaced by a medley of curious sounds. Feet thump, breath rasps, voices explode in a foreign tongue. Visitors curious enough to track these sounds to their source find themselves on the building's second floor, facing a scene that would have been utterly unthinkable to our Yankee ancestors: forty or fifty men, women, and children in white robes (*gi*), bound by belts of white, green, brown, or black, flowing in unison through a sequence of movements that look like a cross between boot-camp warm-up and classical ballet.

As you may have guessed, our explorers have stumbled across a local karate class—one small drop in the martial-arts ocean that is washing across the world.

By one estimate, the United States alone houses some 20,000 or 30,000 dojos, or martial-arts practice halls.

According to legend, modern martial arts began when Bodhidharma (448–527), first patriarch of Ch'an Buddhism, decided to do something about the lazy monks of Shao-lin Temple in China. He designed for them a series of exercises involving physical power, agility, and recollected thought—establishing forever the principle that martial arts strengthen mind as well as body. Ten centuries later, Bodhidharma's teachings reached Japan, where they were rapidly adopted by the *bushi*, the traditional warrior class, giving birth to judo, karatedo, aikido, kendo (sword fighting), kyudo (archery), and a host of other forms. Always in these names one finds the suffix *-do*, a variation on "Tao," underscoring the spiritual nature of these disciplines, with their emphasis on courage, will, and harmonious living.

To learn more about the martial arts, I visited Jeffrey Brooks, director of both Northampton Karate Dojo and Northampton Zendo (a Zen practice hall) in western Massachusetts. Brooks has researched extensively the links between martial arts and spiritual practice, connections that he tries to keep alive in his practice. One senses this in the stability of his form as he conducts a class. As Brooks leads his students in kata, a series of prearranged karate movements against an imaginary opponent, he moves with breathtaking rapidity. At the same time, clad in a white *gi* bound with a black belt, he resembles a rock, a chunk of white granite with a vein of black basalt. A rock that flows: in this paradox we glimpse something of the martial art's remarkable aim, to find peace through the way of the warrior.

For Brooks, kata is the heart and soul of karate: "Through the constant effort of kata, your body becomes balanced and stronger, more connected to your breathing, more integrated with your mind and will." In these respects and others, kata bears a curious resemblance to the short repetitive prayers described in the preceding chapter. Both mantra and kata entail a quick burst of formal activity—whether verbal or somatic—of great precision and delicacy, which results in far-reaching changes in the practitioner. "Through this apparently constrained form," says Brooks, "mind and body become integrated and free."

The process, as Brooks describes it, is gradual. "When you first try kata, you fail. This teaches humbleness. You learn to be willing to make mistakes and to persevere. Many times you are inclined to give up, but you develop perseverance. By acknowledging limits, and their impermanence, you learn about your capacities. At first you are goal-oriented; you work hard to make progress. But later, effort and patience become the poles of a single way of practice. You practice for the sake of practice. You don't seek an outside reward. *This is the condition of my life,* you think. You practice to maintain this condition, and this condition makes you practice. In the advanced stages, the barrier between kata and practitioner completely dissolves. It is no longer you practicing kata, but you embodying kata in a natural and spontaneous way."

Karate, then, may lead to personal transformation. With this in mind, I ask Brooks a difficult question, one that sounds like a drumbeat through this book: "What does kata teach us about ordinary life? Is there any way that I, who don't practice a martial art, can make use of this?"

"Almost everyone has a hobby, a pastime, a family responsibility," he replies. "But very few of us have the experience of undertaking practice. I believe that anything—walking, playing music, doing chores—can be done for practice, as long as you have 'practice mind.'"

But surely, I suggest, different activities offer different types and levels of practice. Mindfulness in one's quotidian existence—while washing the dishes or grooming the cat—isn't the same thing as training in a dojo or praying at a Mass. "The problem," Brooks says, "is that some practices, like karate, have been fully elaborated. The path is marked out, the stages are clear. When you practice on your own, you may choose an easy path that doesn't make uncomfortable demands. This will never lead to transformation."

What, then, of the changes wrought by karate? Anyone who visits a dojo can see that through this rigorous art, bodies and minds are being trained. Advanced practitioners—at least those in the more traditional schools—carry with them an aura of stillness and tranquillity. They have none of the swagger of the bully and much of the grace of the ballerina. How does karate teach one to move with such purity, simplicity, and strength?

"We exist in a body," says Brooks. "You can drag it with you as dead weight, as a series of problems and impediments, or you can fill it with humanity and live in peace. I have found that without moving vigorously, I can't be still or peaceful. The more intense and vigorous my day of training, the more silent I am within. The body has an impulse for movement and an impulse for stopping. Most people live in the middle ground, neither stopping nor moving vigorously. But if you can be truly quiet, or if you can be 100 percent engaged in action, you will find that these two states are very similar. The feeling that arises, which some call *samadhi,* can be transferred into other moments of life. But you can't invent this, it can only come through training practice."

A beautiful aikido throw is sacred

Stillness in Movement

Paul explores the mystery of stillness in movement:

Looming over his training partners in his aikido dojo in Mill Valley, California, George Leonard looks like he is in the wrong trade. He is a bishop pine among poplars, a tall man with the kind of perfectly erect posture depicted on schoolroom wall charts idealizing our evolution into *Homo sapiens*. Yet he masters the swirling energies of a subtle martial art that enables smaller people to diffuse the attacks of bigger people while causing themselves and their attackers minimum harm.

Leonard invites an attack from Charlotte, one of his ablest black-belt students. She strikes at him with punches that increase in velocity and snap. She comes at him again and again. She is very quick. Now, according to street logic, things should escalate into a fierce volley of action and reaction. But as Charlotte's attacks intensify, George grows more quiet. The calmness in his movements is all the more confounding because he appears to be doing less as circumstances demand that he do more.

"Meditation in activity is a hundred, a thousand times superior to meditation in repose," says a Taoist precept. "The stillness in stillness is not the real stillness; only when there is stillness in movement does the universal rhythm manifest."

Watching George convinces me not to dismiss this ancient concept as another shard of paradoxical "Eastern wisdom" but to investigate the promise that, in whatever we do—cooking, driving, sports, dancing—we can manifest a contemplative inner center, one that is simultaneously empty and replete with possibilities.

George begins today's aikido class by having his students sit quietly on the mat and meditate for five minutes. He asks them to simply witness anything that comes into their minds and then to let it pass. It is an exercise in nonattachment to internal images and thoughts. He doesn't want his martial artists to be attached, even to a sound. "Whatever comes, you let it go . . . let it go away," he counsels.

This means that when pushed, you don't need to pull. You have the option of blending with the energy of that push. When pulled, you don't need to pull back. If the attacker strikes, you can step aside. You can, Leonard explains, "become one" with an attacker. Metaphorically, the attacker represents the dynamic world around you. When you blend with your attacker, you open to a greater universe.

George asks his students to question their impulse to throw an attacker who grabs them. To demonstrate, he invites a student to take hold forcefully of his wrists. George and the student lock up, turning round and round in a dance in which it is hard to see who has got hold of whom, who is the attacker and who is the defender. George observes: "From the time we are little children, we've been told that if somebody pushes you, you push back. We live by push and push back. So when someone attacks and grabs your wrists, just join and connect. Don't worry about the throw. Simply be there, in it, witnessing it all. And if you do that right, when you need to throw, you will do it more effectively."

Leonard encourages his students to think that to throw somebody down is the least important thing they do. In fact, the throws that they do without attachment to outcome are by far the most powerful. With a stillness at the heart of movement, your energy is not given over to the attack, or the problem, or the force pushing against you, but rather to the solution. "If you do not take on the problem, you cannot give your power over to it," says Leonard. "When a big problem comes up, instead of giving all your attention to the problem, the alternative is to center yourself and then extend through the problem and past it to the end of the universe. Extend into infinity and the solution will come."

The martial artist is sometimes advised, "Make your mind like water," suggesting that mental stillness will reflect what is actually going to happen rather than what you think will happen. Psychological research shows that our expectations contour the information we take in. A rigid expectation of an outcome can inhibit the natural flow of energy that pours forth when we act. A calm awareness means giving our heads a rest and our bodies a chance.

Much of our culture still teaches us that the body is inferior to our "imperial mind," Leonard observes. "We still teach that the body is this thing full of desires and mischief and that the material world is somehow inferior. Does the Divine Spirit somehow fail to permeate stone and wood?" he asks rhetorically. "Come on . . . who made the flesh? The Divine Spirit, God made the flesh. It's all sacred. A beautifully run race is sacred. A beautiful aikido throw is sacred."

MOVEMENT:
A CONTEMPLATIVE
HARVEST

The Language of the Body

The body, we have said, speaks a language of its own. The customary bodily positions of daily life—standing, sitting, lying down—make up part of its vocabulary; so, too, do more specialized postures and gestures such as kneeling and hand movements. Here is a lexicon of bodily positions, with an eye to their spiritual significance.

STANDING

Only human beings stand erect on two feet. This posture contains an immediate practical advantage, as it frees one's hands to harvest wheat, write novels, or strum the guitar. Purely on the physiological level, then, standing erect is the pathway to civilization. But this posture has spiritual significance as well, for when you stand you plant your feet on earth and raise your head to the heavens; you become, as Black Elk suggests, the axis or link between matter and spirit. Standing thus proves to be a splendid posture for prayer; one variation is the *orans* stance of ancient Christianity, standing with arms outstretched before God.

SITTING

Once a relatively rare position reserved for nobility, sitting has become the most common of all postures. We sit in the car, on the couch, at the desk, at the dinner table. We sit while chatting on the phone, writing a letter, reading a book (it's worth noting that until the sixteenth century, writing and reading were almost always done standing up). Sitting suggests comfort, ease, relaxation—qualities that dictate its spiritual role. For sitting allows us to maintain the essence of standing erect—that is, a straight spine—for long stretches of time without fatigue. As a result, sitting has become, in most traditions, the preferred position for extended periods of prayer or contemplation.

The most famous sitting posture for meditation is the full lotus: legs crossed, right foot on left thigh, left foot on right thigh, knees touching the floor. The posture, once attained (a formidable task—I've never even come close), is reported to offer incomparable stability. A less strenuous variation is the half-lotus: right foot under left thigh, left foot on right thigh, knees touching the floor. Easier still is the "traditional Japanese" or "Burmese" posture in which you kneel with a cushion pushed under your buttocks. This is my preferred position—indeed, the only one in which my remarkably inflexible body can remain still without pain. Many people simply sit in a chair for meditation; the key thing, again, is to keep the spine straight. The face should look straight ahead; an upward tilt leads to fantasizing; a downward one, to sleep.

LYING DOWN

We lie down to sleep. This bodes poorly for the spiritual significance of this posture, for it usually signals inertia or sloth. On the other hand, deliberate prostration—lying fully extended, face down, forehead to ground—is a supremely effective gesture, found in many religions, to indicate submission or surrender, the humbling of oneself before the divine. As we've seen, Muslims prostrate themselves during the *salat*, thus expressing with their bodies the very essence of Islam ("Islam" is Arabic for "surrender"). Similarly, I've known practitioners of the Jesus prayer who prostrate themselves at the end of every verse.

A number of other, more precise postures have found a place in the contemplative repertoire. These include:

BOWING

Through bowing, we honor others by humbling ourselves. In many Asian countries, bowing is a way of life, and minute variations in the bow's depth or duration serve as a precise measure of social status. Bowing discomfits many Westerners, who dislike gestures that suggest servility. Nevertheless, it seems right to bow before that which we respect, honor, and obey: Zen monks and nuns bow to their *roshi*, knights to their ladies, peacocks to their peahens.

It's amusing to imagine how life might change if we encouraged bowing in daily life. Picture the reaction of parents if their children suddenly greeted them each morning with a bow instead of a bark. How might a hard-bitten cab driver react if you bowed to him in thanks for getting to the airport on time? Until this happy day comes to pass, however, I recommend that you simply incorporate bowing into your private devotional life whenever it seems appropriate.

Pilgrimage and prayer, Lhasa, Tibet

Lynn Johnson

KNEELING

Kneeling is, in a sense, a bow extended over time: a voluntary diminution in your own status to honor the greatness of another. In Christianity, kneeling is often the preferred position during long periods of prayer; the physical discomfort of pressing one's knees on a hard surface is sometimes welcomed, as a reminder to the one who prays of the mysterious connection between suffering and grace.

HAND GESTURES

Apart from the face, the hands are the most expressive part of the body. They speak with extraordinary eloquence, as anyone who has witnessed the mudras of traditional Indian dance will testify. No doubt this is why hands play such an important role in ritual, as the channel for blessing, anointing, and consecrating, as well as in core religious symbols like the sign of the cross.

Even in mundane situations, the posture of our hands is important. Where you place them—folded against your chest, resting on your lap, dangling at your sides—carries great symbolic weight and can radically affect your inner life. To take two extreme examples, swinging your arms like an ape will make it impossible to practice walking meditation with any degree of serenity or insight; on

Singing and moving, a communion with the mysterious life within our bodies—
Russian Old Believers, Woodburn, Oregon

the other hand, pressing your palms together in front of your chest is a universal sign of goodwill and a beneficial posture for prayer.

KISSING

While it may seem odd to discuss kissing in a book on spiritual practice, in fact the kiss is a universal gesture of love and respect. A well-publicized modern example is Pope John Paul II's custom of kissing the ground of every nation he visits. But the gesture is hardly limited to pontiffs. Jews kiss the mezuzah, Christians kiss the bishop's ring, believers in almost every faith kiss their holy scriptures. It's a revelation to kiss what you deem sacred, be it an icon, a set of prayer beads, or a photo of a beloved teacher. The bare intimacy of the act destroys any fakery; you'll discover at once whether your devotion is real. We kiss what we love.

Pilgrimage: The Outer and Inner Journey

In December 1968 two men arrive at the Buddhist shrine at Polonnaruwa in Sri Lanka. Man A is amazed by the grandeur of the giant reclining rock statues of Buddha; he remembers the giant Thanksgiving Day balloons in New York, the Lincoln Memorial in Washington. He takes photos and writes postcards. Man B is also stunned. He writes in his journal:

> I was suddenly, almost forcibly jerked clean out of the habitual, half-tied vision of things, and an inner cleanness, clarity, as if exploding from the rocks themselves, became evident, obvious. . . . I don't know when in my life I have ever had such a sense of beauty and spiritual validity fusing together in one aesthetic illumination.[1]

Man A is a nameless tourist; man B is the Catholic contemplative monk Thomas Merton. Both travelers started in America, and both wound up in the same Asian glade. How then can we distinguish between them? In just this way: man A was on a trip, while Merton was on a pilgrimage. For man A, a journey is largely an outward trek, although it may leave an inner residue in the form of pleasant memories. For Merton, however—as for any pilgrim—the journey is inward and outward at the same time. The map of Merton's travels reveals a remarkable double path, one leading to Polonnaruwa, the other to the center of his heart.

We spend our days in movement. Each day we travel through sixteen hours and a good handful of miles—even if we mark off the latter by vacuuming, dusting, and mopping our way through the house. This is our outward journey. We must each ask the question, Is there an inward one as well? How can I make my day a pilgrimage? While there's no simple recipe, this poem by Sir Walter Raleigh suggests some of the ingredients:

> Give me my scallop-shell of quiet;
> My staff of faith to walk upon;
> My scrip of joy, immortal diet;
> My bottle of salvation;
> My gown of glory (hope's true gauge);
> And thus I'll take my pilgrimage.

GOING TO SLEEP

I can still smell the old leather in the reading room, a dry, dusty tang that tickled the nose, compounded of leather-bound books, leather-upholstered chairs, leather-topped desks, and the sourness of human sweat. The reading room, known locally as "the Pit," was tucked away in the

back basement of an elite liberal arts college in southern New England. One entered the Pit through swinging leather-lined doors; once within, the outer world and its vanities vanished, and all that mattered was the life of the mind. It was here that I discovered Plato, Nietzsche, the Koran, the Upanishads—and the mysteries of sleep.

Evening light has a soft luster about it

My initiation into slumber's secrets came as a result of a term paper, assigned by a professor who brooked no excuse for lateness. "A deadline," he proclaimed on the first day of class, "is a confrontation with death." He then pulled himself up to his full height, glared at us over his horn-rimmed spectacles, and declared, "If you miss the deadline, you are dead."

I took this professor at his word; it was verified campus legend that he had once rejected a paper, only ten minutes late, from a student whose mother had passed away the day before. Nonetheless, I was a chronic procrastinator, and before I knew it the paper was due tomorrow. I had to pull an all-nighter. So, fortified with a thermos of coffee, a box of cookies, and a backpack stuffed with paper, pens, and books, I pushed through the swinging doors into the Pit.

All went well until about 2:00 A.M. The coffee kept me awake, and the paper—something on Nabokov—kept me entranced. Then, all of a sudden, my skin began to itch. The sensation started at my shoulders and soon reached my arms and legs. Almost simultaneously, I felt sandbags weigh down my chest and back. The room seemed intolerably hot. I got up and walked around its perimeter, trying to admire the fine Victorian detailing of the wooden molding. Back at my desk, I concentrated again on my paper. "Nabokov's *Pale Fire* suggests a confluence—er—a confluence of ideas, that in toto—wasn't Toto Dorothy's dog?—sujjest the wrapid. . . ." It was hopeless. The room spun around me. The scrape of a chair sounded like a screech, the snap of a light like a pistol shot. What was I doing here? Was I a bat, an owl, a night crawler? Why wasn't I in my warm, soft, pillowy, cushiony, welcoming bed?

In that moment, sleep beckoned in all its beauty. I saw as never before its rightness, its friendliness, its necessity. I understood its essential role in the rhythms of the day, and why Coleridge called it "a gentle thing / beloved from pole to pole!" At that moment, I would gladly have been sleep's consort, sleep's slave.

But for the sake of my paper, I fought off the drowsiness. The next two hours glitter in my memory like torturer's tools: I writhed, moaned, whimpered, scratched, yawned, and stretched through the crawling minutes, the creeping hours. My lips quivered. My arms ached. My eyes blurred and cleared, blurred and cleared, as my pen scratched away.

Then, around four o'clock in the morning, something changed. All of a sudden, I sensed a curious lightness enter my head, as if I were breathing champagne. The clouds dissipated; my mind felt razor sharp. My physical torpor vanished as well; it was as if a thick coating of tar had been removed from my skin. I felt nimble, electric. I glanced at the students around me. In my exhaustion, they had looked to me like living corpses, human slugs, pasty-faced imitations of human beings. But now they looked like gods: radiant in their intelligence, wholly admirable in their scholarly industry. I turned to my paper; immediately I could discern the half-formed links and how to forge them into strong, compelling arguments, how to arrange the words so that they sang rather than stammered. I set to work, whistling.

In that night in the Pit, I received a taste of what the great religious traditions teach about sleep. All agree: sleep is at once demon and demigod. Sleep is friend and enemy, guardian and trap. Sleep is to be welcomed, sleep is to be shunned.

A great Hasidic rabbi put the argument in favor of sleep thus:

> Even sleep has its purpose. The man who wishes to progress in his service always forward, from holiness to holiness, from world to world, must first put aside his life-work in order to receive a new spirit, whereby a new revelation may come upon him. And therein lies the secret of sleep. Yea, even sleep has its service.[1]

Every creature sleeps, in every conceivable medium: human beings in beds, squirrels in trees, swifts on the wing, sharks on the swim. Sleep refreshes body and mind: metabolism slows, breath deepens, muscles loosen, nerves relax; at the same time, the unconscious assumes control of our mental cockpit, steering us into uncharted regions filled with dreams, where we process the events of the day and receive visions that may steer us on our waking course.

Sleep is part of creation's natural rhythm, the out-breath of night to the in-breath of day, the diastole of inaction to the systole of action. It is more than a pause to catch one's breath; it is, as Shakespeare puts it, "great nature's second course," the realm of dreams and visions, nightmares and ecstasies. According to many religious teachings, sleep is a "little death," during which the soul leaves the body and travels in celestial realms; other traditions merely emphasize the importance of a good night as prelude to a good day. In the Psalms we read:

> It is vain for you to rise up early, to sit up late, to eat the bread of sorrows; for so he giveth his beloved sleep.

PS. 127:2

This advice is paralleled by Buddhist teachings on the virtues of sleep. As D. T. Suzuki points out, sleep comes when we are at ease with life and at peace with ourselves; people who struggle with sleep are often irritable, jumpy, high-strung, "those whose spirits are somehow maladjusted to the general scheme of the universe."[2]

At the same time, most traditions look at sleep with a jaundiced eye. A typical warning comes from the Bible: "love not sleep lest thou come to poverty" (Prov. 20:13), equating sleep with sloth and sloth with social ruin.

Even more important, however, is the conviction that sleep leads to spiritual sluggishness. In almost every world religion keeping awake is hailed as a virtuous exercise that sharpens the senses, quickens the mind, and leads one to God. The seventh-century caliph 'Umar said, "What have I to do with sleep? If I slept by day, I would lose the Muslims, and if I slept by night I would lose my soul."[3] Jesus on the eve of his execution bid his disciples to "keep awake and pray." To combat sleep is to embrace life, in all its pain and glory; moreover, sleep deprivation brings with it an exquisite responsiveness of body and mind, in which the ordinary armor that blocks our experience drops away. We become more open to spiritual beauty, to the grace imparted by sacred art, music, and writing. We also feel emotions more keenly; combating sleep thus enables us to learn much about ourselves and others that ordinarily remains hidden. A night without sleep is a night of discovery.

Sleep, then, is a double-edged sword. It cuts away the sludge that begrimes us at the end of every day, freeing us to face tomorrow afresh; but it also cuts away our chance for a deeper life, locking us for eight hours a day in a state that Sir Thomas Browne called "the Brother of Death." Sleep's Janus face is superbly portrayed in this Islamic anecdote retold by Anne-Marie Schimmel:

> Shah Kirmani did not sleep for forty years, but eventually he was overwhelmed by sleep—and he saw God. Then he exclaimed: "O Lord, I was seeking Thee in nightly vigils, but I have found Thee in sleep." God answered: "O Shah, you have found Me by means of those nightly vigils; if you had not sought me there, you would not have found me here."[4]

Obviously we are dealing with a complex issue, one without cut-and-dried rules. At the same time, we can't afford to ignore sleep, for sleep never ignores us: sooner or later, it always pays a visit.

How much sleep is enough? I get by on six hours; more than eight and my mind sags all day. Carol needs at least eight and dreams of ten. Mother Teresa reportedly gets by on less than five. The question of how much sleep you need affords a splendid occasion for discernment, for taking stock, in a sincere and wholehearted way, of your needs, and for balancing them against your desires. Perhaps you believe that you require eight hours a night—but have you tried to get by on seven, or on six plus an afternoon nap? Perhaps you'd like to emulate the fakirs of India and snooze for only an hour or two, spending the rest of the night meditating under the stars—a few nights of experimentation may be enough to burst this illusion, and provide a more realistic sense of your limits.

A Beginner's Exercise

Many of us sleep too much or too little. To determine the right amount of sleep for you, try this simple exercise. Begin with your normal allotment of sleep—and shave away fifteen minutes. Sleep only this amount for one week. Then shave away another fifteen minutes. You may discover, paradoxically, that sleeping less makes you more alert. There's no doubt that too much sleep dulls the spirit. When you arrive at the right amount of sleep, you'll know it: you'll wake up refreshed, and you'll retire with a pleasant heaviness of eye and limb. If you erase yet another fifteen minutes of sleep, you'll find this well-being diminished; simply return to your earlier, ideal level.

Preparing for Sleep

I'd like to return for a moment to Shakespeare's description of sleep as "nature's second course." Human beings have always seen sleep in this light—not so much as an extension of the day but as an entirely new realm with its own landscapes, inhabitants, and rules. Preparing for sleep is thus much like getting ready for a journey, a two-stage affair in which one first tidies up old business and then packs for ports unknown. The first step in going to bed, then, is to put in order the affairs of the day.

Usually, this begins soon after dinner. The day's work is done, and the time has come to slip into a different mode of being. Evening light has a soft luster about it, a silkiness that comes from the sun's rays slanting toward us at a low angle, through thick layers of atmosphere that screen their brilliance and muffle their intensity. All life, ruled by the rhythms of the sun, responds in kind. The body slows, the mind deepens, the spirit opens to a more stately, quiet cadence. This is the time for domestic bliss: for reading, sewing, listening to music. If we wish to complete the day on a contemplative note, there is little room for television or other stimuli that jar the senses. Carol and I decided to unplug our television set five years ago, and we haven't regretted it for an instant; although we miss an occasional good program, this loss is more than compensated by the time we spend together each evening talking, reading, playing games, and going for walks.

The religions of the world have little to say about going to sleep, certainly far less than they do about waking up. No doubt the reason for this lies in the exigencies of traditional life: one worked until the sun went down, ate a frugal supper as the darkness spread, and then slipped under the covers, ready to rise at the glimmer of dawn. Clearly, the artificial restructuring of time brought on by electric lighting and other technological changes calls for a different approach. Happily, some monastic communities have developed concrete programs for closing up the day that will be of great help to us in understanding the spiritual meaning of this last important phase of the daily round. Let us therefore look in at the nuns of St. Scholastica Priory—the sister community to the monks of St. Mary's Monastery, who introduced us to the spirituality of waking up.

CONTEMPLATIVE CLOSE-UP:
EVENING AT ST. SCHOLASTICA PRIORY

Evening at the Benedictine community of St. Scholastica Priory begins with dinner in the refectory. The nuns eat together in silence, while one sister reads aloud from a sacred book. This atmosphere of calm recollection sounds the note for the hours to follow. Once the meal—the last food of the day—is finished, the nuns disperse. Some head to their cells for private reflection, while others gather for quiet conversation. This period of "recreation," devoid of the raucous pastimes that enthrall so many of us, lasts but half an hour. Yet it is a genuine re-creation, an opportunity for the nun to reknit her nerves after a day of vigorous physical, mental, and spiritual labors.

After recreation comes Compline, the last Hour of the Divine Office and the crown jewel in the treasury of the evening's activities. Compline is the mirror image of Vigils, introduced in chapter 2, "Waking Up." Just as Vigils begins in darkness and ends with dawn, so Compline (with seasonal variations) begins with dusk and ends in darkness. It concludes the commerce of the day and introduces the mysteries of the night. Many consider it to be the loveliest of all the Hours, a superbly orchestrated blend of psalms, devotional prayers, and blessings that relaxes the body, quiets the mind, and sweetens the soul.

I asked Mother Mary Clare Vincent, O.S.B., prioress of St. Scholastica, to share with me some of her thoughts about Compline. We talked in the community's small parlor, where she greeted me with typical Benedictine hospitality and a minibanquet of tea, cookies, cakes, and candies; after a few minutes of munching, I felt like curling up right there and taking a snooze. Here indeed, I thought, was a woman who understood the secrets of sleep.

According to Mother Mary Clare, Compline is one end of the "thread of prayer that holds life together." Mother points out that, in common with the rest of the Divine Office, it consists largely of singing the psalms. "The Psalter," she says, "contains everything that we need to say to God. The psalms are expressed verbally and prayed contemplatively. They're not just words; they express the longings of the heart, they take us into union with God. Through the psalms, we join with Christ."

As I mentioned in "Waking Up," St. Benedict recommends that we pray the Divine Office aware of "our place in sight of God and of his angels. Let us rise in chanting that our hearts and voices harmonize."[5] This is a tall order, as I pointed out to Mother Mary Clare. In response, she offered me three tips on how to pray Compline (or, by extension, any set form of prayer):

- *Be patient.* It takes time to get used to the Divine Office, with its wide variety of prayers and blessings. Some people find the array of psalms particularly vexing, both because of content (some "cursing" psalms may offend modern sensibilities) and because of style (composed for an oral culture, the psalms include rhetorical devices and turns of phrase that take some getting used to). Trust in tradition; these prayers have lasted several thousand years for good reason.

- *Expect dry spells.* There may be times when the psalms lose their meaning. Persevere; aridity plays its part in prayer life as surely as it does in life in general; these difficult periods carry their own lessons and rewards.

The interior world blossoms, St. Scholastica Priory

Andrew De Lisle

- *Don't expect fireworks.* "The psalms," Mother Mary Clare said, "are not meant to be charismatic or peak experiences." They are a way of praising, thanking, petitioning, glorifying, and adoring God. On the other hand, she emphasizes, "the psalms are never boring or routine." In fact, when she speaks of reciting the psalms, she glows. It comes as no surprise when she declares, "The psalms are my whole life."

For those interested in experiencing something of the night office of Compline, here is a sampling of the Hour's principal psalms and prayers. Ideally, they would be sung communally, but they may also be prayed privately (at St. Scholastica, most of the singing is done in Latin, whose regular cadences and calm coherence help to create a serene and steady atmosphere of contemplation). Please refer to chapter 2 for specific advice on how to pray the Divine Office.

PSALM 86:1—7

Bow down thine ear, O Lord, hear me: for I am poor and needy.

Preserve my soul: for I am holy: O Thou my God, save thy servant that trusteth in thee.

Be merciful unto me, O Lord: for I cry unto thee daily.

Rejoice the soul of thy servant: for unto thee, O Lord, do I lift up my soul.

For thou, Lord, art good and ready to forgive; and plenteous in mercy unto all them that call upon thee.

Give ear, O Lord, unto my prayer: and attend to the voice of my supplications.

In the day of my trouble I will call upon thee: for thou wilt answer me.

PSALM 91:1–5, 11, 14–16

He that dwelleth in the secret place of the most High shall abide under the shadow of the Almighty.

I will say to the Lord, He is my refuge and my fortress: my God, in him will I trust.

Surely he shall deliver thee from the snare of the fowler, and from the noisome pestilence.

He shall cover thee with his feathers, and under his wings shalt thou trust; his truth shall be thy shield and buckler.

Thou shalt not be afraid for the terror by night; nor for the arrow that flieth by day;

For he shall give his angels charge over thee, to keep thee in all thy ways.

Because he hath set his love upon me, therefore will I deliver him; I will set him on high, because he hath known my name.

He shall call upon me, and I will answer him: I will be with him in trouble; I will deliver him, and honor him.

With long life will I satisfy him, and shew him my salvation.

SCRIPTURE READING (1 CORINTHIANS 13:1–3, 13)

Though I speak in the tongues of men and of angels, and have not charity, I am become as sounding brass or a tinkling cymbal.

And though I have the gift of prophecy, and understand all mysteries, and all knowledge; and though I have all faith, so that I could remove mountains, and have not charity, I am nothing.

And though I bestow all my goods to feed the poor, and though I give my body to be burned, and have not charity, it profiteth me nothing.

And now abideth faith, hope, charity, these three: but the greatest of these is charity.

GOSPEL CANTICLE (LUKE 2:29–32)

Antiphon: Protect us, Lord, while we are awake and guard us while we sleep, that we may wake with Christ and rest in peace.

Lord, now lettest thou thy servant depart in peace, according to thy
    word;
For mine eyes have seen thy salvation,
Which thou hast prepared before the face of all people;
A light to lighten the Gentiles, and the glory of thy people Israel.

CONCLUDING PRAYER

We pray to you Lord, let your holy angels watch over us at night and let your love be with us always, through Christ our Lord, Amen.

BLESSING

May God grant us a peaceful night, a peaceful death, and perfect peace hereafter.

After Compline, the Great Silence descends. This is a stretch of twelve hours or so, lasting until after Mass the next morning, during which absolute silence reigns. Of this strict discipline St. Benedict writes only that "monks should try to speak as little as possible, but especially at night. . . . they are to say Compline, after which no one is to speak."[6] At the priory, the Great Silence is taken literally. All nonessential conversation stops. Phones are switched off, typewriters packed away; no unnecessary noise, whether human, mechanical, or electronic, intrudes upon the stillness. Instead, the nuns turn to the quiet of reading, praying, or visiting the house chapel.

In this silence, a nun meets life as it is, without the buffer of words; as a result, the interior world blossoms. "St. Benedict encouraged those living in monasteries to study and love silence. This is part of our training," says Mother Mary Clare. "We are enveloped in silence and darkness. We hide our voices, and we discover the depths of the cosmos and the immensity of God." But she adds that even silence has its limits: "Silence is relative. Silence is an aid to charity. The one absolute is love." And what, I ask her, is the result of this extended immersion in the world of silence? "The night is sanctified just like the day," Mother replies. "Even our sleep is sanctified. We fall asleep in the arms of God."

GOING TO SLEEP:
A CONTEMPLATIVE HARVEST

Bedtime Practices and Prayers

In many cultures, bedtime rituals ease the transition into sleep. These practices, especially when children are involved, can become as intricate and complex as a

Swiss watch. John, my ten-year-old, takes more than an hour to go to bed, working his way through a bedtime ritual that includes snacking, turning out the gerbil lights, going to the bathroom, changing into pajamas, brushing his teeth, reading, and saying prayers. He's a wizard at dragging out this routine interminably; my wife and I urge him on, but we rarely push it, for we know that he is, in a very real sense, packing for a trip into inner space. Even Andy, the two-year-old, has a routine, which includes saying goodnight to the fish in our saltwater aquarium.

Here is a sampling of bedtime rituals, prayers, and practices from various religions:

ISLAM

The great Islamic sage Abu Hamid al-Ghazali (d. 1111) reminds us that "sleep is the similitude of death" and counsels us to sleep on the right side, for it is in this position that corpses are buried. Sleep not only resembles death, it may even open death's door; the possibility that we will die during sleep is acknowledged in bedtime prayers around the world. Al-Ghazali recommends that we go to sleep with pure heart and clean conscience, preferably with a last will and testament tucked under the pillow. Bed is for sleep, not sloth, al-Ghazali counsels; eight hours will suffice ("It is enough, supposing you live for sixty years, that you lose twenty of these years or a third of your life"). He also recommends that we awaken halfway through the night for a session of prayer.

Al-Ghazali suggests the following bedtime prayer, to be said immediately before putting head to pillow:

> In Thy name, Lord, I lay me down and in Thy name will I rise up. . . . O God, Thou art the first and before Thee there is nothing; Thou art the last and after Thee there is nothing; Thou art the outmost and above Thee there is nothing; Thou art the inmost and below Thee there is nothing. . . . Waken me, O God, in the hour most pleasing to Thee and use me in the works most pleasing to Thee, that Thou mayest bring me ever nearer to Thyself. . . .[7]

JUDAISM

Many Jews recite some or all of the following prayer before retiring for the night:

> Blessed are you, Lord our God, king of the universe, who causes the bonds of sleep to fall on my eyes, and slumber on my eyelids. May it be acceptable in your presence, O Lord my God, and God of my fathers, to cause me to lie down in peace, and to raise me up again in peace; and suffer me not to be

troubled with evil dreams, or evil reflections; but grant me a calm and uninterrupted repose in your presence; and enlighten my eyes again, lest I sleep the sleep of death. Blessed are you, O Lord, who gives light to the whole universe in your glory.[8]

CHRISTIANITY

Here are two Christian bedtime prayers, one anonymous, the other written by a Victorian master of English prose:

> Now I lay me down to sleep,
> I pray the Lord my soul to keep.
> If I should die before I wake,
> I pray the Lord my soul to take.
>
> ANONYMOUS

> May He support us all the day long, till the shades lengthen, and the evening comes, and the busy world is hushed, and the fever of life is over, and our work is done! Then in His mercy may He give us a safe lodging, and a holy rest, and peace at the last.
>
> JOHN HENRY NEWMAN

EXAMINATION OF CONSCIENCE

In many religious traditions, preparations for sleep include an examination of conscience (this is, incidentally, a regular aspect of Compline). Usually the examination entails a mental inventory of the events of the day, with special attention to any failings in behavior toward others or oneself. We confess our inadequacies and resolve, gently but firmly, to do better tomorrow.

Sharon Salzberg on Buddhist Bedtime Practice

Sharon Salzberg, cofounder of the Insight Meditation Center in Barre, Massachusetts, describes two simple Buddhist bedtime practices:

- *Boundless* metta *practice.* When going to sleep, says Salzberg, you might want to modify *metta* practice, directing it "in a global and boundless way." Rather than focus goodwill and compassion upon a particular being, she suggests sending these thoughts toward the entire world and all sentient beings.
- *Mindful passage into sleep.* Salzberg reports that Buddhist practitioners in Burma are sometimes asked whether they fall asleep on the in-breath or the out-breath. "The motive," she says, "is to acquire such supreme mindfulness that you are aware even of something like that"—a physiological event usually invisible to the conscious mind. "I go out on a train of thoughts," Salzberg adds. "I flood my mind with thoughts and it puts me to sleep. But the suggestion here is to fall asleep while mindful. Then you are mindful while you sleep as well."

The World of Dreams

Many years ago I dreamed this dream: I was in a large marble-floored room, like a grand ballroom, standing at the back of a receiving line that stretched as far as the eye could see. As the procession inched forward, I finally made out the guest of honor, who was greeting each person with a hug: it was Pope John Paul II, the newly elected pontiff of the Roman Catholic Church. After an interminable wait, I found myself next to the Pope. He smiled benevolently, bent down his gray head, put his lips to my ear, and whispered, in a sentence of no more than nine or ten words, the secret of life.

Bliss flooded through me, coursing from my head down to my toes. No more doubts, no more fears, no more sorrows: at last, I had learned the great truth that human beings had searched for through the ages. I resolved to remember the Pope's words always—and then I woke up.

Needless to say, I instantly forgot what John Paul had revealed. Oh, I tried to remember. I wracked my brain for days, trying to recapture those golden words. Once or twice I felt them tremble on the tip of my tongue. But they never broke the silence. Nonetheless, the dream remains with me, along with the certainty that for a moment I was privy to the Great Secret of Life.

Almost everyone has a version of this dream, a vision that somehow or other, often in unexpected ways, defines or transforms one's life. Not all dreams carry such a heavy cargo of meaning, however. Some two millennia ago, Virgil observed that

> Two gates the silent house of Sleep adorn:
> Of polished ivory this, that of transparent horn:
> True visions through transparent horn arise;
> Through polished ivory pass deluding lies.

My dream of the pope is, I believe, a dream of "transparent horn." Such dreams are rare, accounting for no more than an infinitesimal fraction of our total dream life. A splendid demonstration of the difference between transparent horn and polished ivory occurs in Charles Dickens's "A Christmas Carol." When the ghost of Jacob Marley first appears to Ebenezer Scrooge, the latter dismisses him as "an undigested bit of beef, a blot of mustard, a crumb of cheese, a fragment of an underdone potato."[9] As events unfold, however, we learn that Scrooge's dream is carved of transparent horn and that his visions will work a miracle.

As all who have enjoyed such dreams know, they can guide one's life. A famous example from ancient Greece involves Aesculapius, the god of healing. For decades, Aesculapius appeared in dreams to a man named Aristides, offering him detailed medical advice. Aristides was kind enough to leave behind a lengthy journal describing some two hundred of these dreams and their aftermath; this document indicates that Aesculapius's nighttime counsel enjoyed an impressive rate of success, even with such vexing ailments as deafness and tumors. Dreams of transparent horn can even guide an entire culture. The Senoi of Malaysia regulate their daily lives by their dreams; one researcher reports that "What did you dream last night?" is "the most important question in Senoi life." These dreams, she adds, make or break friendships, shape religious rituals, and determine where houses will be built. Similarly, for the Beaver of southwestern Canada, sleeping is the portal into absolute reality, for in dreams a Beaver male discovers both his medicines and the true meaning of his life. "The knowledge that comes through dreaming," writes anthropologist Robin Ridington, "is absolute because it comes from a level of symbolic association that is deeper than consciousness."[10]

How, then, shall we approach the world of dreams? Certainly we should learn to discriminate between dreams of transparent horn and dreams of ivory; once in the realm of horn, we should learn to see through the transparency to the truth that lies beyond. Here there are no cut-and-dried rules. Everything depends upon discernment, which depends in turn upon spiritual maturity.

The one bit of practical advice that I can offer is this: keep a dream journal. Store a pencil and pad by your bedside, and as soon as you awaken, jot down your dreams. It's astonishing how quickly dreams vanish if not recorded, as if a cord connects them to some guardian of the night realms who, jealous of their escape, tugs them back. You'll be more likely to recall your dreams if you keep your eyes shut and replay them in your mind before sitting up. Seize on any stray bit that you remember; you may be able to wind it up, like Ariadne's thread, to arrive at the heart of the vision. Keep your journal faithfully. At the very least, the exercise of careful recording will help you to remember your dreams with greater clarity. You will also possess a record that you can return to, days or years later—a footprint, as it were, of your younger, subconscious self, perhaps not as suitable a display as your bronzed baby shoes, but just as fascinating.

A Good-Night Thought

As we snap off the lights, we end the daily cycle. Tomorrow the world will be reborn; will we be there to greet it? Perhaps death will claim us during the night. Let us retire ready to greet whatever comes, in this world or the next. This readiness returns us to the beginning of this book, in which we discussed the practice of the remembrance of death. Only by holding in mind our mortality, our contingency on

Tomorrow, the world will be reborn

a mystery far greater than us, do we reach our full stature as human beings. Only in the awareness of death do we draw the full measure of life.

And if we should join the great mass of people that awakens tomorrow, what will be our response? Will we rejoice like Ebenezer Scrooge, exclaiming "I'm not the man I used to be"? G. K. Chesterton offers a canny observation, directed toward the coming of the New Year, that applies just as well to every morning of our lives:

> The object of a New Year is not that we should have a new year. It is that we should have a new soul and a new nose, new feet, a new backbone, new ears, and new eyes. Unless a man starts on the strange assumption that he has never existed before, it is quite certain that he will never exist afterward.

When the sun rises on a new day, it rises on our new life. The world has been scrubbed clean, and all creation awaits our response. We bring with us our responsibilities and relations; what we make of them is up to us.

Only that day dawns to which we are awake. There is more day to dawn.

HENRY DAVID THOREAU

PART 2

Life

ten

Introduction:

PASSAGES IN THE LIFE CYCLE

*T*he other day, I noticed an ad in an old newspaper for a film called *Jack,* about a boy who suffers from a rare and terrible disease that induces premature aging. The film stars Robin Williams, whose elastic features seem perfectly fitted to this role. The ad plays this up: Williams's face looms in the foreground, his expression a superbly realized blend of astonishment, horror, and impish delight. Studying his image, in which the wrinkles of age clash with a goofy, boyish grin, it struck me that we love to watch films that fiddle with the normal human life cycle. I think of *Big,* in which Tom Hanks plays a boy trapped in a man's body, and *Freaky Friday,* in which a teenaged Jodie Foster switches

Generations   Bill Aron

identities with her mother, and *Cocoon,* in which octogenarians discover the fountain of youth, and *Heaven Can Wait, A Guy Named Joe,* and a flood of others, in which the catalyst for the biological highjinx varies from aliens to reincarnation to a magical curse to heavenly intervention.

Why do we so enjoy these films? No doubt some of it is the thrill of the unknown. What man hasn't wondered what it would be like to be a woman for a day, as happens to Steve Martin in *All of Me*? What woman hasn't longed to relive her high-school years armed with the skills of an adult, as happens to Kathleen Turner in *Peggy Sue Got Married?* Vicarious experience has its rewards. But I suspect that these pleasures, however tantalizing, fail to offer an explanation for the success of these films. To unearth the real reason, we must consider how they end: the boy sheds his beard and becomes a smooth-skinned lad again; the mom-turned-teenager steps back into her middle-aged shoes. *The natural order is reaffirmed.* We watch these films, I believe, for the same reason that we crane our necks when driving past an accident or flip furtively through the pages in the supermarket tabloids: by seeking out the abnormal in other people's lives, we verify the normality of our own. "There but for the grace of God . . ."

We crave this sense of normality, of orderly progression in our lives. We may not ride a bullet train through life, as happens to Robin Williams in *Jack,* or sleep for twenty years, as Robert de Niro does in *Awakenings*—Hollywood likes bold colors on a big canvas—but gentler disruptions of the life cycle crop up all the time, and invariably they throw us off-kilter. An infant dies, and we weep; an eighty-year-old grandmother buys a low-slung sportscar or a low-cut dress, and we blush. We have a sense of propriety about the stages of life. The human life cycle, we believe, does unfold in appropriate phases, according to law or plan or sheer good luck, and each is an essential step in our physical and spiritual maturation. Children don't give birth to nonagenarians; we don't go through puberty in middle age. "For everything there is a season, and a time for every matter under heaven" (Eccles. 3:1).

This isn't to say that all cultures agree on the stages of the life-cycle. Shakespeare in *As You Like It* (Act II, scene vii) declares that "one man in his time plays many parts / His acts being seven ages." These seven ages run from "first the infant, / Mewling and puking in the nurse's arms" to the "last scene of all . . . mere oblivion, / Sans teeth, sans eyes, sans taste, sans everything." A tractate of the Jewish Mishnah known as the *Pirke Aboth* describes fourteen different steps:

> At five years old one is ready for the scripture, at ten years for the Mishnah, at thirteen for the commandments, at fifteen for Talmud, at eighteen for marriage, at twenty for pursuit of righteousness, at thirty for

full strength, at forty for discernment, at fifty for counsel, at sixty for old age, at seventy for grey hairs, at eighty for "labor and sorrow" . . . at ninety for decrepitude, at one hundred he is as though he were dead, and had passed away and faded from the world.[1]

Hindu India reduces the number of phases to four, called ashrama, each with its own obligations, trials, and rewards: brahmachari (student), which entails chastity and instruction under a guru; grihastha (householder), which entails marriage and begetting children; vanaprastha (hermit), during which one leads a life of secluded prayer in the forest; and sannyasin (renunciant), during which one lives as a homeless beggar devoted only to God.

Note that this scheme excludes childhood, adolescence, and other life cycle stages taken for granted by Western psychology and modern pop culture. Even the very terminus of the cycle, death itself—a stage whose reality stands beyond all argument, one might suppose—receives a radically different definition in different cultures. According to the medical standards of modern culture, death arrives when brain activity ceases. But certain peasant societies in Greece deny death its rights until a corpse has been cold and motionless for an entire year, at which time it is exhumed, paraded around the village, and then reburied for eternity.

Even more astonishing, some life cycle stages, to whose reality we can attest from first-hand experience, may be no more than recent social inventions. Historian Phillipe Aries has convincingly argued that the complex state that we call "childhood" is entirely a product of seventeenth-century Europe. Before the Renaissance—and even now, in some traditional societies—children were considered to be nothing more than small, flawed adults. Be this as it may, the fact remains that as I write this sentence, Christmas is less than a week away, and billions of kids around the world await Santa's midnight run with bated breath. Childhood seems here to stay. After studying descriptions of the life cycle in a number of world cultures, Paul and I have arrived at the following basic template:

Birth
Childhood
Coming of age
Marriage and family
Aging
Death

Of course, this list invites all manner of additions and subtractions. For many people, the stage that we call birth begins with conception; for others, death is but a door and the life cycle continues in heavenly realms. Definitions of marriage and family are fluid. As for aging—well, to a child, a forty-year-old teeters on the grave, while to a seventy-year-old, old age begins at eighty. Nonetheless, when all is said and done, Paul and I believe that the six-part cycle presented above can embrace most permutations and serve as a basic map of the universal human life cycle.

Despite wide variations in structure and content, almost all models of the life cycle embrace the following principles:

1. Each phase of life has its characteristic pitfalls and rewards. This idea has been explored most fully by psychoanalyst Erik Erikson, who divides the life cycle into eight stages and discerns in each a task to complete, a vice to avoid, and a virtue to cultivate. Thus infants must learn to trust, avoid withdrawal, and cultivate hope; toddlers must learn autonomy, avoid compulsion, and cultivate will; and so on up to the elderly, who must discover their own "integrity," avoid disdain, and cultivate wisdom. Erikson's model is open to revision, depending upon cultural expectations and one's tolerance for psychoanalysis,

Frank Ward

Pilgrims navigating the stages of life

but his basic idea seems sound: that throughout life we are faced, like the heroes of old, with dragons to slay and treasures to gather before we can return home in triumph.

Not everyone succeeds in meeting the challenges. We've all known people who stalled along the way: the fourteen-year-old girl who sucks her thumb, the fifty-year-old man who haunts teenage dance clubs. We've all known those who take a wrong turn and fall prey to Erikson's "vices": the bitter retiree, the reclusive aunt, the child too bored to play. To some extent, successfully navigating the stages of life is a matter of meeting each day in the right frame of mind, a task addressed in part 1 of this book. However, each stage of the life cycle also contains singular events—for instance, birth—for which specific preparation is needed and specific counsel is available. Much of the material contained in part 2 deals with these special moments in life.

2. The transition between stages of the life cycle is a time of promise and peril. This important idea comes from Arnold van Gennep, the anthropologist who first studied the life cycle in depth and who coined the term *rites of passage* for those religious ceremonies—marriages, funerals, and the like—that mark the transitions between life's stages.

These rituals serve multiple purposes. Consider, for example, a typical Christian wedding ceremony. Flowers, music, liturgy, church architecture, priestly vestments, even the throwing of rice (through which the community bestows its fertility upon the couple), all carry a rich cargo of symbol and meaning. The ritual connects bride and groom to universal spiritual truths and to the community in which these truths find concrete expression. In part 2, you will encounter many such rituals. Indeed, if we can define meditation as the fundamental spiritual act of the daily round, then ritual can be defined as the fundamental spiritual act of the life cycle.

3. The life cycle is, as its name implies, a cycle. At fifteen years of age, life stretches straight ahead of us, a highway to riches and fame. But as we mature, so does our understanding. Sooner or later, it dawns upon us that our trajectory is anything but a straight line. We zig and zag, double back upon ourselves, tie ourselves in knots, branch out in new directions. And as we approach death, we may discover that life's two ends meet. Certainly infant and elderly share a common frailty, dependency, even a tendency to nod off. The life cycle (from Greek *kyklos*, "circle") ends where it begins. Moreoever, each stage along the way "recycles" its material into the next; an adult doesn't emerge full-born, like Athena out of the head of Zeus, but unfolds naturally from the lengthening limbs and thickening muscles of adolescence. Our life is a coming-into-being, a gradual disclosure of our true self.

Spiritual Rebirth

What is the aim of this coming-into-being? Thomas Carlyle expressed it well:

> Let each become all that he was created capable of being; expand, if possible, to his full growth, and show himself at length in his own shape and stature, be these what they may.

And here we encounter the great paradox of human development: that in order for each of us to "become all that he was created capable of being," it is necessary to reverse the life cycle, go against the grain, run the film backward, and become a child again, even die and be born again.

The best-known summation of this extraordinary teaching, which can be found in almost every religion, comes from the Gospel of Matthew:

> At the same time came the disciples unto Jesus, saying, Who is the greatest in the kingdom of heaven?
> And Jesus called a little child unto him, and set him in the midst of them,
> And said, Verily I say unto you, Except ye be converted, and become as little children, ye shall not enter into the kingdom of heaven.
>
> MATTHEW 18:1–3

This advice seems linked to another mysterious teaching of Jesus:

> "Verily, verily, I say unto thee, Except a man be born again, he cannot see the kingdom of God."
> Nicodemus saith unto him, How can a man be born when he is old? can he enter the second time into his mother's womb, and be born?
> Jesus answered, "Verily, verily I say unto thee, Except a man be born of water and of the Spirit, he cannot enter into the kingdom of God."
>
> JOHN 3:3–6

We must die and be reborn. We must abandon the mode of being that has trapped us, enchained us, held us back. Almost all cultures cherish this idea in one form or another. Indian male Brahmans speak of themselves as "twice-born," experiencing through the upanayana ceremony a second birth into a new, inner life. Buddhist texts speak repeatedly of spiritual rebirth, sometimes referring to it as "breaking the eggshell." In some African cultures, for example along the Loango coast, boys between the ages of ten and twelve undergo symbolic burial, during which they are painted white like ghosts, and then return to life to learn the eso-teric traditions and sacred language of the people.

The idea of a second birth appears in less explicitly religious arenas as well. Consider, for example, the Twelve Steps for Alcoholics Anonymous: what are these but a prescription for spiritual death and rebirth? Of particular importance are the first three steps, through which the alcoholic dies to his previous life and seeks rebirth in God's tender love by deliberately emulating the openness, dependency, and trust of a newborn:

1. We admitted we were powerless over alcohol—that our lives had become unmanageable.
2. Came to believe that a Power greater than ourselves could restore us to sanity
3. Made a decision to turn our will and our lives over to the care of God as we understood Him.[2]

When reborn, we become as children. Every tradition has its childlike saints—Mullah Nasr Edin, the Baal Shem Tov, Ramakrishna, the Myokonin. What do we mean by calling these holy ones "childlike"? The adjective has nothing to do with childhood's darker side, with the incessant ego gratification, the constant refrain of "I, me, mine" that we find irritating in kids and intoler-able in grown-ups (whom we accuse of acting "like spoiled children"). What we love in the saints is their eagerness, their innocence, their sense of wonder, their radical openness to life at every turn. St. Francis kissed lepers and lectured to birds; who but a child—or a great saint—would act like that? East Asian Bud-dhists speak of "beginner's mind," of approaching everything in a fresh, open spirit. To "become like children," as Jesus asked, is to recover the primordial trust that lies at the very beginning of human life.

The symphony that is life contains two intermingled melodies: one wrought of becoming, accomplishment, success, procreation, leaving one's mark upon the world as a person of stature; and the other wrought of being, accepting, surren-dering, erasing oneself to make room for God. There need be no conflict between these two melodies, between the outer life cycle in which we grow ever older, passing from childhood to adulthood to old age, and the inner life cycle, in which we grow ever younger, more supple, more eager to learn. Our task is to unite the two, to join the wonder of infancy to the wisdom of age. The result, we may hope with confidence, will be a music worth hearing and a life worth living.

eleven

BIRTH

$\mathcal{A}$ friend of my wife's, whom I'll call Sophie, swears that this story is true: She was in labor with her first child, writhing in pain and longing for relief, when suddenly the heavens opened up above her and she saw revealed the secrets of the cosmos. In a flash, she learned the true nature of all things and came face-to-face with the living God. Then the vision clouded over and all her special knowledge vanished. Why? cried Sophie, why show me this and then snatch it away? This answer came: that this revelation is granted to all laboring mothers so that they may guide their children by its invisible influence, even if the details are forgotten.

Consider now this talmudic legend: At the moment of conception, an angel escorts the soul from its abode in heaven into the womb and there unites it to the embryo. The angel tutors the new being in the mysteries of the world, transporting it to heaven and hell to see the heights and depths of creation, revealing to it the ways of beauty, truth, and goodness, disclosing every detail of its future life on earth, even to the time and place of death. As the child matures within the womb, it ponders the wonders that it has seen. Then, at the instant of birth, the angel touches the child on the mouth, erasing all memory of these marvelous revelations.

In these two parallel tales we glimpse the unfathomable mystery of birth, so profound an event that both mother and child are vouchsafed a knowledge that we would ordinarily call divine. Then, in dramatic fashion, the knowledge is removed (an act of great compassion, I suspect, for who could bear to know the terrifying secrets of the cosmos, or the date and details of one's death?). Yet a trace of the numinous remains. Just as we can still see at pilgrimage sites in India the footprints of the Buddha, although he has long since passed on, so does the imprint of divine knowledge, the watermark of the sacred, rest forever in the heart of mother and child:

> *Not in entire forgetfulness,*
> *And not in utter nakedness,*
> *But trailing clouds of glory do we come*
> *From God who is our home:*
>
> WILLIAM WORDSWORTH,
> "Intimations of Immortality"

We know nothing of the exact composition of these "clouds of glory"; our meteorology of human origins is still in its infancy. Indeed, we can fairly say that we know next to nothing about what birth really is, just as we know next to nothing about what death really is. The origin of every human being—of you and me and the grocer down the street—is as mysterious as the origin of life itself. The very birth of the universe remains a mystery; the most fundamental of questions, neatly formulated by Leibnitz as "Why is there something rather than nothing?," looms as large as ever.

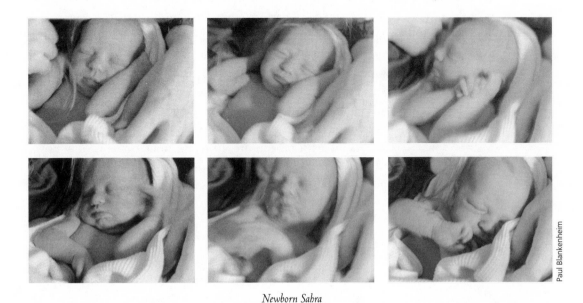

Newborn Sahra

Paul Blankenheim

What we can say with certainty is that every birth is an event of momentous proportions. This is true whether the newborn be humble or exalted. Many religions rejoice in the nativity of a god, sage, saint, or founder, which they often paint in miraculous terms. Thus the first-century Indian poet Ashvaghosha, describing the Buddha's birth, declares that "his limbs shone with the radiant hue of precious gold, and lit up the space all around," while the Gospel of Luke (2:13) reports that at the birth of Christ, shepherds witnessed "a multitude of the heavenly host" appear in the skies, singing and praising God.[1]

But the real wonder of birth, as any new mother or father will attest, is that every infant inspires this same sense of miracle, of exaltation, of heaven reaching down to kiss the earth. The mystery writer Janwillem van de Wetering, a lifelong student of Zen, once remarked to me that "every time a new baby is born, I believe that he might be the one to save the world."

No doubt raw animal (or at least mammalian) pleasure plays a part in our happiness, for chipmunks and chimps, antelopes and zebras treasure their offspring as well. But there exists a special reason for our rejoicing. Human beings, all religions agree, occupy a unique position in the cosmos. Buddhism teaches that every living being must be reborn as human before achieving enlightenment; Christianity describes human beings as created "in the image and likeness of God." In other words, every human birth is a holy birth.

No wonder, then, that birth is an occasion for great celebration, and a time to renew, through contemplative and ritual practice, our ties to the sacred processes that govern the cosmos. In most cultures, this process extends over months or even years; the child's departure from the womb is but the centerpiece of a long table, heaped with spiritual activity, that extends from the moment of conception to the last rites of infancy. Chinese and Ibo prenatal practices, Sikh and Eskimo naming practices, the delightful Jewish custom of the weaving of the wimpel—all are part of the spiritual treasury of human birth, to be encountered in the pages that follow. Indeed, although our discussion of birth stops at the gates of childhood—around the age of one, when infants begin to be toddlers—I've no doubt that this is an artificial rupture. In truth, none of us is fully born. We are caught between darkness and light, conception and fruition. To witness a birth is also to know something of the mystery of our own life struggling to emerge.

Paul reports on the experiences of women seeking a more conscious and fulfilling childbirth.

Contemplative Close-up: Mirabai, Nora, and Libby

Childbirth is a sacred process that washes through your body.

NORA

The labor and delivery of the baby . . . is a journey to another shore.

MIRABAI

Birth presents us with a deep mystery: the one becoming two and the two becoming one.

LIBBY

My daughter Karen was born thirty-three years ago, emerging into the world as her mother exclaimed with the exquisite logic of one carried beyond mere joy: "It's . . . it's . . . a baby!" The doctor placed Karen in my arms. Ours had been a conscious birth, considered a bit experimental at a time when mothers were

A time of quiet gestation

routinely put into "twilight sleep" before the baby was delivered. Anaesthetized, the mothers woke up with a baby, recalling nothing of the birth itself.

The struggle of women to give birth in a deeply nourishing emotional and spiritual setting has been hard and often lonely. Still, a contemplative approach to pregnancy and birth has been like a gathering stream, into which has flowed a variety of secular and sacred sources of inspiration and practice.

This is a story about several women who have explored ways of bringing heightened awareness to birth, viewing it as a time when, as one tradition puts it, "The Book of Life is open." During pregnancy, many women become more reflective and philosophical not only about birth but about death as well. Birth and death are intimate partners in the dance of consciousness, and in a strange and miraculous way, one teaches the steps to the other. As evidence for this, consider the experiences of a young British army surgeon, Grantly Dick-Read, whose World War I service included the notorious bloodbath at Gallipoli.

Dr. Dick-Read survived the war—only barely—to become a founder of the natural childbirth movement. What he learned in the trenches about fear and death, he transmuted into lessons about awareness and the emergence of new life. At the risk of doing an injustice to the scope and poignancy of the madness he lived through, one can highlight some events that transformed his consciousness.

The first occurred on the beach at Gallipoli where, at his aid station, he was surrounded by hundreds of wounded men who were shivering and dying in the night air. "From time to time," he recalls in his memoirs, "death seemed to reach down from the empty space and seize this man or that."[2] Resting on a mound of sand within earshot of his flock, he is suddenly engulfed by a feeling of "utter loneliness." Back home, as a resident obstetrician in a London hospital, he was to bring this deep understanding of fear, apprehension, and loneliness (and the compassion generated by his own experience) to women about to give birth.

"Perhaps this is why," he wrote, "I shudder when I pass the door of those wards where women lie alone, enduring the first stage of labor with no understanding of what is taking place, fearfully imagining what greater agonies await them."

Dr. Dick-Read had a second battlefield experience from which he drew insights into childbirth. In Belgium, a young woman entered the British trench seeking a doctor's help. She was "very pregnant." As he placed her on a stretcher and examined her, he was profoundly struck by her lack of discomfort. "She seemed oblivious to the noise of war all around us," he remembers. After the baby was born the woman sat up on the stretcher, laughed, and took the baby in her arms. The doctor "could not forget the look of joy on her face."

Even for the contemporary reader, immersed in a culture that is coming to accept a dynamic relationship between mind, body, and spirit, Dr. Dick-Read's insights must seem quite extraordinary. Besides finding some heaven in hell, so to speak, he becomes aware of the relationship between the mother's emotions and how well or how poorly her body will perform in labor. Moreover, he realizes that what is "natural" about natural childbirth is for the mother to be clear and conscious, attending with all her senses to the birth; that her awareness and positive emotional responses inform the physiological processes. Conversely, fear and anxiety introduce unwanted muscular tension and resistance into the mother's body. Nature, it would appear, has designed a subtle system for birth that works best when the mother's mind and spirit are supported with unconditional love, warmth, joy, and awareness.

In the 1960s, the counterculture—infused with Hindu and Buddhist traditions and newly awake to indigenous practices and midwifery—began to expand the meaning and import of awareness during pregnancy and birth. Mirabai Bush, who had lived in India for several years, kept a journal when she was pregnant with her son Owen in 1971. The pages capture an evolution from the psychological attentiveness advocated by childbirth pioneers such as Dr. Dick-Read toward a mindfulness replete with spiritual awareness.

On a page headed "Meditation" she writes:

> *During pregnancy, meditation is being simple.*
> *Doing only a few things each day, so you can be conscious of them.*
> *Meditation is easier when you are pregnant,*
> *Because your body is stilling itself.*
> *Using its energy for child growth.*
> *Through meditation you are creating*
> *a spiritual womb that surrounds and protects*
> *the physical womb. It must be continually created.*
> *Be graceful.*
> *There is no where to go*
> *So go slowly and gracefully.*
> *Toes are popping,*
> *Heart is beating,*
> *Hair is curling,*
> *Arms and elbows and finger and round buddha belly*
> *All is happening just as it should.*

"The labor and delivery of the baby," writes Mirabai, "is a natural ritual, a vehicle that takes you from one consciousness to another. It is a journey to another shore and when you reach the end it is the beginning. . . . The more fully you participate in the birth, the more conscious and aware and present you are during the ritual, the more clearly you see the pain and doubts and fears and faith and love and strength manifesting, the more ready you will be for the child."

The physiological shocks and hormonal changes of pregnancy and birth seem to be nature's uncanny way of preparing women not only for the physical act of birth but for an initiation into the mystery of life's wider meaning and purpose. The emergence of a new, living body from within the body of another is not only the birth of a baby but an illumination. The spiritual essence of relationship, the heart of I and Thou, can now be understood with greater clarity and immediacy. According to Jewish custom, the period between Rosh Hashanah and Yom Kippur is a time during which the Book of Life is open. Your slate is momentarily clean and, if you are deserving, God will inscribe a new beginning for you. During pregnancy and birth, the Book of Life is similarly open to new ways of looking at the world and acting in it. This holds for the father and other family members, as well.

How do the new mother and her family seize this golden opportunity? One way, according to psychologist Libby Colman, is to take a more contemplative approach to pregnancy, birth, and the postpartum period, the aim of which is clarity and balance. Three decades of work with new mothers have confirmed her own experience that pregnancy, birth, and the postpartum period can create opportunities to change a woman's overall level of awareness, to reframe her sense of meaning and purpose in the world, and to increase her resilience in the face of future traumas. Contemplative practice can also reduce the mother's anxious efforts to control things and can help her surrender to the flow of events from pregnancy, through birth, and into the postpartum period.

One of the things that a woman can benefit from in the early stages of pregnancy, Libby suggests, is a quiet attention to the changes going on in her body. During such a reflection, a woman may become more sensitively attuned to the initial swellings in her breasts or the tingling sensation in her nipples. When she brings this awareness of what is happening to her body into a healthy perspective, it can set a good course for her entire journey.

Early in pregnancy, women experience the fetus more like an organ of their own bodies, often describing early fetal movement as "a butterfly fluttering in the womb" or "a little fish swimming around." In late pregnancy, they can feel specific limbs and an increased presence of the other being. In effect, a dialogue with the baby has begun, one that can be shaped by the mother's awareness.

Libby remembers being in labor with her third child and on her way to the hospital: "We stopped at an overlook near the Golden Gate Bridge. The panorama was particularly apt: the bay felt like a uterus, the Golden Gate like a birth canal, all fluid and open—but then a tanker came along and I was overwhelmed with the sense that the tanker heading toward the Gate was the baby heading toward the outside world and that I had better get to the hospital in a hurry because if I watched that tanker go under the bridge my baby would crown right there in the car."

Libby recommends keeping a journal so that the sequence of images that come in dreams or during meditation can be tracked and reflected upon: "You'll be able to see the development of your inner growth as a parent. Being open to the images that your own inner being is creating is the most powerful practice that you can develop during pregnancy."

Some women describe birth as pushing them to the edge, forcing them to make a kind of leap of faith. Nora Bateson, a new mother, recalls such a moment: "It was the pivotal moment in transition, when I was very tired, very uncomfortable and scared. I just wished that someone else could take over for a while, or that I could do it tomorrow, or that there was some other way to get to the end of the journey without going through this. Then I realized that there was only one way out, and that was through the door that I stood before, stalling. To get through meant I had to let go of the last strings of my old life, to go through the pain, through the chaos, and to trust the natural process. At that moment, I suddenly felt connected to every other woman in history. There was no one but me and the baby to do the work, but I was not alone. I will always have this experience to draw on."

Nora gave birth at home, with her husband, Dan, at her side. She was assisted by midwives and surrounded by family and friends. "I wanted as much openness as possible," she says, "and I wanted to share the birth with others, to create a community around the birth of the baby."

Over time, Nora has come to understand that the inclusive way she chose to give birth to her daughter, Sahra, echoed the most powerful event of Nora's adolescence: the death of her father. Suffering from cancer, Gregory Bateson declined chemical treatment that promised to extend his days in favor of remaining clear-minded to the end. "He died a conscious death. His death was shared, open. It changed people's lives. It was a sacred event."

For a woman to treat pregnancy, birth, and the postpartum period as sacred means that she will invest her time and attention in these events. "Finding time simply to be with pregnancy is hard in our culture," says Nora. "The only real tradition we have is the baby shower and the layette.

"The most important thing I did in pregnancy, the best thing I did," she recalls, "was to sit on my bed, look out the window, and do absolutely nothing. Not read, not write, not try to get to some ecstatic place. Just sit still. Just be there in quietness. That really opened up communication between myself and the baby."

For the first-time mother, birth is a great unknown. And, while there is no way to rehearse the experience, Nora believes that mothers can use pregnancy as a time to become more familiar with the source of peace within themselves. In this regard, yoga and breathing practices can be particularly helpful in reducing both physical discomfort and anxiety.

According to Libby Colman: "Early in pregnancy many women discover that the anxiety is coming from their relationship to their own bodies and the fear of their bodies getting out of control. So, here is an opportunity for a woman to meditate on her body image and her need to control things rather than surrender to natural change."

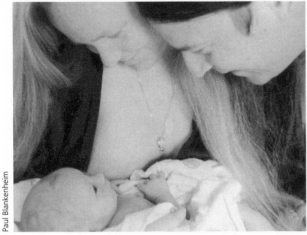
Nora, Danny, and Sahra

To be fully present throughout pregnancy and birth and into the postpartum period, Nora was forced to take a hard look at what she calls "the insanity of our daily lives." She chose not to continue business as usual but to honor her time with her baby: "So what if the dishes aren't done. This is a moment of peace and its value is immeasurable." Nora's godmother had advised her, "Don't do or say anything in this house that you wouldn't do or say in a temple." Nora felt that the new baby filled the home with the kind of sacredness she has experienced in a place of worship.

Nora is weaning Sahra and is pregnant again. She regularly attends a prenatal group with other mothers. "We have four hours just to be pregnant. In the adventure of pregnancy and birth it is so easy to become lost in the medical complexities and to get distracted from the deeper work. This is the work that acknowledges and nourishes the spirit."

BIRTH: A CONTEMPLATIVE HARVEST

Prenatal Spiritual Practices

I began this chapter with two prenatal tales: one about my wife's friend Sophie and her heavenly vision, the other about the adventures of the embryonic soul according to talmudic lore. As these stories suggest, the nine months preceding birth are a spiritually charged and precarious time for both baby and parent. Many religious cultures respond to this time with a complex set of prescriptions and proscriptions governing life in the womb. For example, the Ibo believe that if a pregnant woman eats snails, her child may suffer from weak nasal membranes, while Malaysian tradition holds that acts of cruelty by the father during the mother's pregnancy will result in a deformed infant.

Some prenatal taboos, such as the Ibo's ban on snails, may be based on direct observation of the effects of food upon pregnancy. Others, such as the worldwide belief that a pregnant woman risks miscarriage if she glimpses a funeral procession, can be classed as sympathetic magic. But what is sympathetic magic? Although we may doubt that sketching a successful hunt on a cave wall will ensure a bountiful real-life hunt, as the Picassos of Lascaux may have believed, we can recognize the genius of the underlying vision, which acknowledges the interconnectedness of all creation. Sympathetic magic may be poor science, but it reveals an acute sensitivity to the symbolic and analogical kinship of all things. Among the Chinese of rural Taiwan, for example, it is believed that Tai Shen, the deity who oversees pregnancy and birth, takes up residence in the bedchamber of every expectant mother and dwells there until the moment of childbirth. Can there be a lovelier expression than this of the spiritual nature of pregnancy? The image suggests, at the very least, that one should accord respect to the perceptions of pregnant women, for they dwell in a special realm, with its own modes of knowing and experiencing.

COUVADE

If you want to watch a grown man squirm, tell him about couvade (from the French *couver*, "to hatch"). The effect is quite extraordinary. He'll wince, sputter, and groan; he may even bolt out of the room. No topic short of castration produces so dramatic an effect. While it may discomfit macho sensibilities, the custom of couvade persists worldwide. Details vary from one culture to the next, but the kernel remains the same: the father takes to his bed before or at the birth of his child and proceeds to mimic the mother's symptoms of labor and birth. The following is a description of some aspects of couvade as practiced in British Guiana:

> No sooner is the child born than the father takes to his hammock, and, abstaining from every sort of work, from meat and all other food, except weak gruel of cassava meal, from smoking, from washing himself, and above all, from touching weapons of any sort, is nursed and cared for by all the women of the place.... This continues for many days, and sometimes even weeks.[3]

I'm hardly suggesting that readers of this book begin practicing couvade. Not only is it entirely beyond the cultural reach of most modern males, but it would be an artificial imposition at best, the grafting of an oak twig onto an elm tree. Like the prenatal regulations discussed above, however, couvade springs from an exquisite awareness of the spiritual power of childbirth. At the very least it reveals:

- The deep relationship between father and mother, so that the father shares in every possible way in the mother's pregnancy, labor, and childbirth. (I should mention here, with some discomfort, the delight of my female students at Smith College when I describe, during my course on Native American religions, a parallel practice among the Huichol of Mexico. During the delivery of a child, the father sits in the rafters of the house, a rope tied around his scrotum; the ends of this rope are clutched by the pregnant woman, who tugs on them as the contractions come, so that her husband will share in her pain.)
- The equally deep relationship between father and child, so that, as we saw in the case of couvade in British Guiana, the father is fed and comforted at the same time and in the same manner as his offspring. Although physically separate, father and child may thus share parallel experiences from the moment of birth (a weak but genuine counterpart to the breast-feeding shared by mother and child).

Realistically, couvade stands no chance of becoming a common form of paternal participation in twenty-first-century pregnancies. Today, a father is more likely to join in the birth process in the guise of labor coach. Nonetheless, the impulse behind these practices remains the same: to welcome the father into the sacred circle of intimacy in which mother and infant dwell. As such, couvade and its analogues will always be valued.

Postpartum Spiritual Practices

Postpartum practices, like prenatal ones, mark and consecrate the emergence of a new human being. While variations flourish from one religious tradition to the next, almost all place great weight upon two particular events: naming and coming out into society.

NAMING

Nothing matters more than a name. My son Andy, now two, walks around the house pointing at objects and chanting their names at the top of his lungs, as if taking part in an exuberant religious rite. When he spots his mother, he chants

"Momma!" "Momma!" "Momma!"; the same for "Daddy!" and "Da!" (John) and "Pooh!" and "Yerbi!" (gerbil) and other inhabitants of our crowded household. At other times he chants our names even in our absence, not as a summons but as a mantra to accompany his ceaseless round of activity. All this is the stuff of genuine religion (from the root *religare*, to bind); by reciting names, Andy is binding his inner being to the outer world, uniting both into a meaningful whole.

Names not only tie us to the world; they affirm the very existence of that world and everything in it. In Pueblo mythology, Thought Woman thinks the world into being and then immediately names its contents, thereby confirming and defining their existence. In Genesis, naming both initiates and concludes God's seven-day labor of creation. Nothing is real until it receives a name, and thus its own identity in the welter of being.

Names contain multiple dimensions of meaning. When a friend announced that her new son would be named Fred, someone asked, "And is he just like a Fred?" This question recognizes one of the most mysterious powers of a name: although Freds come in all shapes and sizes, nonetheless the name "Fred" conjures up an image that most of us share, a sense of "Fredness" brewed from all the Freds that we've known or heard of, a Fred-like way of being that will mold this newborn babe as surely as it has Fred MacMurray, Fred (Mr.) Rogers, and all the other celebrated Freds of history. One wonders how Friedrich Nietzsche might have turned out if his parents had called him "Fred"—or better still, "Freddy." N. Scott Momaday remembers his grandfather saying that "a man's life proceeds from his name, in the way that a river proceeds from its source."[4]

Acknowledging the spiritual importance of names scarcely makes the final choice any easier. Generally speaking, one should make use of whatever clues are offered. When the birth of our first son approached, my wife and I followed local custom and compiled a long list of potential names. That list sits on the desk before me as I write. Some of the names on it I now find inconceivable— Bartholomew? Nehemiah?—while others, like William and Michael, continue to ring true. My wife and I worried the issue endlessly but could come to no conclusion, beyond agreeing that we preferred a name from the Bible. To our delight, the solution came to us in classical biblical fashion—in a dream. My mother phoned one morning to say that our soon-to-be-born son had appeared to her while she slept and had announced, "My name is John." And so John he was, and John he remains. It doesn't hurt that John is a beloved family name, worn by my maternal grandfather and one of my maternal uncles, that it means "God is gracious," and that it is the name of saints and sages whose memories we venerate and of friends whose company we enjoy. Common the name may be, but now that John bears it, it seems uniquely his own.

Every tradition has its own way of naming a child. Among the Eskimo, the name is bestowed at birth. A trusted female relative recites potential names during the last stages of labor; when the correct name is uttered, the baby rushes forth from the womb. The Blackfeet choose names that reflect the circumstances of birth. Traditional Sikhs select the infant's name at a *gurdwara* (place of worship): a holy man recites a prayer and then opens the Sikh scriptures at random; the first letter of the first word on the left-hand page of the opened book becomes the initial letter of the child's new name.

But what, you may wonder, can I learn from such rituals, which arise in a culture that is not my own? What can they teach me about the process of naming my baby?

The answer, I believe, is: a great deal. I may discover that my own tradition includes a naming ritual of which I knew nothing, which can be recovered to the great joy of my family and myself. I may find that another tradition offers a practice that I can adopt as my own without violating its integrity (for example, there's no reason why the Sikh method of choosing a name, with its reliance on "randomness"—which really amounts to reliance on God's providence—can't be adopted by people of any tradition). Eskimo, Sikh, and Blackfoot rituals differ radically, but a single spiritual principle—that seemingly chance events may be profoundly meaningful—infuses them all. The howl of a wolf, a letter from scripture, the timing of a baby's departure from the womb: each is a sign, apparently random but nonetheless significant, that reveals the infant's true nature and his appropriate name.

When it comes to naming my own baby, then, I can make good use of this principle and remain alert for signs that will help me to choose the right name. The choice may come in a dream, or through family tradition, or by opening a beloved book at random. The key is to be as open as possible to the life of my child, the life of names, and the mysterious relationship between the two.

COMING OUT INTO SOCIETY

The ritual of coming out into society, an infant version of a debutante ball, presents the newborn to society and to the divine. Often this ceremony is linked with naming. For example, seven days after an infant's birth, some Muslims introduce the newborn to family and friends through the *aqiqah,* a combined naming and coming-out-into-society ritual thick with symbolic actions. These include shaving the infant's head to signal his nakedness before God; weighing the shorn hair and donating gold of equal weight to the poor; and placing a piece of date in the baby's mouth, symbolizing the sweetness of God. Similarly, the Wolof of Africa hold a naming and coming-out-into-society ceremony one week after a birth, beginning at exactly the same moment during the day that the delivery took place. This ceremony, as the timing suggests, serves as a second birth, in this case into the social and spiritual realms.

One of the most famous of all coming-out-into-society ceremonies is the Jewish *brit milah*, or rite of circumcision. Performed eight days after birth, the *brit* initiates the infant boy into his community and into the Jewish covenant with God. For all its bloodiness, a *brit* contains a rich sense of the numinous. An empty chair sits beside the participants, reserved for the prophet Elijah, who is invisibly present as God's representative and acts as the child's spiritual guardian. The *brit* resonates with blessings, born from an acute awareness of God's abiding presence:

> Blessed are you, O Lord our God! King of the universe, who sanctified us with your commandments and commanded us regarding circumcision.

> Blessed are you, O Lord our God! King of the universe, who sanctified us with your commandments and commanded us to initiate [the infant] into the covenant of Abraham our father.

> Blessed are you, O Lord our God! King of the Universe, who kept us alive, sustained us, and brought us to this time.

Just as the biblical Abram, at the time of his circumcision, received from God the name of Abraham, so does the infant, immediately following his circumcision, received his Hebrew name. By reenacting Abraham's circumcision, the *brit* reconfirms the original covenant between God and his people, and thus immerses the infant in the great stream of Jewish history and belief.

THE WIMPEL
A wonderful Jewish custom from western Europe involves the wimpel, the piece of cloth that swaddles the baby during circumcision. After the *brit milah*, the wimpel is cleaned, cut,

Baptism

Bill Aron

and sewn into a twelve-foot-long strip that is embroidered by mother or grand-mother with the infant's name, date of birth, zodiacal sign, and wishes for a life of Torah, marriage, and good deeds. These decorations can grow quite elaborate, until the wimpel resembles a cross between a medieval tapestry and a Shaker spirit drawing. On or about the child's first birthday, the parents bring the wimpel to the synagogue, where it is wound around the Torah scrolls as a ritual binding, while a special prayer is recited, asking God to shower the child with purity, grace, strength, and love. The wimpel is then donated to the synagogue.

As all these rituals suggest, we respond to the birth of a baby with a rebirth in our own lives, a joyous surge of creativity and celebration. Different cultures celebrate this renewal in different ways; the variety of symbols, rites, rituals, and other prac-tices applied to birth staggers the mind. As we will see, this pattern of abundance repeats in every stage of the life cycle. Always, these practices have much to teach us. As an imaginative exercise, let us stack all the ceremonies, rites, and practices that we have encountered in this chapter atop one another. We will find that certain truths about human birth shine through from top to bottom. These include:

- Birth is more than two or twenty hours of labor; it extends across many months, before and after delivery.
- Birth involves not only the mother and her child, but also the father, the extended family, and the entire community.
- In sum, birth is more than the coming into being of a new human being; it is the means whereby parents, family, friends, and society renew their ties to the sacred and to one another. *The birth of a child is, potentially, the rebirth of us all.*

t w e l v e

CHILDHOOD

*A*friend of mine reports that her eight-year-old daughter recently took up the cello. My friend dutifully arranged for private lessons, and a few weeks later she drove out, daughter and cello in tow, to an immaculate ranch house surrounded by roses and rhododendrons in the affluent suburbs of Boston. The teacher ushered them into the house and then excused herself for a minute, leaving my friend and her daughter alone inside a large, lavishly furnished living room. The daughter scrutinized the polished parquet floors, the glass coffee table topped by flowers and a spray of magazines, the immaculate lace curtains on the French windows, the Moroccan and Turkish carpets, the delicate vases on the mantel. She then turned to her mother, wrinkled her nose, and said, "Hmmm . . . no children."

This anecdote tells us a great deal about a child's capacity for observation; it tells us even more about a child's capacity for life. Children are vital, vibrant, bursting with juice; children are messy, disruptive; children are *real*. Anyone who

Priscilla Carrasco

Anna Kutsev and her sisters, Russian Old Believers, Woodburn, Oregon

reads much utopian fiction will sooner or later utter the same observation as my friend's daughter: "Hmmm . . . no children." Often little ones are entirely absent, or nearly so, as in the depiction of the elysian Eloi in *The Time Machine* (where Wells devotes two skimpy sentences to kids), or else they are programmed and pigeon-holed until they are no longer children, as in Skinner's *Walden II.* In real life, children explode all expectations: an elementary school dunce becomes a brain surgeon, while the best violinist in the high-school orchestra winds up singing on a chain gang.

In this quicksilver quality, we find the essence of a child's spiritual life. Give a child a stick and it becomes a ray-gun, show her a dragonfly and she sees a dragon. Hinduism celebrates Krishna the Butter Thief, the blue-skinned god who as a young man steals the hearts of milkmaids south of Delhi and, as a cherub-faced toddler, steals butter from his mother's cupboard. According to John Stratton Hawley, Krishna is "a god of love, and love is at the heart of his story. Butter itself is love." And why does Krishna steal love? Because "God is not to be limited, and neither is love."[1] Children break all boundaries; they live unfettered by the irons that we adults forge for ourselves and wear with pride.

As the tale of Krishna suggests, children possess, in some mysterious embryonic form, the wisdom of the ages: "Truly I say to you, whoever does not receive the kingdom of God like a child shall not enter it" (Mark 10:15). Wallace B. Clift aptly calls the child an image of wholeness. Yet this is not a static wholeness; the child is still baking in the oven, and all the culinary arts at our disposal are needed to ensure a successful outcome. Childhood has no radical transitions, such as we witness in birth, puberty, or marriage; few religions, if any, have rituals to mark various stages of childhood. Rather, childhood is a time of slow evolution, of gradual gain in strength, knowledge, and understanding.

How to nourish this gentle unfolding? This problem is, I believe, the most difficult and important task of human life. On the one hand, we must learn how to encourage the natural spontaneity, freshness, and insight of children. We must let them be what they are, without excessive adult restraint. On the other hand, we must learn how to train children to make the best use of their resources both inner and outer. We must teach them to become what they are not, by giving to them the knowledge of the past. I'm describing a process of letting go and reining in, of fertilizing and pruning—in a word, cultivation. As any parent knows, this husbandry has many turnings and traps. One needs a good flashlight to see one's way. As we discussed in part 1, this flashlight—for all human beings, but perhaps especially for children—is attention. There is no more important job for an adult than teaching a child how to be attentive. Without attention, no child can play, no child can pray, and no child can love. "Not only does the love of God have attention for its substance," writes Simone Weil; "the love of our neighbor, which we know to be the same love, is made of this same substance."[2]

To foster attention in children, we should take certain precautions. We should beware of television programs—some of them supposedly designed for children—whose images flicker past too quickly for assimilation or digestion. We should watch out for computer and video games that replace real life with ersatz experience. On the other hand, we should encourage the reading of books, which stimulates the imagination. We should encourage painting, building, dancing, cooking, music making, and other forms of active engagement with the world. Our aim isn't to bombard kids with excitement—if that were so, we could simply wire them to a circuit board that directly stimulates the brain. Nor is our aim to lull them with comforts—if it were, we could just feed them a steady diet of tranquilizers. Our aim must be to make each life an epic voyage from truth to truth, to teach each child how to take two sticks and make a fire, how to take two words and make a poem, how to take the earth and make of it a heaven.

CONTEMPLATIVE CLOSE-UP: TRUSTING THE LIFE WITHIN

"Every child is an idea of God," writes Eberhard Arnold, a founder of the Protestant spiritual community known as the Bruderhof, or Society of Brothers. He goes on to explain this bold declaration:

> God knows what this child is intended for; He has conceived an idea for
> him from all eternity, and He will hold to it. The service which parents,
> teachers and community must render the child is to help him become what
> God's original idea meant him to be. . . .[3]

Whatever our understanding of God may be, Arnold's claims ring true. The child has an inner life, born in the sacred ("trailing clouds of glory") and pointing toward an unknown destiny. Our task is to nourish this inner life, to bring this precious crop to spiritual harvest. The Aztecs of Mexico had a phrase for this: "to find one's face, to find one's heart." Let us explore some of the ways in which this may be accomplished.

The Ultimate Thing

Children, most of us believe, have a special relationship to the divine. We see this in their spontaneity, their sense of awe, their very closeness in years to the origin of life and thus to the Mystery from which it springs. The Bruderhof make much of this divine impulse within the child. Like the Amish, their close spiritual kin, they value large families—to visit one of the Bruderhof agrarian settlements scattered around the United States and Canada is to glimpse the world as it was before the widespread availability of birth control—and thus have much experience upon which to draw.

A child's educational development, the Bruderhof teach, must be in accord with the child's inner life. Arnold writes that "we should not force on [the child] anything that has not been born into him, awakened from within, or given him completely new by God."[4] The goal of education is "awakening the child to the essential and ultimate thing that lives in the depths of his heart."[5] Put into daily practice, this becomes a threefold process consisting of:

- *Trust in the child.* Parent and teacher must have complete faith in the child's essential goodness, seeing the child as a precious manifestation of God's love. This doesn't mean a laissez-faire approach to child-rearing; children can be scamps as well as charmers. The parent's task is to let the good in children shine through, by fostering an atmosphere of love and reverence. "Love for the child affirms and intensifies his childlikeness and constantly strengthens it with forces of good, so that the child does not fall victim to an intentionally bad action," writes Arnold.[6]
- *Trust in the family.* To the Bruderhof, the family is the center of the child's life, the primary culture in which the child will grow and flourish. "The child's being is rooted in the home and in father and mother," suggests Arnold.[7] The parents have been given a sacred task, that of guiding the development of a new human life. In a home resplendent with love, this guidance will nourish in the child security, happiness, and reverence toward life.
- *Trust in the community.* The Bruderhof introduce children to communal living from the first days of life. No child is raised in isolation; even infants spend their time with other infants, learning to play, eat, and explore together. This emphasis on shared experience continues throughout the child's education. In kindergarten (which lasts two years) and elementary school, children celebrate religious holidays together, garden together, make music together. Nature study teaches them the community of all living things, just as diverse training in pottery and mathematics, woodworking and writing, teaches them the community of human skills.

This emphasis on trust is not, of course, limited to the Bruderhof. Traditional Quakers, for example, hold dear many similar precepts and practices. A variation on the Bruderhof belief in the child as "an idea of God" can be found in the key Quaker teaching of the "inner light," which a renowned early Quaker, Isaac Pennington, defined as "that which shineth from God in the heart, wherein God is near to men, and wherein and whereby men may seek after God and find Him"—a teaching that naturally invites the believer to contemplation and prayer.[8] The practice of attending to the inner light bestowed on many Quaker children a reliable moral compass, as one nineteenth-century text testifies:

Jan Watson

Learning by experience and example

> I could say with thankfulness of heart, the Lord was my morning light; for I well remember to have been favored with that Light in very early life as a reprover for sin, even in childish transgressions and disobedience to parental injunctions. Thus it was with me when very young, that I was made renewedly sensible of the love of Him who first loved us. . . . I am certain that if the necessity of attending to the inward monitor were impressed upon children, they would not so often grow up in hardness of heart.[9]

Like the Bruderhof, Quakers understand that the inner light cannot shine in a vacuum. The good in the child needs to be nurtured at every moment. Listen to how successfully this can be accomplished through regular contemplative practices, as exemplified by the early years of the great Quaker leader Rufus Jones:

> I was sprinkled from morning till night with the dew of religion. We never ate a meal which did not begin with a hush of thanksgiving; we never began a day without a family gathering at which mother read a chapter of the Bible, after which there would follow a weighty silence. These silences, during which all the children of our family were hushed with a kind of awe, were very important features of my spiritual development. There was work inside and outside the house waiting to be done, and yet we sat there hushed and quiet, doing nothing. I very quickly discovered that something real was taking place. We were feeling our way down to that place from which living words come and very often did come. Some one would bow

and talk with God so simply and quietly that He never seemed very far away. The words helped to explain the silence. We were now finding what we had been searching for.[10]

Singing up the Children

The Papago Indians of southern Arizona have an expression, "singing up the corn," that refers to the process of song, prayer, and ritual that ensures a healthy annual corn harvest. I believe that this is what we do with children as well when we remain open to their needs and offer them an abundance of attention and love. We sing up the children. The Bruderhof and the Quakers offer some ways to nourish the inner life of children; for other suggestions, let us now turn briefly to the cultures of native North America.

Until the last century, Native American spiritual formation always took place through oral transmission, face-to-face. Teaching was immediate, flexible, and spontaneous, and thus well suited to the chameleonlike nature of a child's attention. Often, the child was expected to learn through his own initiative. Anthropologist Thomas Buckley asked an elderly Yurok canoe maker if he had served an apprenticeship. The man replied:

> Naw, nobody taught me nothing. I just watched and picked it up. That's how you used to learn everything; you watched and figured it out and went ahead and did it. Nobody taught you.[11]

As Buckley points out, Yurok education for this elderly man involved more than learning how to make a canoe; by relying on his own resources, he learned the nature of facts, of cause and effect, of relationship—lessons of the first importance.

Even when an adult intervenes in the learning process, the child may be expected to extract the lesson for himself. Buckley quotes another Yurok who remembers how he overcame his fear of the sea:

> I was afraid of the ocean. I was born that way I guess. When I was about eleven, my uncle made me go sit on a big drift-log that stuck in the beach and hung far out over the surf. I wanted to come in right away, but he made me stay. I sat there all night. Slowly I began to see the water, to see what the important things about it were. And when I saw this, I started to see the facts of my fear about it. . . . I studied the water, and I studied the fear, and I swam a great deal.[12]

Among the Indians of the Great Plains, children participate in activities especially designed to bring out desired characteristics. Thus—at least in the olden days—boys from an early age were expected to fast, plunge into ice water, and go without sleep, thus building fortitude and strength, qualities that would make them effective warriors later in life. Girls learned all the domestic skills expected of them, as well as female virtues like honesty and courtesy, and they, too, underwent ordeals to ensure their stamina and courage.

CHILDHOOD: A CONTEMPLATIVE HARVEST

The Excitement of the Unknown: A Conversation with Richard Lewis

To learn more about the spiritual life of children, I talked with Richard Lewis, director and founder of The Touchstone Center, a nonprofit organization in New York City that for nearly thirty years has explored the inner world of the child. Lewis, a friendly man with an air of whimsy, laughed when I asked him to begin by defining childhood. "It's been the victim of romanticizing," he said. "People see it as a blissful world. But actually the process of growth isn't easy. Look at an infant—see how much struggle there is just to survive."

Part of the romanticizing, Lewis suggests, springs from ignorance. We simply know very little about the inner life of children. "It's a very difficult field to investigate," he says, "because we can't speak to kids about everything that's happening inside them. We're dealing with lack of vocabulary and lack of articulation. Vast areas within the child remain unknown."

This is where Lewis's own work begins, in trying to explore these nearly inaccessible pathways within the child's psyche that have to do with creativity, sensitivity, spirituality. As Lewis points out, this cuts against the grain: "The emphasis in schools isn't on the inner life of the child, but rather on what the child has learned. Those modalities of feeling that are the essence of the individual are not what education is concerned with. Teachers are not allowed to venture into this territory." The irony, Lewis says, is that when we bother to ask children about themselves, they respond gladly: "Children are amazed when you talk to them about the marvelous qualities of their own thought. Many children have been told that they're not good students or good creators. When you tell them about the marvel of their own thought, it changes their ideas about themselves."

According to Lewis, encouraging children to discover and reveal their inner world is the obligation of every parent. "You have to praise where a child's life seems to be moving. Each inch of the way, you must say to the child, 'That's wonderful, what you have done. I appreciate that.'" Lewis warns that enthusiasm can't be feigned. Children are very sensitive to adult moods and immediately detect a lack of parental interest. The only solution is to surrender to the life of the child. Lewis believes that this submission brings ample reward. "It's a very humbling thing, for it brings us down to the child's level. This is of great benefit to us, for it puts us in touch with the phenomenon of life itself, and especially with those aspects of life that we usually don't take the time to notice."

Just as parents need to encourage the spiritual life of children, so do children need to cultivate their own inner gardens. This is done through play, which Lewis defines as "the essence of a child's ability to discover its own way of looking at the world." But play must involve the right materials. Ready-made toys, Lewis believes, destroy the creativity of real play and can be as mind-numbing as television shows. He frowns on giant toy stores that have "materialized play," and he criticizes the film *Toy Story* for celebrating the accumulation of products that neither inspire nor instruct. I mention that when my son John receives a new Lego set, he builds the prescribed rocket ship or submarine and then immediately dismantles it and uses the plastic blocks to construct objects of his own invention. This, Lewis agrees, is how a child's imagination ignites. He suggests that parents keep simple objects— sticks, stones, buttons—lying around the house. In no time, children will turn them into fairy castles.

Another important tool in education, as we saw in chapter 7, "Words," is storytelling. Lewis encourages the telling of tales, but he adds that often it's the children's story that needs to be heard. "It is important," he says, "to listen to what the child is telling you as his story. This is very fragmentary at times—a couple of sentences, a few references. But children are anxious to share this with us." This has particular importance, he suggests, because storytelling is a way of discovering the reality of relationships. "Have you noticed how children always continue a story by saying 'and'? 'And' is a footbridge from one event to another. I believe that a story is another kind of 'and' for children, a way to connect the different parts of their lives. For a child, the telling of a story is a way of making relationships come alive, as well as helping to explain them."

At the same time, Lewis believes that explanations sometimes block a child's sense of wonder. "One of the great things that I've discovered about getting older," he says, "is that you get to enjoy the wonderful unknowns that surround us. The question mark keeps getting larger. In school, children go to the known all the time. I want to let them see that the unknown is equally as exciting." Lewis's lifelong affection for Basho, Issa, and other Zen poets seems a part of this; in their haiku he finds the spontaneity and openness of childhood, sustained even into old age. Chinese and Japanese cultures, says Lewis, have a useful view of childhood: "it isn't something that you grow through into adulthood; rather it's a permanent part of

Un Rebozo, Pueblo, Mexico

life. As you grow older, you don't leave childhood; you recycle it. Growing older is coming into deeper aspects of childhood. Childhood isn't a stage of life but a way of life."

Training the Life Within

Just as a climbing rose needs a trellis, so a child needs a tradition to support the upward journey. Let us look now at two traditional approaches to the formal spiritual education of the child.

THE LIFE OF TORAH

The Hebrew word for education, *hinukh,* means not only instruction but also consecration. To educate is to make sacred; to educate a Jewish child is to escort that child into the sacred precincts of the faith. Rabbi Hayim Halevy Donin has identified four ways in which this is accomplished:

1. By teaching the moral precepts of the Jewish faith.
2. By teaching active observance of the Jewish commandments.
3. By instilling a sense of solidarity with all Jews.
4. By teaching the Torah (the Bible as interpreted by rabbinic authorities).[13]

While attending to the child's immediate needs, traditional Jewish education—formerly limited to boys, although this is changing—also emphasizes the need to learn a profession. The Talmud reminds us that "a father is obligated to teach his son a skill. He who does not do so, teaches him to steal."[14] Nonetheless, the primary concern of parent and community is to deepen and widen a child's experience of God. Religious instruction begins immediately after birth. During the seven days between birth and circumcision, schoolchildren visit the newborn's home to recite the Shema, the basic Jewish declaration of faith, thus instilling the essence of Judaism in the child's nascent psyche.

Jewish education unfolds with an eye to the individual child's needs, capacities, and place in society, in conformity with the scriptural injunction to "train the child in accordance with his way" (Prov. 22:6). Customarily, the mother teaches the domestic prayers, such as the Shema, the blessings over food, and so on, while the father imparts the basic tools of scholarship, such as reading and writing, as well as the ways of congregational worship and the meaning and practice of festivals, holidays, and rituals.

Pride of place belongs to Torah study. While still in the crib, children hear their mothers sing lullabies encouraging them to hasten to their teacher's house, there to learn the Torah. According to the *Pirke Aboth*, Torah study is the very reason for existence. Education in Torah leads to happiness in all things ("Whoso receives upon him the yoke of Torah, they remove from him ... the yoke of worldly care);[15] it is the very bedrock of culture; it brings one into the presence of God. Formal Torah study begins at the age of five or six, and demands extraordinary concentration on the part of the child. Great emphasis is placed on analysis of texts as well as prodigious feats of memorization. The child learns Hebrew, studies Mishnah and Talmud, and eventually, it is hoped, becomes a teacher to the next generation, transmitting not only the technical skills but also the distilled wisdom of the tradition.

THE REALM OF VIRTUE

For a hundred generations, until the Maoist revolution, child-rearing in China revolved around filial piety. This term covered a number of different behaviors, but above all, it meant the reverence of children toward parents. An early Confucian text, *The Classic of Filial Piety*, discusses filial piety in the form of a dialogue between Confucius and his disciple Tseng-tzu. Confucius makes no bones about the importance of filial piety for the social fabric, calling it "the root of virtue and the source of civilization."[16]

Filial piety between child and parent, Confucius tells his disciple, is a model for all human relationships, even those outside the family. Every stratum of society—lords, ministers, scholars, commoners—ideally practices a form of filial piety. Filial piety is, in fact, the perfect expression of the interdependency of the cosmos. It is "the pattern of heaven, the standard of the earth."[17] Kings respect their fathers and thus serve heaven; they respect their mothers and thus serve the earth. Children respect their elders, and as a result elders respect their underlings. Even ghosts and spirits respond well to the trust and reverence generated by filial piety. Virtue rules in every sphere.

This is, no doubt, an admirable social portrait in the abstract, but how is it realized on the canvas of life? Confucius imagines filial piety as a five-stage process lasting a lifetime, during which a child reveres his parents, brings them delight, nurses them when they fall ill, mourns them when they die, and prays for them after death. The *Li Ki,* or *Book of Rites,* sets out these obligations as well as every other aspect of a child's maturation. At six, children learn numbers and compass directions. At eight, they begin to walk behind their elders. At nine, they learn the calendar. At ten, the sexes live apart and receive different educations. Boys learn music and dance; girls, sewing and weaving.

This precise rule of life is matched by an even more exact code of behavior. A thirteenth-century guidebook written by disciples of Chu Hsi establishes the appropriate behavior of students for every moment of the day and every conceivable activity, from dress ("even in the hottest days of summer you should not take off your socks or shoes at will")[18] to deportment ("Do not step on doorsills. Do not limp. Do not lean on anything").[19] It's pleasant to imagine how such a rule book would go over in a modern American high school!

What results from this immense weight of rules? According to Confucius and his followers, nothing less than spiritual insight and moral rectitude. "Generally speaking," reads one Confucian text, "that which makes man man is the meaning of his ceremonial usages."[20] The ancient Chinese used jade, a precious mineral found in caves and dragon lairs, as a metaphor for the human soul. "The jade uncut will not form a vessel for use, and if men do not learn, they do not know the way," reads one venerable text.[21] By cutting the jade, by shaping the person through an intense indoctrination in proper decorum, the radiance of this precious substance—the beauty of one's true nature—is allowed to shine. "If you can follow the above regulations closely," concludes a Confucian treatise on education, "you are approaching the true realm of virtue."[22]

Classical Jewish and Confucian educational systems may strike some of us as stern, unyielding, and insensitive to the inner life of the child. But is this really so? Certainly they differ from the gentle massaging of the spirit favored by many educators. But their strictness, which expresses itself in an emphasis on rote learning as much as an adherence to moral rules, brings its own rewards. These ancient educational systems teach us, at a minimum:

- *A deep respect for the intellectual abilities of the child.* In Jewish and Chinese tradition, a child is expected to learn at a pace and depth that would cause many modern high-school students to throw up their hands in despair. Even today, millions of young Muslims in Egypt or Saudi Arabia manage to memorize the Koran in its entirety. As a result, the sacred texts that shape the culture cease to belong to some foreign precinct, that of the home bookshelf or school library, and become part of the child's own store of knowledge, a treasure nestled at the center of his or her being. Are traditional systems demanding too much of their children, or are we demanding too little of ours?
- *A deep respect for the child's sense of responsibility and judgment.* Instead of manufacturing excuses for bad behavior, these classical societies expect good behavior and set out, with no ambiguity, the rules of community life. Again, are they asking too much of their children, or are we too lackadaisical with ours?

No doubt, we need to arrive at a golden mean. The teachings of Bruderhof, Quaker, Jew, and Chinese provide parts of the puzzle. By piecing them together, by finding the balance between trusting and teaching, between sugar and vinegar, we will learn how to make childhood both a joy for our children and a fitting prelude to adulthood.

The Altar of the Home

The shared spiritual life of parent and child begins at home. This remains true even if the child joins in a formal program of religious training. One example of how this may be accomplished comes from my friends Dechen and Eileen, who have raised their children, Jigmed and Pema, in the principles and practices of Tibetan Buddhism. From their earliest years, the children joined their parents in grace before meals, always recited in Tibetan. Dechen often lulled them to sleep by chanting Buddhist mantras as nursery lullabies. As the children grew older, they prayed each morning and night with prostrations and chanting at the family altar. Also of primary importance, Eileen believes, were the answers that she and Dechen gave to the inevitable probings of young children: Why am I here? What happens after death? Where does the universe end? Rather than blank stares, embarrassed silences, or the door-slammed-in-the-face answer of "Nobody knows"—a terrifying response for many young children—Dechen and Eileen offered their children a traditional anchor, forged of Buddhist doctrine and insight.

Every tradition offers the same opportunity to blanket children in the security of sacred knowledge and the bliss of sacred practice. Thus my wife used to sing John to sleep each night with the Salve Regina, the last prayer in the Office of Compline; now he enjoys his own nightly routine, a medley of traditional prayers and his own private intentions for family and friends, while baby Andy nods off to Salve Regina. Our Jewish friends make sure that their children recite the Shema every morning and evening; our Native American friends accompany their children with prayers drawn from their own traditions.

Perhaps the surest, and certainly the coziest, way to nourish family spirituality is through reading. There exists a delightful moment in the 1984 version of *The Razor's Edge* when Larry Darrell, a young man in search of illumination, falls into a conversation about books with a coal miner who has just emerged from a day of backbreaking labor in the bowels of the earth. The talk turns toward religious texts. Suddenly the older man, whose porky, soot-blackened face suggests a fan of Saturday-night wrestling rather than of studious prayer, turns incredulously toward Larry. "What!" he exclaims. "You've never read the Upanishads?"

No, Larry had never read these wonderful Vedic scriptures; if he had, the film seems to suggest, perhaps he wouldn't now be scouring the world for scraps of truth. Reading, as we saw in the chapter on "Words," is a royal road to the contemplative life. Who can fathom the extraordinary graces that may enter a child's soul if he or she were read, from the earliest age, excerpts from sacred books? At the very least, such reading would ground the child in spiritual realities and provide a vigorous soil for the growth of meditation, mindfulness, and prayer.

Of course, this sort of reading needn't be limited to scripture. The quickest way to a child's heart is through a cracking good story. A few years ago, Carol and I read C. S. Lewis's Narnia Chronicles out loud to John; as the narrative unscrolled, we could see great truths—the eternal conflict of good and evil, the beauty of sacrifice, the power of faith—take seed within him. A different sort of fruit, equally satisfying, comes from the composition of homegrown tales. For several years now John—and lately Andy as well—has clambered into bed with Carol and me first thing each morning, where I spin a "one-minute story," conceived on the spot, about the adventures of Egbert the egg, Roberto the magic rabbit, and their kin. Telling these tales, I see my children's sense of wonder come alive, bringing with it a conviction that life, for all its turbulence, has shape and meaning.

Ben Aron

The Duties of the Parent

Child-raising entails the cultivation of parent as well as child. I hold dear a nameless and anonymous Amish text, written during the late nineteenth century and published in a German-language newspaper,[23] that suggests several reasons why education fails and children grow disobedient. This work, which I've read several times in the course of raising my children, places much of the responsibility for children's failures, correctly I believe, upon the parents. It cites three major ways in which parents let their children down:

- Parents engage in inconsistent behavior. Promises are made and broken; punishments are stated and rescinded; rules change depending on mood.
- Parents fail to explain the deeper meaning of actions. As the Amish see it, rules exist for the same reason that the body has a skin— because every created thing needs a boundary.
- Parents fail to pray. Rules, say the Amish, need the support of God as well as parents. Prayer and work will save the day.

These three points rest, it seems to me, upon one fundamental premise: that the spiritual life of children depends upon the spiritual life of parents. As Alexander Elchaninov writes, "In the education of children, the most important thing is that they should see their parents leading an intense interior life."[24] If we are upright, honest, generous, and open to the sacred, so will our children be. The child must understand, through the parent's example, that the simplest things—cleaning up a dirty bedroom or doing homework on time—have profound significance. If parents and children share a regular religious practice, be it attending church, synagogue, or temple, or simply allowing a moment of silence before meals, so much the better. Instead of fists clenched in anger, let us offer our children hands folded in prayer.

COMING-OF-AGE

"*P*rofessor Zaleski," the young woman asked, "how did you celebrate your coming-of-age?"

The question came from a Smith College senior, one of the brightest students in my course on Native American religions. She had a wistful, almost desperate catch in her voice.

How did I celebrate my coming-of-age? I understood the source of the question; in class, we had been discussing the *kinaalda*, the girls' puberty rite of the Navajo Indians. This joyous ceremony, with its dancing, candy-throwing, and music had delighted my students. Here, they felt, was a ritual that made sense, an acknowledgement of the newfound power to create life, to bear children. Then I had asked them what comparable ceremonies they could point to in their own lives, and I had watched their faces sag with dismay.

How did I celebrate my coming-of-age? I glanced out of my office window and saw in the distance the small figures of other students sprawled on the spring grass at the edge of Paradise Pond or tugging on the oars of the white rowboats that plied the Mill River. Fifty years ago, many of these young women would have been debutantes, participants in a gala ritual that ushered them simultaneously into high society and eligibility for marriage; that, I thought, was a coming-of-age ceremony of sorts. But today? I thought back to my own adolescence. What was my coming-of-age ritual? My first sip of Budweiser? My first puff on a Camel? My first peek at Playboy? The first night I spent away from family and hearth, on a cold, dreary camping trip with the Boy Scouts, an adventure that ended prematurely when our campsite was invaded by millions of inch-worms raining down from the skies?

How did I celebrate my coming-of-age? I told my student the sorry truth. "I didn't."

Nothing reveals the spiritual problems of our age more than our lack of a genuine coming-of-age ceremony. For most of us, the transition from childhood to adulthood is a study in chaos, a series of unplanned and usually painful events: cigarettes behind the bushes, joyrides in the parent's car, sexual fumblings at the mall cineplex. These are rites-of-passage, but they have been bled of all sense of the sacred.

How different it is in a traditional culture. Among the Maori of New Zealand, the !Kung San of the Kalihari, the Navajo of the American southwest, sacred coming-of-age rituals still thrive, and they bring with them a bouquet of blessings. A young man or woman enters into adult society under the tutelage of elders, who offer firm guidance and loving support every step of the way. The community as a whole benefits as well, for coming-of-age rites reaffirm its sacred origins and destiny, its own intimate bonds with the divine.

Our culture's lack of a sacred coming-of-age ritual has had dire effects, most noticeable a serious disruption of the normal life cycle. Children are cast adrift in the surge toward maturity, and the results are plain to see. On the one hand, vast numbers of people undergo an extended adolescence, floating aimlessly in their late twenties or early thirties, happy to be perpetual students or to hold a series of low-level, low-paying, low-responsibility jobs. On the other hand, many people— often the same ones who become slackers—suffer from an early onset of adolescence, spewing out four-letter words at ten, puffing pot at eleven, and having sex at twelve.

Fortunately, there are still pockets of sanity around. Large numbers of Jews celebrate bar mitzvah, the only religious coming-of-age ceremony still widely practiced in America. But even here limitations arise. The bar mitzvah is exclusively male; attempts to develop a female version, the bat mitzvah, have not been very successful. And as Jewish scholar Miles Krassen points out below, in many communities the bar mitzvah has been stripped of its numinous mystery and turned into just another social event, albeit one of grand proportions.

What to do about this ritual vacuum? In the following pages, you will find an array of coming-of-age ceremonies from cultures around the world. These rituals are still in daily use, and often rival in pomp and circumstance more familiar ceremonies surrounding birth, marriage, and death. Clearly, these rites play a vital role in the life cycle; indeed, many of the participants would insist vehemently that without a coming-of-age ceremony, they would never have reached adulthood.

At the same time, little can be gained by slavishly imitating these ceremonies. They belong to particular cultures or specific religions. Recently, American Indians have unleashed a barrage of protest against non-Indian New Agers who head to desert or mountains, drum and smudge-stick in hand, on a "vision quest" modeled after that of the Lakota Sioux, Ojibway, and other indigenous peoples. To many Native Americans, this smacks of cultural desecration. Whatever the truth of this charge, it seems clear enough that if I—a middle-class white American—were suddenly to adopt, say, Navajo ways for a weekend, I would only succeed in making a fool of myself.

Nonetheless, I believe that great rewards lie in store for those who study the coming-of-age practices of other cultures. At the very least, the meaning of these practices can spark a spiritual revolution in our own lives. The vision quest, for example, speaks eloquently of the need to find a guiding light, a higher meaning in life that gives it authenticity and meaning. When a Lakota Sioux "cries" for a vision, he is brother to an ancient Greek consulting the oracle at Delphi, a Hindu donning the golden thread in the upanayana ceremony, or a Christian receiving the chrism of confirmation. In each case, the participant opens himself to divine guidance and help. This is something we all must do, whether we spend our time on isolated mountain peaks or amid a swarm of children clamoring for dinner.

In some cases, traditional coming-of-age ceremonies can be exported in whole or in part to new circumstances without violating cultural boundaries. For example, one compelling element of the Navajo *kinaalda* involves the cooking and eating of an enormous cornmeal cake. This is a moment of great happiness for all participants—who doesn't love a feast?—and also one resonant with meaning, as pinches of the cake are offered to the cardinal directions and to Mother Earth. In our culture all manner of events—birthdays, anniversaries, promotions—are celebrated with a cake. It seems to me entirely possible to mark some aspect of a child's coming-of-age—perhaps turning thirteen, the beginning of the adolescent gauntlet—with a cake, accompanied by prayers and blessings. Certainly, I wouldn't recommend linking such a celebration to a specific biological marker like first menses, unless you enjoy watching your daughter blush every shade of red from alizarin to vermilion. Nor would I work myself into a lather over the celebration. Home-brewed rituals should be simple and relaxed. By their very nature, they can never have the power of those that come from the gods—but I believe that they're a step in the right direction.

Another approach to coming-of-age ceremonies that seems to be growing in popularity is the secular variant on sacred rites. One example of this is the current passion for "orienteering" and other wilderness adventures, such as those sponsored by Outward Bound (see below for more on these programs). Wittingly or not, these activities bear striking similarities to Native American vision quests and, judging by the reports of participants, may offer some of the same rewards. They make no claim to be religious, except in the fuzziest generic sense, but they do testify to our unquenchable thirst for a ceremony to mark that cataclysmic and miraculous event, the transformation of boy into man, of girl into woman.

CONTEMPLATIVE CLOSEUP:
COMING-OF-AGE IN NATIVE AMERICA

"Men are from Mars, women are from Venus," exclaims a popular book title. Coming-of-age ceremonies for the two sexes are also planets apart. Generally speaking, male ceremonies cultivate traditional masculine virtues like courage and strength, while female ceremonies cultivate traditional feminine virtues like fecundity and tenderness. We can see the rationale in this; it's difficult to picture a female Hercules or a male Aphrodite. Nonetheless, the generalization is simplistic, for all traditions recognize the value of female qualities in the male and vice versa. Among the Sioux, for example, female bravery is much admired, as is male compassion. We'd hit the mark better by saying that coming-of-age ceremonies help the young man or young woman—who are often as bewildered as newborn infants—to define and fulfill their different but complementary adult roles. With this in mind, let's examine two coming-of-age ceremonies, one for men and one for women, as they are practiced to this day in Native America.

A Male Ceremony: Crying for a Vision

The most famous Native American religious rite, found among the Eskimo of the far north, the Salish of the west coast, the Huron of the east, and a hundred Indian

John Collier, Jr.

Son of a Navaho healer

nations in between, is the vision quest. Usually, but not always, the ritual is undertaken by an adolescent male. While details vary from one region to the next, a basic pattern can be discerned: a boy retreats to the wilderness, where he fasts and prays until he receives a message from the spiritual world. He then returns home a man.

Among the Sioux, a vision quest can be undertaken by man or woman, at any stage of life, for any number of reasons, such as to cure an illness, solve a problem, or simply to worship the Creator. Whatever the motive, the method remains the same: to encounter what the Sioux call wakan, the sacred—the word is both noun and adjective—and thus to establish personal communion with *Wakan Tanka*, a term that has been translated as the Great Spirit, the Great Mysterious, or simply, God. Petaga, a Sioux medicine man, offers this explanation to Arthur Amiotte, a young man about to embark on his first vision quest:

> From the holy goodness of Wakan Tanka a way was given us—for he loves his children and this creation—that we may pray, and have a glimpse, a little knowledge, of the Great Mystery that is this life. He has given us a way that we may be reminded regularly of our obligations as ikce wicasa— original man—and what we must do in this life to be good people, men, women, and children, and how to remember our origins and to honor our creator.[1]

Amiotte undertook his vision quest after he had attended university. Often, however, the rite takes place at puberty. As the great Oglala Sioux prophet Black Elk describes it, crying (or "lamenting") for a vision begins when a boy seeks advice from a *wicasa wakan*, a holy man. They pray together, the older man calling upon all created realms—sky, earth, and water—to help the boy in his quest:

> All the Powers of the world . . . all things that move in the universe . . . all the sacred peoples of the universe: Listen! A sacred relationship with you all will be asked by this young man, that his generations to come will increase and live in a holy manner.[2]

The boy purifies himself and all that he will take on his quest—pipe, knife, tobacco, and so on—in a sweat lodge. He then travels to a remote location, usually a mountainside, where he strips off his clothes in order to meet Wakan Tanka in a state of nakedness, poverty, and humility. We see the same impulse at work when Moses removes his sandals during his first ascent of Sinai; like a barefoot child, the supplicant before God must be in an aboriginal state, unprotected, open to everything that comes.

Once prepared, the boy and his elderly guide hike up the mountain to a clearing, where they construct an altar of forked sticks. Then five cherry poles are erected, one in the center of the area, the others ten paces away toward each of the cardinal directions. The four perimeter poles are encircled with a rosary of tobacco bags, sealing off the sacred space. The elder then departs.

What follows is prayer, intense and unremitting, reminiscent in many ways of the repetitive prayer-practices, like the mantra, dhikr, or Jesus prayer, described in the chapter on "Words." The "lamenter," as Black Elk calls the boy, stands at the central pole and then walks toward the west, stopping when he reaches the outer pole with its rosary border. As he walks, he may cry out, "O Wakan-Tanka, have pity on me, that my people may live,"[3]—thus underscoring the communal importance of his actions—or he may keep silent. He returns to the center pole in the same manner, and then continues on to the northern, eastern, and southern poles in turn. Walking and praying are done slowly and contemplatively; a single circuit of the field may take an hour.

Throughout the vision quest, the lamenter never eats or drinks. He may smoke, and he may sleep—indeed, the answer to his quest may come through a dream—although the closeness of the supernatural often keeps him awake. He must arise in the middle of the night for another round of prayer, and again before dawn to beseech the morning star for help. At every moment, he meditates on the meaning and purpose of his quest. Along with incessant praying, then, the lamenter offers his thoughts, solitude, hunger, thirst, nakedness, and fatigue to Wakan Tanka. Sooner or later, a response may come, often in the form of an animal visitation:

> Perhaps a Spotted Eagle may come to him from the west, or a Black Eagle from the north, or a Bald Eagle from the East, or even the Red-headed Woodpecker may come to him from the south. And even though none of these may speak to him at first, they are important and should be observed.[4]

No one knows what the lamenter will discover on his vision quest. The Sioux speak of acquiring "power," of joining in some way the divine processes that govern the cosmos. To achieve this goal, the lamenter may have to undergo several more solitary retreats. In the long run, however, success is assured; as Black Elk writes, if the seeker "is always sincere, and truly humiliates himself before all things, he shall certainly be aided, for *Wakan-Tanka* always helps those who cry to Him with a pure heart."[5]

A Female Coming-of-Age Ceremony: Kinaalda

All people recognize the importance of first menses, which signals the sudden emergence in a girl of the awesome powers of child-bearing. In many traditional cultures, however, this event is greeted, like the sudden advent of a new comet, with fear and foreboding. The woman is isolated from the community while her blood flows, out of fear that her newfound powers will lead to pollution, illness, or even death.

One happy exception is the *kinaalda* ceremony of the Navajo of the American Southwest. Among the Navajo, a girl's first menstruation is perceived as the eruption of female power that complements that of the male. To be sure, taboos are enforced; the girl is barred from eating salt or meat, touching water, and so on. But these restrictions—which constitute a complex symbolic language reflecting the interdependency of all creation—exist not so much to ward off pollution as to show respect for power. To the Navajo, encountering a woman during her menstruation is akin to touching an electric wire; the force is beneficial (where would we be without electricity?) but possibly overwhelming.

The Navajo rejoice in a girl's coming-of-age; rather than banish the girl to an isolation hut, as do so many other cultures, they throw a party. This celebration is based on the puberty rites of Changing Woman, the spirit being who created the Navajo people. The first menstruation of every Navajo girl is thus seen, not as a profane occasion for shame and fear, but as a sacred re-enactment of the coming-of-age of a goddess. When Changing Woman arrived at first menses (or "became kinaalda"), the myths report, her fellow spirit beings devised a ritual for her. According to Navajo storyteller Frank Mitchell,

> They did this so that she would be holy and so she could have children
> who would be human beings with enough sense to think for themselves
> and a language with which to understand each other. [6]

The *kinaalda*, then, confers both holiness and the gifts of civilization. Navajo myth records every detail of Changing Woman's *kinaalda*, from the clothes she wore to the manner of baking the ceremonial cake. In time, these ritual instructions were followed by the first Navajo to celebrate *kinaalda*, and they are still followed today, as Changing Woman directed:

> [Changing Woman] said, "After this, all the girls born to you will have
> periods at certain times when they become women. When the time comes,

you must set a day and fix the girl up to be kinaalda; you must have these songs sung and do whatever else needs to be done at that time.[7]

A modern *kinaalda* usually stretches over four days and nights and concludes with an all-night sing. The usual pattern, somewhat abbreviated, runs as follows:[8]

- *Day one:* The girl dons ceremonial dress, including sash, necklaces, and bracelets, and enjoys a hair-brushing by an "aunt" (older woman). She then lies face down on a pile of blankets, while the aunt presses her limbs and torso into the womanly shape of Changing Woman. One or more sessions of running outside the hogan ensue, in order to enduce strength and stamina. The day culminates in a long session of vigorous corn-grinding.
- *Days two and three:* These days are filled with more runs and corn-grinding.
- *Day four:* This day begins with a run, but soon attention shifts to the major event: the digging of the oven pit, mixing of the batter, and cooking of the *alkaan,* or ceremonial corncake. An all-night sing follows, attended by a crowd of relatives, friends, and ritual chanters. Dawn witnesses another run and a ceremonial hair-washing. The cake is removed from the pit, cut, and distributed. A mix of white clay and water is painted in an upward motion, symbolizing growth, on the girl's body as well as the faces of other participants. Finally, the girl undergoes a final molding at the hands of her aunt.

While *kinaalda* ceremonies vary in details, all display extraordinary fidelity to the original *kinaalda* of Changing Woman. As a result, the pubescent girl acquires the stature of a mythic being as well as that of a fertile woman, and the sacred origins, customs, and destiny of the Navajo take on new life and meaning.

COMING-OF-AGE:
A CONTEMPLATIVE HARVEST

Other Ways

The Sioux vision quest and the Navajo *kinaalda* can be found, by and large, only in specific locales: the American southwest for the Navajo, the American great plains for the Sioux. Some coming-of-age ceremonies, by contrast, are practiced around the world. Sometimes this is the result of a forced diaspora, as in the case of Judaism, and sometimes the result of missionary zeal, as in the case of Buddhism.

BAR MITZVAH

As noted above, the most widely practiced coming-of-age ceremony in the West today is certainly the bar mitzvah, celebrated by Jewish boys at thirteen years of age in response to the Talmudic decree: "At thirteen, he is ready for the commandments" (*Aboth* V:24). At this age, males assume the responsibilities of adult religious life—fasting on Yom Kippur, wearing *tefillin*, and so on.

The Jewish celebration differs from its Native American counterpart in one crucial specific: while crying for a vision initiates a boy into adulthood and in some sense triggers maturity, bar mitzvah does nothing per se to spur his development. At the age of thirteen, a male Jew becomes a young man, bar mitzvah or not. The ceremony serves, however, to confirm the boy's new status in his own eyes and those of his community.

The core of bar mitzvah consists in being "called up to the Reading of the Torah"; that is, in reciting a blessing before and after the weekly Torah reading in the synagogue. The script for boy and congregation goes as follows:

Before the Torah reading:
BOY: Bless the blessed Lord.
CONGREGATION: Blessed be the Lord who is blessed for ever and ever.
BOY: Blessed are you, O Lord our God!, King of the universe, who has chosen us from all the peoples and given us your Torah. Blessed are you, O Lord, Who gives us the Torah.

After the Torah reading:
BOY: Blessed are you, O Lord our God!, King of the universe, who has given us the Torah of Truth, and planted life eternal in our midst. Blessed are you, Lord, Who gives us the Torah.

As the boy is called to the Torah, the father utters a saying from an ancient midrash on Genesis: "Blessed be He who has freed me from responsibility for this child." From now on, the boy is responsible

Bar Mitzvah, Temple Beth Am

Bill Aron

for his own religious conduct. Following the ceremony, the entire family holds a gala celebration, likened by the Zohar to a wedding feast. In some social circles, bar mitzvah festivities have swelled to colossal proportions, with Brobdingnagian mounds of catered food, gaudy decorations, professional musicians, and the like. To some, this well-intentioned excess blots out the real significance of the event. How many Jews, they ask, know of the teaching, also recorded in the Zohar, that at the bar mitzvah twin marvels occur: the boy receives a new soul, and two guardian angels descend from heaven to offer him life-long protection? What can be done, they ask, to ensure that the sacredness of bar mitzvah remains intact for the next generation? These questions, which parallel those asked by parents in every tradition—how can we keep our practices vital, so that our children will rejoice in them instead of rejecting them?—invite serious consideration, as Miles Krassen suggests in the sidebar interview in this chapter.

A NOTE ON BAT MITZVAH

Traditional Judaism has no coming-of-age ceremony for girls, as such a rite receives no sanction in the Talmudic laws and rabbinical ordinances that govern Jewish life. In recent years, however, some Jews, especially in the more liberal congregations, have developed a rite of passage known as the bat mitzvah as a female counterpart to the bar mitzvah. Because girls mature more rapidly than boys, the celebration usually takes place around the twelfth birthday. In most Reform and Conservative synagogues, the bat mitzvah echoes its venerable counterpart in every respect, including being "called up to the Torah" and throwing a lavish party afterward. Among those Orthodox synagogues that do allow the bat mitzvah, the resemblance is more muted and the girl never offers Torah blessings.

In the limited success of the bat mitzvah, we can read the tensions that afflict all contemporary religions. Here, two admirable impulses find themselves at loggerheads: on the one hand, the wish to bring girls into full equality with boys; on the other hand, the wish to preserve the traditions that bestow meaning and purpose to life, that in the case of Judaism have been the bedrock of identity throughout millennia of persecution. This is a painful conflict, without an easy resolution. At the very least, it should make us appreciate the need for careful discernment in balancing traditional ways and modern needs.

Tasting the Honey:
A Conversation with Miles Krassen

According to Miles Krassen, assistant professor of religion and Judaic and Near Eastern studies at Oberlin College, something remarkable happens to a boy at the time of his bar mitzvah, something not recognized by modern psychology or by most Jewish parents. "It is only at the age of thirteen," he says, "that one becomes responsible for the *yetzer hara,* the negative impulse. In classical Jewish psychology, there is a tension between good and bad urges within every person. But we are not responsible for our propensity to follow bad urges until the age of thirteen. There is a sense of innocence until that time."

Once a boy undergoes bar mitzvah, he "takes on the yoke of the commandments," as the saying goes. According to Krassen, this "deep transformation" entails following all of the 613 commandments of classical Judaism, which include 365 prohibitions and 248 positive actions. Some rabbinical authorities believe that the 613 commandments are connected to the 613 parts of the body, including tendons, bones, muscles, circulatory system, and so on, as enumerated in traditional Jewish medicine; assuming the yoke of the commandments may

thus in some mysterious way elevate the body into a new physio-spiritual whole.

Isn't it ironic, I ask, that the bar mitzvah has surged in popularity just as our culture—and a large segment of the Jewish community—has become sharply secularized? Krassen agrees and points out another irony, that thirteen is still deemed to be an appropriate age for the ceremony. "The bar mitzvah doesn't correspond to adulthood in this culture," he argues, "where thirteen-year-olds are still deep within childhood. In ancient times, a thirteen-year-old was a genuine adult and ready to take on adult responsibilities."

In truth, the growth of the bar mitzvah and its attendant festivities may have more to do with social expectations than with devotion. "In modern times, the bar mitzvah has become a party. The deeper meaning of it is not even recalled in some denominations, usually those denominations where few people take the obligations of the commandments seriously." Indifference to the ceremony's real significance is widespread, and even the boy himself rarely cares. Krassen remembers his own childhood: "My bar mitzvah was a significant moment for the community. I said a blessing and read the Torah, and that was important to my elders. To me, however, it seemed the end of involvement in religion. I had no sense of obligation to God."

What of the future? Clearly Krassen hopes that Jewish teachers and parents will discover the full meaning of the bar mitzvah and pass their knowledge on to children. Hope may lie in recapturing the practices of the past, even if it results in a diminishment of the ceremony's role in Jewish life. "In a traditional community, the bar mitzvah is not as big a deal as it is in much of contemporary Judaism, because there are so many stages that a young boy passes through before his bar mitzvah. For example, there is a custom among some Jews that the boy gets introduced to the Hebrew alphabet by seeing letters written in honey. He licks the honey and thus gains a sense of the sweetness of the Hebrew scriptures. By the time of his bar mitzvah, a boy has accomplished something. And in the years to come, he will go far beyond it."

SHIN-BYU

Buddhism, too, at least in its Burmese manifestation, offers a spectacular coming-of-age ceremony for young boys known as the *shin-byu*. The heart of the ceremony, like that of *kinaalda*, involves the reenactment of a holy being's life—in this case, that of the Buddha. To prepare for the shin-byu, a boy's family constructs an "palace," a simulacrum of the royal dwellings in which Prince Siddhartha, the Indian nobleman who became the historical Buddha, passed his childhood. In this model palace—much smaller than the original, but still inhabitable—the boy ascends a throne and dons royal robes. He then processes with a crowd of family, friends, and monks to a nearby monastery, a journey that recalls the travels of the Buddha from his childhood home to the place of his enlightenment.

After this excursion, the boy returns to the palace. There the heart of the ceremony unfolds, a blend of sacred rites and secular entertainment, the latter including jokes, chants, sermons, and songs under the direction of a master of ceremonies. The boy's eyebrows and head are shaved, symbolizing his rejection of worldly values. He recites the Ten Precepts, the Buddhist code that forbids killing, stealing, sex, lying, intoxicants, theater, perfume, excessive food, sleeping on luxurious beds, and the handling of money. This is followed by the recitation of the basic Buddhist pledge (Buddham saranam gacchami):

> *I take refuge in the Buddha.*
> *I take refuge in the Dhamma.*
> *I take refuge in the Sangha.*
>
> *For the second time, I take refuge in the Buddha.*
> *For the second time, I take refuge in the Dhamma.*
> *For the second time, I take refuge in the Sangha.*

For the third time, I take refuge in the Buddha.
For the third time, I take refuge in the Dhamma.
For the third time, I take refuge in the Sangha.

The boy then returns to the palace a penniless monk. Next morning, he receives a new Pali name and moves into the monastery to receive a thorough Buddhist education before returning to resume normal life.

There are striking parallels between the *shin-byu* and the bar mitzvah, most noticeably in the confluence of sacred and secular elements. The cost of a *shin-byu* can be staggering, to such a degree that many families can't afford the ceremony. In yet another parallel, there exists a Burmese coming-of-age ceremony for girls that amounts to a muted variation of the boy's ceremony. At the same time that their older brothers undertake the *shin-byu*, young Burmese girls—usually below the age of ten—also dress in royal robes and ascend the throne in the imitation palace. The climax of their participation comes when their ears are pierced by the master of ceremonies.

The Spiritual State of Adolescence Today

All successful coming-of-age ceremonies have this in common: they ignite in the celebrant a sense of the sacred. With the aid of this new sense, the world is transformed. Life is no longer a playground, for it has become a pilgrim's path. The boy is no longer a boy, but a man. The girl is no longer a girl, but a woman. The new adult may possess a new name, speak a new language, manifest a new power over life and death (as child-bearer or enemy-slayer).

I think it is fair to say that we have little experience of this in our contemporary culture.

The first lesson to be drawn, then, from the coming-of-age ceremonies described above, is this: that we need to do whatever we can to preserve those ceremonies that exist today. As Miles Krassen indicates, this means more than simply enacting the rites; it means cherishing the symbolism and absorbing the meaning. One drop of honeyed scripture in the mouth of a child is worth a thousand sermons. We should also remain open to the possibility of creating new coming-of-age ceremonies, when this can be accomplished with skill and sensitivity. The fledgling bat mitzvah, constructed on the firm foundation of the bar mitzvah, may point the way, for it shows how a new ritual can achieve some success if it answers a felt need and if it arises, not from individual whim, but from the collective wisdom of the people.

The truth remains, however, that for many people in today's deritualized culture, a coming-of-age ceremony is out of the question. What then? All is not lost, for the coming of age unfolds nonetheless; the magic wand of time still transforms each child into an adult. What we need to do is to sustain in the child a sense of the numinous throughout the long teenage years. Every young boy or girl believes in Truth; our task is to ensure that the capital T is not decapitated by the age of eighteen or twenty-one. In a sense, then, our job is to create a slow-motion coming-of-age ceremony, one that takes six or eight years to accomplish, one so subtle that it blends effortlessly into the tribulations of adolescence, yet so powerful that it produces an adult ready to revere, as the Sioux medicine man said to Arthur Amiotte, "the Great Mystery that is this life."

How might this be achieved?

One step, if you are raising a child in the traditions of a specific religion, is to introduce the child to that faith's deeper levels of practice and belief. More than once, I've been visited in my college office by students who have burst into tears while declaring dissaffection for their family religion. After some discussion, it usually turns out that these students are rebelling, not against the tradition itself—with which they are hardly acquainted—but against some pale shadow of it that they've encountered in Sunday school or Hebrew school or some other religious education program. The failure to reveal to our children the astonishing spiritual wealth of the world's religions is a stain upon us all.

A second step, allied to the first, is to introduce adolescents to the complex map of the world's spiritual paths.

At Smith College, I teach an introductory course in Native American religions, during which my students become familiar with the basic vocabulary of all spiritual systems, including myth, symbol, and ritual. As we discuss the sacramental use of the sacred pipe in Plains Indian religion practice, I can see the light dawn in the eyes of my students, as they grasp for the first time the basic meaning of a sacrament, and then apply that knowledge to their own religion. Nothing cures spiritual myopia more effectively than a lens borrowed from a foreign faith.

A third step is to accept as inevitable the benign but irksome (to adults) adolescent impulse to reject the familiar and explore the unknown. A plant sends out new tendrils and thus ensures its growth; so, too, does a young adult. It's a sorry truth, of course, that exploration often leads to brick walls or unfenced cliffs. But it also leads many a teenager into discoveries that keep alive, or even heighten, the spiritual quest. Especially noteworthy in this context are programs that place a youth in the silence and stillness of nature. As Norman Boucher reminds us in our discussion of simple pleasures, the wilderness may be a cathedral of bark and boughs to a young adult, a fit place to ponder the mystery of life.

Beginning to nurture the world

Such programs are sprouting up everywhere. The most famous on American shores is probably Outward Bound, a nonprofit organization that locates its roots in the experience of young British sailors in World War II. Time and again, when German submarines torpedoed British merchant vessels, the youngest and fittest men suffered the heaviest casaulties. Kurt Hahn, a British educator, investigated this mystery and discovered that despite their vigor, these sailors suffered from panic and lack of will. In response, he developed a program to instill courage, trust, and self-reliance.

A half-century later, Outward Bound puts ten thousand people each year through a program of teamwork, problem solving, and risk taking designed to produce mature adults. One aspect of the program is the "solo," a one- to three-day sojourn alone into the wilderness, to be spent in writing, thinking, and contemplation; the parallels to a classical religious retreat are obvious.

Another popular activity these days is "orienteering," where the participant—again, often a boy or girl on the brink of adulthood—navigates the wilderness with the help of map and compass. The challenges of orienteering, like those of Outward Bound, mimic classic initiation rites—threading a maze, crossing a perilous bridge—and achieve some of the aims of a coming-of-age ceremony, by infusing in the adolescent a sense of strength and self-reliance.

A fourth step toward awakening a sense of the numinous in adolescents is to realize that the spiritual impulse, especially during the teenage years, often appears in disguise. A young woman may not worship God, but she may worship the young man sitting next to her in chemistry class. A young man may not know a Tibetan tanka from an Italian pieta, but his girlfriend may be for him an icon of absolute beauty, truth, and goodness. Nor is romantic love the only costume that the sacred wears. A passion for civil rights, for the environment, for rock 'n' roll, all may be sublimations of religious yearning. We should encourage them whenever possible. At every moment, our aim should be to keep alive in youth a sense of personal spiritual worth. The world, to everyone, but to teenagers above all, is but their own hearts writ large. If young adults sense their intrinsic beauty, yet without falling prey to narcissism, then they will befriend the world and glorify the beauty of all creation.

fourteen

MARRIAGE AND FAMILY

*B*rowsing around the Internet this morning, I stumbled across some happy news: Zuzu and Mike have entered the ranks of parenthood. Zuzu, reports CNN, gave birth to a healthy male baby late Tuesday night in Lop Buri, a town seventy miles north of Bangkok, Thailand. But why, you may wonder, did this blessed event catch the eye of the world's most prominent news service? For the simple reason that—hold onto your hats—Zuzu and Mike are Thailand's only married orangutans.

That's right, married orangutans. The couple tied the knot in early April, after Zuzu, then six years old, had been flown from Taiwan, no doubt blushing as furiously as any mail-order bride, to marry Mike, an irascible bachelor. According to CNN, the marriage was "a lavish, widely publicized ceremony that was called the wedding of the year in Thailand."[1] Nine months later, the marriage reached a new crescendo of happiness, as Zuzu and Mike found themselves "well on their way towards forming a full-fledged nuclear family."[2] A photo showed an infant, its spindly arms extended toward its mother's breast. According to CNN, hundreds of people turned up to cheer the new parents; the orangutans' keepers passed out cigars; one doctor declared, "We had champagne and a big celebration."[3]

In this story, and especially in our reactions to it, we can discover some fundamental truths about marriage and family. We smile benignly at the news of

Zuzu and Mike's nuptials, for marriage is a universal good: an occasion of joy, a sign of love, a promise of prosperity. We smile, too, at the news of a little orangutan, for reasons both biological and spiritual: children mean continuation of the species (in this case, a species under grave assault); children also bring the possibility of familial bliss.

At the same time, most of us wince at reports of a lavish orangutan wedding. Cigars, champagne, feasting, and frippery: this strikes us as play-acting and not entirely in good taste. Did Zuzu wear a wedding gown? Did a minister preside? It calls to mind those disquieting reports of elaborate pet funerals, complete with miniature mahogany caskets and pint-sized tombstones. We draw back from such accounts, sensing instinctively that some things should be reserved for human beings. Copulation, like death, belongs to all animals; but weddings, like funerals, belong to us alone. Marriage is a sacred ritual; it divides us from the beasts and binds us to the gods.

Nearly everywhere we turn in the world of religion, we find marriage acclaimed as a sacrament, a visible sign of invisible divinity. In Judaism, marriage returns the couple to Eden; thus the *huppah*, or wedding canopy, has been likened to a second womb, from which bride and bridegroom emerge reborn in the paradise of marriage.[4] Marriage crops up frequently in mystical writings, where it serves as a metaphor for the union of human and divine, as well as for the reconciliation of opposites, of cold and hot, darkness and light, active and passive, masculine and feminine.

Marriage then is a sacramental union that reflects God's own unity and goodness. But perhaps this seems too rosy a portrait. After all, people marry for sex, cash, power. From an economic standpoint, marriage ensures the circulation of money by way of dowry and inheritance; from a Darwinian standpoint, it mixes genetic stock, prevents inbreeding, and leads to a healthy evolutionary ecology; from a political standpoint, it binds scattered families, ends wars, and welds long-term alliances. All this is true—but none of it contradicts the sacred meaning of marriage. A rose is a rose, whether it adorns a grand piano or a grave. Just so, a marriage remains a sacrament, whatever mundane purpose it may serve. In addition, we should never forget that in the eyes of tradition, every activity, from making money to making love, has its higher aspect. Washing a fork may disclose the sacred and so may a marriage of convenience.

From the sanctity of marriage springs the sanctity of the family. This sanctity applies to the smallest of all family units, that of husband and wife; to the larger nucleus of father, mother, and child; and to the extended company that includes all manner of relatives near and far.

The sanctity of marriage and family has enormous implications for daily life. Above all, it means that for each of us, whether spouse, parent, or child, *the family is the principal arena for spiritual growth.* The family is the laboratory in which we unearth the

From the sanctitiy of marriage springs the sancitity of family

secrets of the soul. Domestic life offers incomparable opportunities for self-reflection and intimacy. In the haven of the home, we enjoy a degree of openness and trust unattainable in the outer world. Our social masks drop away; we have a better chance to come to ourselves. By the same token, domesticity offers many opportunities for self-overcoming. It's easy enough to be compassionate toward a stranger; it's quite another thing to be compassionate with your husband when he ignores a sinkful of dirty dishes or with your children when they whine and whimper. If you can anchor yourself in the domestic maelstrom, you can do it anywhere.

Domesticity, then, holds out the possibility of genuine spiritual transformation. The twentieth-century Orthodox priest Alexander Elchaninov sees the life of marriage and family as:

> a revelation and a mystery. We see in it the complete transformation of a human being, the expansion of his personality, fresh vision, a new perception of life, and through it a rebirth into the world in a new plenitude.[5]

Through marriage, we discover the essential mystery of other people. To the encomium quoted above, Elchaninov adds that "only in marriage can human beings fully know one another—the miracle of feeling, touching, seeing another's personality—and this is as wonderful and as unique as the mystic's knowledge of God."[6]

It's well known that married people suffer fewer heart attacks, depression, and obesity than do single people, and that parents enjoy greater physical health than childless couples. These blessings are but the outward signs of inward grace, a reflection of the deeply felt need within the human soul to love and be loved, a need that marriage and the family exist to fulfill. At the same time, we know all too well that the divorce rate has reached 50 percent, that domestic violence is rampant, and that many marriages remain intact only through the Scotch tape of legalities and inertia. To a great extent, we've failed to live up to marriage's promise. What is this failure but spiritual sleep, a willful refusal to awaken to the divine call? As Elchaninov says:

> In marriage the festive joy of the first day should last for the whole of life; every day should be a feast day; every day husband and wife should appear to each other as new, extraordinary beings. The only way of achieving this: let both deepen their spiritual life, and strive hard in the task of self-development.[7]

CONTEMPLATIVE CLOSE-UP: THE WEDDING CEREMONY

Alexander Elchaninov's reflection on marriage, found above, reveals the three sacred functions of the wedding service and its role in spiritual life:

1. The wedding sanctifies the marriage, bringing it under the shelter of the divine. This is the source of the "festive joy" to which Elchaninov refers. What couple would not rejoice, knowing that their union is inscribed on their souls and in the annals of heaven, as well as in the county register?

2. The wedding provides a template for the marriage, from the seal of the kiss to the seal of the grave ("the festive joy of the first day should last for the whole of life"). Just as the morning sitting sets the tone for the day, providing a touchstone to which we can return throughout the hours, so does the wedding set the tone for married life, providing a touchstone through the long years of marital ups and downs.

In this light, the wedding day can no longer be written off as a one-day carnival followed by a life of drudgery. Every detail of the ceremony—gathering food, erecting tents, inviting guests, choosing the gown, securing reservations, celebrating the ritual with as much grace as one can muster—becomes a prototype for the events of later years, for the shopping and washing and stitching and scheduling of married routine. The wedding day is life distilled into a single, and singular, event. This doesn't mean, of course, that a wedding day of thunderstorms, drunken guests, and wilted corsages presages a failed marriage. It means that love should rule the wedding day; that if bride and groom bear in their hearts the meaning of marriage, then they will meet the humdrum aspects of the ceremony—and, by extension, of married life—with recollection and grace.

3. Through the marriage ritual, bride and groom acquire not only new wedding bands but new eyes, and thus they come to see each other as "new, extraordinary beings." This transformation is expressed through costume: the bride's gown, like a giant white blossom; the tuxedo, as grave and elegant as a sword; archetypal symbols of woman and man, rising from the soul to be worn upon the skin. The sacred ceremony, too, emphasizes the "extraordinary being" of bride and groom. In the Orthodox wedding of which Elchaninov writes, the married couple no longer see themselves simply as John and Jane, but as Alpha and Omega in a cosmic drama with its roots in the primordial past (the nuptials of Adam and Eve) and its final flowering in God's heavenly kingdom. In weddings on the island of Java, where Islam and folk religion blend into one, this transformation is literal:

Bill Aron

The festive joy of the first day should last for a while life

the evening before the wedding, a bride sits in absolute stillness for five hours, while an angel descends from heaven and enters her, gracing her with its holy presence for the next five days. "Thus it is," says anthropologist Clifford Geertz, "that all brides look so much more beautiful on their wedding day than on any other."[8]

You will find a number of traditional wedding ceremonies described below. I've selected those rituals that seem to answer most directly the spiritual needs of contemporary men and women. Space prohibits detailed accounts; rather, I've highlighted a few aspects of special interest. Some readers may discover specific ceremonial elements that they would like to incorporate in their own celebrations; everyone, I hope, will discover in these rituals the essence of the wedding day: the love, dignity, and mutual respect that husband and wife should find in each other whatever struggles their future life together may bring.

Gazing at the Polestar: The Hindu Wedding

In classical Hinduism, marriage is esteemed as the highest sacrament, the greatest of the *samskara*s, or life-cycle rituals. The wedding date is fixed by an astrologer, who consults the stars to find an auspicious day. While reliance on horoscopes is a regular feature of Indian daily life, it carries special importance here: every detail of the wedding must be in rhythm with the movements of the heavens.

The wedding itself takes place in a booth, erected about a week before the ceremony from mango and banana leaves and green bamboo sticks (symbols of fertility). In this booth, a sacred womb of sorts (much like the Jewish *huppah*), a mystical transformation takes place, as for the duration of the ceremony bride and groom become deified, transformed into gods. The precise nature of this change depends upon local religious custom. In some cases, the bride becomes the goddess Parvati, a supernatural being of all-pervading consciousness, the consort of Shiva. The groom becomes the great god Shiva himself, lord of creation and destruction.

To sanctify their union, the spouses-to-be undertake ten "gestures," which include honey sipping, rice throwing, and present giving, all symbols of fruitfulness and prosperity. One of these gestures includes the lovely act of "binding with the cord," wherein a string wound from twenty-four white cotton threads is looped around the necks of bride and groom, making of them one unit, one family, one being.

The wedding concludes with two evocative rites. The first is the "seven steps" (*saptapadi*) to the north of the sacred fire, embodiment of Agni, the god who presides over the phases of the life cycle. Bride and groom take one step together, while he exclaims, "Take one step with me, and I promise to feed you as long as you live: Vishnu is witness." A second step follows, while the groom exclaims, "Take a second step with me, and I promise to behave in such a way that your face shall always shine with inner health: Vishnu is witness." Subsequent steps promise wealth, well-being, and abundant cattle. Finally the groom makes his greatest pledge:

> O friend, take the seventh step with me and become my friend in reality and follow me.[9]

The ceremony climaxes with a return to the realm of the stars, under whose benign influence the wedding ceremony began. Bride and groom go out into the night to gaze upon the polestar, Dhruva—the one that never moves, symbol of constancy and faithfulness. The groom says, "Look at the polestar"; the bride responds, "I see the star." To this, the groom declares, "You are faithful; I regard you as faithful; be faithful to me and to those for whom I provide."[10]

Anointing with Oil, Washing with Water: African Weddings

Marriage lies at the heart of African culture. Marriage brings children, peace between neighbors, communal prosperity, even a secure afterlife; African-born theologian John S. Mbiti describes elderly Africans admonishing their grandchildren, "If you don't get married and have children, who will pour out libation to you when you die?"[11]

Inevitably, African weddings teem with special activities. Among the Batoro of Uganda, as the ceremony winds down, the newlyweds enter a courtyard where they find a basin of ice-cold water, left by the bride's sister. The couple disrobe and wash each other in the frigid liquid, erasing all traces of their earlier life—including any sins that cling to their skin—leaving them as innocent and naked as newborn babes. A similar ritual occurs among the !Kung San of the Kalahari Desert. The morning after the wedding feast, female relatives anoint the newlyweds with oil and red ocher (a blood-red mixture of clay and iron oxide). Oil symbolizes fecundity; ocher, the life force. This ritual dabbing, like the Batoros' ice-water ablution, transforms the couple, whisking them from the barren, childless world of the unmarried to a new realm of offspring and abundance.

A Crown of Fine Gold: An Orthodox Christian Wedding

An Orthodox Christian wedding consists of two ceremonies, performed back-to-back. First comes the rite of betrothal, the ecclesiastical equivalent of a civil service, sealing the marriage through prayers, petitions, and the exchange of rings. The betrothal is followed by the remarkable crowning ceremony, which has no precise counterpart in any other religious tradition. The couple walks to the altar while the chorus sings Psalm 128, praising the joys of marriage. Now comes the ritual apogee, as crowns of pure gold or wreaths of flowers (in Russian and Greek ceremonies, respectively) descend upon the heads of bride and groom. These crowns, the nuptial counterpart of saints' halos, reveal the glorified state attained through marriage and foreshadow the "crown of righteousness" (2 Tim. 4:7–8) worn by the just in heaven. Marriage is an intimation of eternity, a reflection of paradise.

The ceremony concludes with two notable activities. First comes the sharing of the cup, during which bride and groom sip wine from a single vessel. Henceforth, marriage means sharing with one's spouse the humblest, most ordinary aspects of life. Finally comes the "dance of Isaiah," in which the married couple process three times around the lectern. This "dance" symbolizes the course of married life, a graceful advance through the year, with the lectern—God's word, his holy presence—as the center of gravity. The dance traces out on the church's floor a circle: the circle of life, which finds its beginning and end in holy things.

I am my beloved's and my beloved is mine.

Shendl Diamond

Making New Worlds: A Jewish Wedding

The *Zohar* declares that "God creates new worlds constantly. In what way? By causing marriages to take place."[12] This saying has, I believe, two meanings, for "new worlds" refers to the union of husband and wife into a single spiritual being and also to the children produced by this union. In either case, marriage consecrates our most profound creative powers; and this is why marriage is expected of all Jews.

A traditional Jewish wedding is a spectacular affair, unfolding through dozens of phases before the delighted eyes of hundreds of well-wishers. Some aspects of the wedding are raucous, others contemplative. Those that emphasize silence, stillness, or the sense of sacred presence include:

- *Fasting.* Bride and groom fast throughout the wedding. Like the cold-water wash of the Batoros, this fasting cleanses body and soul. It serves, too, as a sacrifice to God, a thanksgiving for his blessings on the marriage.

- *Bedeken.* Before the couple gather under the *huppah,* the groom and his male companions dance over to the bride, who is seated on a throne. The groom veils the bride while saying:

> Thou art our sister! Be thou the mother of thousands of millions (Gen. 24:60).

  This saying brings to mind the highest blessings that God can bestow on a marriage: a friendship between husband and wife so deep that the spouses can call one another "brother" and "sister," and fertility for untold generations. The veil suggests modesty and sanctity, two qualities befitting a bride, two jewels in anyone's spiritual treasury.
- *Huppah.* The *huppah,* or Jewish wedding canopy, consists of an embroidered or plain cloth, supported by four poles, that shelters bride and groom throughout the ceremony. The *huppah* represents the perfect marriage of material and spiritual worlds, for in it the most mundane of substances, cotton cloth, becomes a sacred bower, the first home of the married couple, a dwelling place especially blessed by God.
- *Circling the groom.* In this practice, with its remarkable affinities to the "seven steps" of a Hindu wedding, the bride circles seven times around the groom. From now on, Jewish tradition teaches, the groom will be the bride's center of gravity, while the bride's love will encompass the groom. A more esoteric explanation holds that through this sevenfold circumambulation, a wife penetrates the seven spheres of her husband's being to his very core. Henceforth, nothing can come between husband and wife.
- *Sheva berakot.* Under the *huppah,* the rabbi proclaims the *sheva berakot* or seven blessings, from the first,

> Blessed are you, O Lord, our God! King of the universe; who creates the fruit of the vine,

to the last, a rapturous proclamation of the blessings of marriage:

> Blessed are you, O Lord, our God! King of the universe, who has created joy and gladness, bridegroom and bride, delight and song, pleasure and hilarity, love and brotherhood, peace and friendship; speedily, O Lord, our God! let there be heard in the cities of Judah and the streets of Jerusalem, the voice of joy and the voice of gladness, the voice of the bridegroom and the voice of the bride. . . . Blessed are you, O Lord! who causes the bridegroom to rejoice with the bride.

- *Breaking of the glass.* In this famous ritual, the groom wraps a glass in a napkin and stomps it with his foot, to shouts of "Mazel Tov!" The shattering glass symbolizes, no less than the Batoro lavation or !Kung San anointing, the end of old life and rebirth into the new.
- *Yihud.* At the end of the wedding ceremony, bride and groom retire into a private room for a few minutes of quiet recollection (*yihud* is Hebrew for "seclusion"). Here the newlyweds break their fast; the abundance that marks the married life has begun.
- *Gladdening the bride.* This delightful custom, carried out during the wedding feast, involves male guests dancing before the bride and praising her beauty. In traditional Judaism, gladdening the bride is a *mitzvah,* a divine commandment. It fills the bride with joy, and it echoes the *Simhat Torah,* the last day of the annual Sukkoth feast, when Jews dance in jubilation around the Torah. Thus it unites, in the hearts of every guest, marriage and scripture, the two pillars of traditional Jewish life.

Candles and Flower: A Modern Japanese Wedding

The modern Japanese wedding is a rococo blend of Shinto, Buddhist, and Christian elements. At times, the main intention seems to be to make a gigantic splash, with a cavernous banquet hall, lavish decorations, tables groaning with food, unlimited sake, and costumes galore. In this nuptial extravaganza, two ceremonies stand out for their essential beauty, tenderness, and tranquillity:

- *The candle service.* The newlyweds enter the banquet hall, each carrying an unlit candle. The groom lights his candle from a taper burning at his parents' table; the bride does the same with a taper at her parents' table. Bride and groom then circle the hall, lighting together the candles that sit atop each dining table. Finally they proceed to a two-foot-tall "wedding candle" at their own table. Both light it at the same time, two flames merging into one, while a master of ceremonies praises this gracious action as a symbol of the new marriage, the melting of two beings into one.
- *The flower presentation.* At the end of the ceremony, bride and groom stand at one end of the hall, holding an enormous bouquet of flowers. A voice fills the hall, proclaiming the couple's immense love and gratitude to their long-suffering parents. As the peroration ends, bride and groom cross the room to the parents, bow deeply, and present the floral thank-you.

Become What You Are: A Conversation with Dr. Petroc Willey

The banquet hall has been swept, the plates scraped and scrubbed, the guests dispersed to their homes. The wedding is over. What now?

From the standpoint of most traditions, marriage is a sacrament that lasts a lifetime. The purpose of a sacrament, as the term suggests, is to sanctify, to purify our hearts and bring them to God. Marriage means hard spiritual work, a lifelong search for holiness in the context of domestic life.

Such an understanding of marriage, I thought, must have enormous practical implications. Dr. Petroc Willey, a British educator who has written widely on the spirituality of marriage, agrees. He quotes Pope John Paul II: "Married couples, become what you are!" According to Willey, this statement points directly to the real task of a marriage, which he believes is intimately linked to the understanding of a sacrament. "A sacrament," he says, "is not a thing but a person. In marriage, the couple themselves are the sacrament. Each is the sacrament for the other." This has tremendous significance, Willey says, for "sacraments are signs of God's presence and love. To realize that you are a sign of God's presence for other people is very important. In married life, husband and wife transmit to one another the sense of God's love."

This is, I point out, a heavy responsibility. How may it be accomplished? Willey suggests that the first job in any marriage is to take nothing for granted. "In the old days, we called a sacrament a 'mystery.' Every person is a mystery. The biggest killer in any marriage is the belief that when you marry someone, you know them. To see your spouse as a mystery helps you to feel reverence and awe. There's a wonderful line by Rainer Maria Rilke about this. It goes, 'I hold this to be the highest task of a bond between two people: that each should stand guard over the other's solitude.'"

Respecting the integrity of one's spouse sounds easy on the surface. But in the storms of marriage, precepts like these are easily washed away. Willey believes that some practical activities do much to keep alive the sanctity of marriage. Above all, he says, we are called to a work of self-observation and self-discipline. He mentions the desert fathers, Christian monks who fled to the Egyptian sands in the third and fourth centuries, and observes that "by spiritual life, they meant controlling the passions. This is what marriage is about, controlling the passions." Although in our sex-drenched culture passion is a synonym for lust, Willey uses the term in a broader sense. "To succeed in marriage, we must learn to handle our emotions, whatever they might be. We must learn to guard our hearts. Cassian [an early Christian monk] said that you need to discover which passions afflict you, and then you need to talk to someone else about your affliction. This can create a wonderful relationship in a marriage. Husband and wife can talk to one another, offer support and advice, and become soul-friends."

What a lovely term, "soul-friend." Surely this must be the aim of marriage, to bring man and woman into intimate friendship. "Marriage is basically a call to unity," says Willey. "This is tricky, though. Most people think that they will plow their way to God, by themselves, rather than get to God as a couple. But in the spiritual life of marriage, husband and wife find God together. I depend on God's love, and in marriage I depend on the way that my spouse communicates God's love to me. Marriage is not something that I do; it is something that I accept as a gift."

MARRIAGE AND FAMILY:
A CONTEMPLATIVE HARVEST

Stepping into a Fairy Tale:
The Spirituality of Family Life

When I was a boy, my family seemed as wide as the world. This world began with my house, my suburban street, and the well-trodden path to my elementary school; beyond these familiar precincts stretched the mysterious outlands, filled with knights and brigands, angels and dragons, all the marvelous beings that I had learned about in Andrew Lang's green and red fairy-tale books. My family, too, began at home, in the shelter of my mother's warmth, my father's strength, the companionship of my brother and sister. Beyond stretched a world, vast and largely uncharted, filled with relatives of every stripe: actors and homemakers, musicians and soldiers, mystics and tycoons.

The size of my family amazed me: my maternal grandmother gave birth to nine children, my paternal grandmother to six. These siblings brought into the fold fistfuls of husbands and wives and bushel baskets of kids. Over the years, I learned to recognize and love many of my kin, but the greater part of my family remained a mystery. Every so often a previously unknown relative—great-aunt Cha-Cha from Warsaw, great-uncle Sam from Malta—would flash across my field

The kiss

of vision like a new comet for an exciting day or two, bringing sweets from the old country and that musty smell peculiar to the elderly, and then vanish forever into the family mists. Mostly, however, this continent of relatives was terra incognita. Even today, I can't name many of my first cousins—there must be forty or fifty of them, perhaps more—and wouldn't recognize them if they appeared on my doorstep for a surprise reunion. But if they introduced themselves as relatives, I would yelp with joy.

In this variegated landscape, lies, I believe, the value of family. Above all, the family is the hearth, the warmth and solidarity of home. Where would we be without its intimacy? At home we can take off our shoes, stretch, snuggle; we can be ourselves. But the family is also the outlands, where strangers roam and surprise rules. As G. K. Chesterton observed, we choose our friends, we even choose our enemies; but God chooses our family. We have no hand in the matter, and for just this reason we can learn more from our relatives than from our friends. Christ told us to love our neighbor, but the supreme challenge is not to love that charming woman who lives to the south or that handsome man who lives to the north, but to love cantankerous, warty Aunt Gretchen who lives in the basement. This, as Chesterton also said, amounts to the grandest of all adventures:

When we step into the family, by the act of being born, we do step into a world which is incalculable, into a world which has its own strange laws, into a world which could do without us, into a world that we have not made. In other words, when we step into the family we step into a fairy tale.[13]

Like a fairy tale, the family teems with tests and gifts: tests, because our love may founder upon the family's reefs, its sharp edges and hard cases; gifts, because by navigating every day the white water of family turmoil and tension, we arrive at the harbor of family love. The family, like the fairy tale, offers both hearth and hills, comfort and challenge. Like the fairy tale, the family never dies, although it changes conventions from age to age. We may reject our friends, repel our neighbors, lose our jobs, our savings, our very minds, but the blood of the family never runs dry.

The great religious traditions have little to say about family. Family is the medium in which life unfolds, as taken for granted as the air we breathe. When teachings do emerge about domestic life, they usually take the form of advice about child-rearing (see chapter 12, "Childhood," for more on this subject).

There is, however, one notable exception to this widespread taciturnity: Confucius perceived the family as the key to religious life, and his disciplines excel in practical counsel on family spirituality. One Ming manual of "Family Instructions" offers, amid typical advice about child discipline, parental responsibility, daily schedules, and the like, the following two nuggets:

- *Families should share a vigorous religious or spiritual practice.* In Confucian culture, this means scrupulous attention to ritual life, including coming-of-age and wedding ceremonies, sacrifices to the ancestors, and so on. We may apply it more generally. In the home, a family might say grace together, join together for morning or evening prayers, or sit together in silent meditation. Outside the home, a family might attend religious services together; a shared weekly visit to church, mosque, or synagogue not only renews the family's dedication to the spiritual life, but reminds both parents and children of the family's sacred origins and destination.
- *Twice a month, the entire family should gather for a meeting.* The Ming manual recommends a sunset meeting, in which everyone "from the honored aged members to the youngsters" participates.[14] Leadership of the meeting rotates among the adults. At these gatherings, all who are assembled—both young and old—report on their experiences during the past weeks, describing what they have done to improve themselves, solve family problems, and promote family

Great Egrets nest building

harmony, and making suggestions for the future. Others offer support and advice. "The purpose of these meetings," reads the text, "is to encourage one another in virtue and to correct each other's mistakes."[15]

Such meetings, or variations on them, are a staple in many contemporary homes. Children adore them, for they get to act like grown-ups, proffering advice with impunity. This is no small thing. Through such meetings, children learn to help the family and themselves; on occasion, they even come up with invaluable counsel. Adults, too, benefit from the give-and-take. If regular religious practice is the hearth that warms the family, regular meetings may be the mortar that holds up the hearth.

Grandparents—the Reverend and Mrs. Crenchaw, Little Rock, Arkansas   Lewis Watts

f i f t e e n

AGING

Why some things exist is beyond imag-
ining. Everyone has a list of favorite imponderables: mine starts with soap operas,
mosquitoes, and bell-bottom pants. But the greatest mystery of all, at least for
many middle-aged men, is male-pattern baldness. Curiously enough, this phenomenon bedevils scientists as well. Every evolutionary biologist and family physican
has a pet theory, but no one's quite sure why some men, and not others, suffer
mid-scalp hair-loss in that circular pattern that resembles a landing pad for miniature helicopters and shouts unequivocally "I'm aging." The good news is that
male-pattern baldness, at least in theory, attracts potential mates, for to say "I'm
aging" is to say "I survived the rocky reefs of adolescence, I'm navigating the
straits of adulthood, I'm strong and reliable." The bad news is that this theory
doesn't impress too many females, who prefer mop-tops to skin-tops (and usually
abhor rug-tops, the bald male's pathetic attempt to cover up, quite literally, his
evolutionary goof).

   This equivocation extends beyond baldness to the larger event of aging itself.
To put it bluntly, growing old is both blessing and curse. Aging's drawbacks are
plain to see; in fact, plainness is one of its chief characteristics, for the years snatch
the bloom from beauty and the edge from wit. Old age means pain, sorrow, loss,
and imminent death. In "Growing Old," the Victorian poet and critic Matthew
Arnold paints a picture of old age as a dark, cold state, a sort of premature burial
within the sepulchre of failed powers:

What is it to grow old?. . .

It is to spend long days
And not once feel that we were ever young;
It is to add, immured
In the hot prison of the present, month
To month with weary pain.

It is to suffer this,
And feel but half, and feebly, what we feel.
Deep in our hidden heart
Festers the dull remembrance of a change,
But no emotion——none.

It is——last stage of all——
When we are frozen up within, and quite
The phantom of ourselves,
To hear the world applaud the hollow ghost
Which blamed the living man.

I can see no comfort here, no hope of grace. Pain grows, memory fades, resentment triumphs. Every aging person shares, at moments, Arnold's moroseness and despair. But his dark colors convey only a portion of the truth. Old age should be painted in bright tints as well. At the very least, it brings a sense of triumph. The aged are survivors, veterans of that strange feeling, half sorrow and half pleasure, that comes from watching friends and acquaintances fall before the Reaper while one remains unscythed. But this is the least of old age's charms. It comes bearing gifts, wisdom above all. To be sure, there's no guarantee; some souls constrict into hard knots with age. But for the most part, aging brings to human beings, as surely as to cheese or wine, a certain maturity, a pleasing depth and mellowness. It brings, too, an immense gratefulness for the gift of life. While Arnold settles into frigid silence, Whitman gives thanks:

Thanks in old age——thanks ere I go,
For health, the midday sun, the impalpable
      air——for life,
mere life,
For precious ever-lingering memories

> *(of you my mother dear*
> *—you, father—you, brothers, sisters,*
>   *friends,)*
> *For all my days—not those of peace*
>   *alone—the days of*
> *war the same,*
> *For gentle words, caresses, gifts from foreign*
>   *lands,*
> *For shelter, wine and meat—for sweet*
>   *appreciation. . . .*
> *Thanks!—joyful thanks!—a soldier's,*
>   *traveler's thanks.*

In these lines, we sense (as always with Whitman) an animal exuberance so powerful that nothing, not even death itself, can trample it down. But few of us live as lustily as Whitman. Perhaps more apropos are these famous lines by Robert Browning from "Rabbi Ben Ezra":

> *Grow old along with me!*
> *The best is yet to be,*
> *The last of life, for which the first was*
>   *made:*
> *Our times are in His hand*
> *Who saith, "A whole I planned,*
> *Youth shows but half; trust God; see all,*
>   *nor be afraid!"*

Browning, you'll note, never specifies the pleasures awaiting the aged. He is all optimism and openness, ready to embrace whatever comes. But that old age will be grand, he never doubts. Why so? Because life is a whole, shaped by God ("A whole I planned . . ."). It would contradict God's kindness, mercy, and intelligence for him to fashion human life in such a way that it climaxes at thirty, followed by a long, slow slide into the grave. In truth, insists Browning, old age surpasses youth as a statue surpasses its pedestal. Our early years are but apprenticeship; old age is the time of mastery, the "best . . . for which the first was made." God, the consummate artist, always saves the best for last.

In Browning and Whitman, we find a spiritual approach to aging. Faced with this bewildering, terrifying, exhilirating process, which produces wrinkles and wisdom in equal measure, the only sensible response is absolute, unmitigated *trust*. All religions approach aging in this way. They teach the young to trust in elders, and the elders to trust in God.

However, this trust remains largely implicit. Few religions have significant rituals associated with aging. To some extent this is because old age is a modern invention. It's not that ancient cultures didn't have its elders—Abraham, Socrates, Confucius and a host of others sported white hair and wrinkled brows. But old age remained a rare event, far rarer than in today's world of heart-transplants and artificial knees: perhaps there just weren't enough old folks around to justify a sacred ritual. Few ancient societies offered safety nets for the aged: death soon snatched any old person unable to fend for himself. You lived a full fruitful life— farming or hunting or cooking or teaching the young—or else you died. In some cultures, the aged were deliberately turned out to the elements; in others, they just couldn't keep up. The end result was the same.

The same practical considerations, however, gave to the elderly a special dignity and importance. Old people weren't shuffled off to nursing homes or hospital wards, to spend their days watching soap operas or snipping paper doilies. They remained active members of society, with more experience in their belly and more wisdom in their hearts than anyone else. Thus arose the traditional role of the elder. In almost every society, elders counseled, cajoled, taught, and directed the younger generations. Few of the great traditional cultures say anything explicit about the office of elder— it was so woven into the fabric of society that it needed no special comment—but, as we will see, elders enjoyed tremendous influence and prestige.

Aging, then, is a study in contradictions. It brings wisdom, balanced by worries. It brings the bone-weariness of accumulating years, balanced by the lightness of freedom from the tyranny of hormones and social expectations. It brings the desire to teach others, along with concern over one's own final destiny. "Aging is inherent in all living things. Work out your salvation with diligence," said the Buddha. Let us see now how the great religions approach this curious state of physical decay and spiritual growth, and how they understand its relationship to what the Buddha calls "salvation."

CONTEMPLATIVE CLOSEUP:
THE FINAL LIBERATION

"A man of fifty is responsible for his face," the saying goes; one might say, with equal justice, that a man of fifty is responsible for his soul. One shouldn't demand too much from the young, who may be too dazzled by the world around them to pay much attention to the world within. But by middle-age, the center of gravity

John and Mary Collier—grow old along with me!

Linda Connor

begins to shift; the rush of blood quietens, and one begins to hear what the Bible calls "the still, small voice" of the spirit.

Of all religions, perhaps Hinduism makes the most of this truth. Certainly it goes beyond other faiths in enunciating the spiritual role of the elderly, or at least of those elderly men who wish to follow the inner quest to its limits. Hinduism, as mentioned earlier, divides the life cycle into four stages, or *ashrama*: student, householder, forest dweller, and hermit. Since this system evolved, about two thousand years ago, the last two *ashrama* have belonged to the aged.

A classical Hindu life proceeds strictly according to formula. A man becomes a student and then a householder. He fathers children, builds up his estate, performs household rituals, tastes the pleasures of life. As time passes, perhaps he hungers for something more. Sex, food, and money no longer satisfy. He pays more attention to his daily practice; he meditates faithfully, pores over sacred texts, and struggles with his appetites. Things may go on this way for years or even decades. Then one day comes a catalyzing event: a creak in the bones that signals the onset of old age, a death in the family, a business collapse, the way the light shines through the window casement on a fine spring morning. The call sounds, the heart responds, and the householder drops his comforts and cares, takes up saffron robes, staff, and begging bowl, ready to spend the remainder of his life in the single-minded pursuit of wisdom.

The Hindu scriptures describe the appropriate time for this personal earthquake, which cracks open a man's life and puts a unbreachable crevasse between all the years that have come before and the few that remain. It comes "when a householder sees his (skin) wrinkled, and (his hair) white, and the sons of his sons"[1]— that is, when he is a grandfather. The man begins his new life by entering the third *ashrama*, that of the forest dweller. The scriptures continue with an account of this arduous way of life:

> Abandoning all food raised by cultivation, and all his belongings, he may depart into the forest, either committing his wife to his sons, or accompanied by her. . . .
>
> Let him wear a skin or a tattered garment; let him bathe in the evening or in the morning; and let him always wear (his hair in) braids, the hair on his body, his beard, and his nails (being unclipped).[2]

Sometimes the asceticism reaches heroic pitch. The holy texts recommend that the daily plate be laden with "flower, roots and fruit alone."[3] As for clothing, the rule of thumb seemed to be discomfort at all costs, as the forest dweller wears the ancient equivalent of flannel in summer, shorts and T-shirt in winter: "in summer let him expose himself to the heat of five fires, during the rainy season live under the open sky, and in winter be dressed in wet clothes."[4] And what does he do during his retreat? He prays, meditates, gives alms, performs rituals. If that doesn't suffice, he is invited to make the final sacrifice: "Let him walk, fully determined and going straight on, in a north-easterly direction, subsisting on water and air, until his body sinks to rest."[5]

Incredibly, these hardships mark but the beginning of the path. Eventually the forest dweller, sufficiently purified, graduates into the fourth *ashrama*, that of the homeless wanderer:

> He shall neither possess a fire, nor a dwelling . . . (he shall be) indifferent to everything, firm of purpose, meditating (and) concentrating his mind on Brahman.
>
> A potsherd instead of an alms-bowl, the roots of trees (for a dwelling), coarse worn-out garments, life in solitude and indifference towards everything, are the marks of one who has attained liberation.[6]

Thus the Hindu achieves his final lot: a penniless, homeless mendicant, abandoning all for the sake of all. These days, the third *ashrama* is invariably skipped, and devout Hindus leap directly from the householder stage into the last *ashrama*. A dramatic ceremony may mark the occasion: the new *sannyasin* bids farewell to his family, distributes his wealth, and then quits home, his son at his side. After walking a little way, father and son halt and put their backs to each another. The son heads toward to the village, and the father—who will never see his family again—strides forward into the unknown.

What do we make of such a regime? I suspect that most of us are simultaneously fascinated and repelled, filled with admiration at austerities voluntarily shouldered in the search for wisdom, yet dismayed by the suffering and loss of family involved. In our modern culture, bound hand and foot by the silken cords of comfort, we can scarcely imagine such sacrifices, much less undertake them ourselves. Yet over the past two millennia, millions upon millions of Hindus have chosen the path of renunciation, and it continues to be a viable option for many elderly men today.

Let us at least give praise where we can. The renunciant follows a strict moral code that does much to enhance the inner life:

> Let him be always industrious in privately reciting the Veda; let him be
> patient of hardships, friendly (towards all), of collected mind, ever liberal
> and never a receiver of gifts, and compassionate towards all living creatures.[7]

To follow such a set of precepts is in itself a magnificent achievement. As for the essence of the third and fourth *ashrama*—separation from the parent culture, and, at least for the *sannyasin*, a life of absolute solitude—surely this constitutes a frightening prospect for elderly Indians as well as young Americans or Europeans. To understand why so many have accepted this burden, it helps to remember what is at stake. I spoke earlier about the difficult spiritual terrain of family life, where many a good intention comes to shipwreck on the Scylla of one's spouse or the Charybdis of one's children. In the Hindu *ashrama* system, we find a radical solution to this problem, one that places the seeker, at the proper moment of his life, in conditions propitious for rapid spiritual advance—leading, in this lifetime or another, to final liberation.

And that goal—escape from rebirth, union with the infinite Spirit, absolute knowledge and unconditional freedom—may be worth any sacrifice. We get a foretaste of what it brings in various passages from the scriptures, which describe the renunciant as being "free from sorrow and fear," "delighting in what refers to the Soul," "reposing in Brahman alone." These phrases remind me of those used to describe St. Antony, one of the first great Christian saints, when he emerged from twenty years of solitude in the Egyptian desert:

> The state of his soul was one of purity. . . . when he saw the crowd, he was not annoyed any more than he was elated at being embraced by so many people. He maintained utter equilibrium, like one guided by reason and steadfast in that which accords with nature. . . . he consoled many who mourned, and others hostile to each other he reconciled in friendship.[8]

The tranquillity of bearing and presence ascribed to the *sannyasin* of India and the desert fathers of Egypt reflects a profound degree of spiritual attainment. We sense that these men have made good use of their lives; they have won, in the words of Proverbs, the "crown of the wise."

Now, let us take a deep breath, swallow our self-satisfaction, and compare this way of life to that of elderly men—and women—in the industrial nations today. As I said above, old age today for many people amounts to hours staring at the television set, or playing bingo in a church basement, or looking forward to a social worker's cursory visit a week from Thursday. It's glaringly obvious that such activities do little to warm the heart, much less feed the soul. Perhaps we need to learn a lesson from traditional India. The ancient Hindu system that I have described takes old age seriously. It respects the elderly. It believes that wrinkles are a road map toward the Absolute. It believes that white hair is a signal to start, rather than stifle, the search for God.

The *ashrama* system will never find a home in contemporary industrial societies. It is culture-specific, embedded in the heritage of India. In any event, we don't tolerate beggars well in our society. But adaptations are possible. In fact, we find such accommodations in India itself.

For reasons we can well imagine, many Hindu men prove unwilling to sacrifice the fruits of lifelong labor, not to mention the love of family, in order to become *sannyasin*. Some of these men establish a middle ground between spiritual aspirations and earthly attractions by moving into a hut close by the family dwelling, where they live a semi-hermetic life. Others continue to live with their families, but retire from active employment in favor of a regime of meditation, ritual, and scriptural study. That is, they adopt the daily practices, but not the dwelling, of the renunciant. Others take on the *sannyasin* ideal of ceaseless movement, but rather than meander as beggars from village to village, they travel as householders from one sacred pilgrimage site to the next, where they offer worship, praise, and thanksgiving. Women, too, although in lesser numbers than men, have successfully undertaken all of these alternatives to the orthodox, and exclusively male, fourth *ashram* of complete renunciation.

These are Indian solutions to the problem of how to keep alive the essence of the *ashrama*, the search for the absolute. As each one of us, tomorrow or in fifty years, faces our own old age, the questions loom: Can we emulate this wonderful Hindu system and discover, in the language of our own culture, a way to keep the spirit aflame from birth to death? Can we find in old age the means to "delight in what refers to the Soul," as the Vedas put it?

One possibility is the development of elderly communities, or even nursing homes, that encourage contemplative practice. Such homes—the principle might even be extended to hospices—would allow the aged to engage in serious inner work into their final days. Certainly, on the individual level much can be done. There's no apparent reason why retired people can't, if they choose, adopt a quasi-*sannyasin* manner of life in Toronto or Tokyo, living in modified hermitages attached to the family home. If this seems too radical a step, a retirement devoted to pilgrimage, prayer, and the study of sacred texts may appeal instead. If it works in New Delhi, it can work in New York.

These proposals may sound quixotic, but the problem remains: secular culture offers the aged no spiritual role. To begin to grasp this situation and catch a glimpse of possible solutions, I believe that we need to ponder *the meaning of the elder*. Society needs to ask itself what it means to have an elderly population—a vast reservoir of knowledge and experience that remains largely untapped. Elders themselves need to ask what responsibilities this tremendous fund of skills entails, both in their own lives and in those of the younger generation.

AGING: A CONTEMPLATIVE HARVEST

The Elder

The other day I was watching, for the sixth or seventh time, Frank Capra's *Lost Horizon*, a magical movie about a magical kingdom in the heart of the Himalayas. The film has much to recommend it: Ronald Colman as a dashing British diplomat, marvelous neo-Tibetan sets, spectacular mountain scenery, the wonder of Shangri-La itself. But what won my heart—what most people remember about the film—is Sam Jaffe's astonishing portrayal of the 200-year-old Father Perrault. His soft voice, commanding mind, and dignified bearing sum up everything that we mean by the word "elder."

The universal acclamation accorded Jaffe's performance is good evidence, I believe, that the idea of the elder resides deep in our psyches. We need elders desperately, for guidance and support. When an older person of genuine spiritual force appears—Mother Teresa is an obvious example—the world shouts its joy.

Alas, we have few such people to turn to; our so-called "elder statesmen" are usually tired politicians, retired generals, or the like. For the most part, we stand bereft.

Elders insure the spiritual well-being of the community—Lama Gyurme and pilgrims, Drepung Monastery, Tibet

In many traditional cultures, by contrast, the role of elder befalls most men and women who attain a certain age. In the eyes of tradition, age and wisdom are nearly synonymous ("no wise man ever wished to be younger," said Jonathan Swift). Elders teach the young, heal the sick, mete out justice, declare war or peace, and tell the stories that reveal the meaning of life. In sum, they ensure the spiritual well-being of the community. Let us examine a few of these activities in greater depth:

TEACHING

Perhaps you remember the scene in the film *Independence Day*, where an elderly Jewish man, long estranged from his faith, dons his yarmulke, picks up his Bible, and brings comfort to the children huddled around him while alien spaceships attack. We don't know exactly what he is reading to the children, but it may well be this passage from Psalm 92: "In old age they still produce fruit; they are always green and full of sap." This is the quintessential task of the elderly: to produce the fruit of wisdom, which the younger generation will eat; to succor; to instruct.

Among the !Kung San, grandmothers care for grandchildren while the mothers forage in the bush. This care involves not only ordinary tasks like feeding and clothing, but that of instilling in children the essential !Kung San virtues of kindness, industry, and humility. In nearly every culture, grandparents undertake this task of imparting to the young the moral and religious precepts that sustain society. For the !Kung San and many other peoples, this education takes the form of storytelling, and skilled storytellers earn high respect. Among the Coast Salish Indians of Washington State and British Columbia, almost all elders serve as storytellers at one time or another, transmitting to a new generation the cultural treasury of the people. Indeed, one scholar comments that "the archetype of the pitiful figure in Coast Salish mythology is the child without grandparents to instruct him."[9]

HEALING

The image of the wizened healer, a staple figure in Western pop culture (from Marcus Welby, M.D., to Dr. Ruth Westheimer), proves to be an accurate reflection of the elder's role in many cultures. With age accrues knowledge, in particular of ailments and how to cure them. Elderly !Kung San, both men and women, freed from the onerous chores of hunting and gathering, devote much of their time to perfecting the healing arts. This often involves entering a trance state in order to communicate directly with the spirit world. To the Kirghiz of Afghanistan, no one under thirty has the insight to perceive the world of spirits; thus the role of *bahkshi*, which involves curing afflictions caused by malevolent spirits, falls upon the elders.

LEADERSHIP

If we could gather all the world's leaders on a single stage—all the presidents, prime ministers, generalissimos, supreme chairmen, kings, and queens—we would notice, amid the inevitable squabbling and squawking that come when different tongues and ideologies mix, one constant: they all have wrinkles. By selecting older men and women to rule, if in few other ways, the modern world conforms to the wisdom of the traditions.

Among the Coast Salish, at least until European contact, all political and economic leadership with the exception of warfare (the province of young men) belonged to the aged. The Asmat of New Guinea give power to the *tesmaypits*, old men who excel in woodcarving and other skills. But we needn't restrict ourselves to traditional societies. The five major world religions—Buddhism, Christianity, Hinduism, Islam, and Judaism—all put their trust in the elderly. An apparent exception arises in Tibetan Buddhism, where the current Dalai Lama assumed his title at the age of three. But this extreme youthfulness is deceptive, for Tenzin Gyatso is held to be the reincarnation of a long line of earlier Dalai Lamas, stretching back six centuries, and to possess the accumulated wisdom of the intervening years. Even here, in veiled form, we find that age, wisdom, and leadership coalesce.

What can we conclude from this glance at elders in various religions and cultures? That the aged have special contributions to make in a number of fields, especially health, education, and government; that these contributions draw on precisely those spiritual resources that the elderly possess in abundance; and that we have failed miserably to find a parallel work for the elderly in our own culture. A great resource languishes, and the question presses: what will we do about it?

Paul visits Ram Dass to talk about consciousness and aging.

A Visit with Ram Dass

Before his illness, Ram Dass was a familiar sight tooling around his hometown of San Anselmo, California, in his vintage MG convertible, his white hair puffed out by the breeze. He was not wistful about the dying of the light. Yet, like so many others, this seemingly ageless counterculture personage and spiritual teacher had grown old. Although he was in the midst of writing a book about aging, I sensed that he came late to a strong personal identification with the older set. A little while ago, doing a personal interview on a British television program, he used the pronoun *they* to refer to aging folks. I looked forward to teasing him about this slip and hearing his views on a subject in which he has invested a good deal of thought. We met over apple juice in his Victorian house, where he launched right into the subject.

"When I go to India," he began, "and I go to a village and somebody says, 'Ram Dass, you are looking much older,' I instinctively feel impoverished by what they've said. Then, I listen to the tone of their voice and I hear that they are really honoring me. India is a traditional society in which aging means wisdom and passing on the lineage. I'm to be valued now, rather than to be disposed of. So the first thing we can do to bring consciousness to our aging is to contemplate what our culture has done to us."

The fear of aging, of losing one's powers, of becoming marginalized and obsolete, is so deeply rooted in our modern Western culture that even when we celebrate older people, we do so in terms of their undying youth. "Hey, did you hear about Linda? She's seventy and she's got a new lover." Or, "Wow! Ed is eighty-two and he is still climbing mountains." There is a tendency to celebrate youth and that kind of energy, says Ram Dass, "because we do not know what else there is."

To find out what else there is, Ram Dass suggests that we begin by focusing our awareness on our views of time and change and the possibility of living more in the strange and wonderful timelessness of the present moment. If aging causes us to obsess over the past and the future (which, for most of us, looks both shorter and less appealing with age), the key is to have one's consciousness remain in the present moment.

"Our egos train us to be time-binders," Ram Dass observes. "From the time we are little children, we live future-oriented lives. Then, when we age and the future doesn't look so attractive, we flip into the past and dwell in memories. We miss where all the statement is, which is in the moment."

Dwelling in the past, going back to a moment in the past, pulls us back into the consciousness we experienced at that time. We are flooded with the feelings we had then, even though we are not the same person now. We need to bring our recollections forward into present consciousness and to sit with them in the light of awareness. "As you do this," says Ram Dass, "history loses its control over you."

Ram Dass recalls that when his mother died, he felt terribly guilty that he had not spent enough time with her or done enough for her. "I've carried the guilt with me and now, if I go back there, into the memories, I start to have the old feelings I had, the feelings that belong to the person I was then. But if I just sit with all of that and bring it into the present moment, something interesting happens. I begin to see why she was the way she was and why I was the way I was. Or why my father did what he did. When I sit mindfully with all of this, I develop a compassion toward the whole situation. The past images don't have the same kind of power over me that they did before, because I have updated them in the moment, in my present consciousness."

If we can live with the full past in our present consciousness, we can also bring our thoughts about the future into the present and attend to them in a similar spirit of appreciation and nonjudgment. The future primarily involves fears of future suffering, including fear of losing physical and mental powers and fear of dying.

Ram Dass believes that when we bring these fears into present awareness and examine them consciously, when we meditate on them rather than avoid them, they become less dark and shadowy. While we may not like the prospects before us, our very courage to be open to them marshals the resources of our spirit and enables us to examine more clearly the roots of our suffering. What is the fear all about?

Although our speculations are rich in metaphors, we really don't know what happens after death. The questions are, How do we deal with things we don't know? How does one prepare to face the ultimate uncertainty with a sense of adventure and joy? "The best preparation," says Ram Dass, "is to live each moment."

Last Days

Sooner or later, old age becomes decrepitude. Vim and vigor may remain at eighty, or even ninety, but few centenarians escape the wheelchair or the bed. Most of what I've said about the aged applies to the physically and mentally fit, those able to don the mantle of responsibility that comes with the office of elder. But what of those whose arms tremble too much to lift the mantle? What of those afflicted by exhaustion, blindness, senility, or the other myriad woes of extreme age? Here, a special phase of life begins, a work based in courage and hope.

John Neihardt, poet laureate of Nebraska and amanuensis of Black Elk, tells of a Sioux friend of his who recalled in old age a vision quest conducted decades earlier. For three days, Neihardt's friend remembered, he had prayed, fasted, and awaited a vision. But nothing happened. Anticipation gave way to despair, and he thought of running away in shame. Then at the height of his agony, when all seemed bleak, a voice sounded above his head. Looking up, he spied an eagle wheeling in the wind, and this is what it said:

"Hoka-hey, brother—*Hold fast, hold fast; there is more!*"

The old Sioux, remembering this moment, said to Neihardt, "As I listened, a power ran through me that has never left me, old as I am. Often when it seemed the end had come, I have heard the eagle's cry—*Hold fast, hold fast; there is more. . . .*"[10]

This counsel to "hold fast," which comes from the eagle—and thus from *Wakan Tanka*, or God—becomes the cry of all old people who see their powers slip away into the impenetrable night of decay and death. This is raw courage, pure grit, braced by a lifetime of experience that teaches always that "there is more." When everything shouts "stop!" one forges on. As the body wilts, the heart blossoms anew. Here is a description of the surgeon Sir James Paget in his final years of decline, written by his son:

> Paget had to give up everything: the companionship of his wife, and the sight of his friends; the very power to stand, or to write his own name, or to speak above a whisper. These last two years of his life are nothing short of a miracle; they cannot easily be reconciled with any natural interpretation of things . . . he surrendered every vestige of his old life with a sort of courteous, half-humorous gentleness. So long as he could hear a note of it, he delighted in music; so long as he could see a word of them he read his books of devotion . . . the longer he lived, the higher he went.[11]

Paget's perseverance, in the light of the progressive death of all his powers, moves us deeply. Here is courage, just as Neihardt's friend prescribes, but of a special kind, neither fierce nor frightened, but with "a sort of courteous, half-humorous gentleness" at its heart. The only possible response to the final calamities of old age, Paget's story suggests, is one of loving surrender, in the knowledge that "there is more."

I am reminded here of an old woman whom I knew some twenty years ago, afflicted by cancer, who watched helplessly, like Paget, as all her ordinary pleasures were snatched away by the relentless progress of the illness. No longer could she stroll in the Boston Arboretum, or join her friends for a tea and muffin at her favorite Harvard Square cafe, or even read a book—the last a sacrifice of incomparable proportions, as she delighted in the written word, and especially in poetry, all her life. As my friend's world disintegrated, I saw a change come over her, especially in her final year: her features sharpened, her eyes brightened, and her skin turned translucent; her face seemed to glow with an inner light. "All this," she said one day, propped up in bed, waving her hand at some stained poetry chapbooks and, by implication, at the forests and fields, friends and food that were also denied her, "All this . . . I miss it terribly. But what does it matter? Behind it is something else."

What is this "more" of which the aged Sioux spoke, this "something else" in which my friend found solace? No one can say exactly, and perhaps it varies from one person to another. For many, certainly, it involves the discovery of something in the inner life that seems safe from the ravages of age. Listen to the Rev. George Congreve, deaf and wracked by pain, writing as death approached:

> If I find no home any longer in this world, it is because God has been withdrawing me, my love, my treasures, my remembrances, my hopes, from a place where the frost-wind of death touched every precious thing, where no good can last, but night falls, and only icy solitude and silence remain. This is no home, this is but a lodging. . . . I must begin to long for home. I seem almost asleep, but my heart is awake. . . . Memory sleeps, action sleeps, thought sleeps, but love is awake; it is withdrawn from the surface of life to the center."[12]

Congreve, too, finds the familiar signposts of life vanishing before his eyes. He, too, responds with acceptance, and he defines for us the real nature of Paget's "courteous, half-humorous gentleness": it is love. Love is awake when all else sleeps; love gives to aging, to its horrors and deprivations, meaning and grace. This love lies at the "center," says Congreve; it is the same love that we encounter in our daily sittings, prayers, and meditations, in our quotidian efforts to return to the source of being. Here, in extreme old age, it becomes the anchor not only of our daily round, but of our very life.

sixteen

DYING

The churchyard of Christ Church, New Brunswick, New Jersey

Christine Knodt

$\mathcal{D}$riving to church last Sunday, my family and I passed one of our local graveyards. It's a classic New England burial ground, a patch of sandy soil holding thirty or forty listing, lichen-etched slabs, their inscriptions badly eroded by wind and acid rain. I slowed the car to point out my favorite marker, a blackened stone with a grinning death's-head, the ubiquitous Puritan symbol of mortality. Just then my ten-year-old son John piped up.

"I want to be buried next to Mo Vaughn," he said. I should explain that Mo Vaughn, an athlete of Olympian power and grace, plays first base for the Boston Red Sox.

"Why?" I asked.

"Because," he answered, "then my soul can play baseball with him in heaven, and my body can play baseball with him under the ground."

I laughed and wondered, *Does it happen as early as ten?* In this juvenile wish, unlikely to be answered for any number of reasons, my son had summarized our species' troubled relationship with death. On the one hand, anxiety: the fear that death is the end, that our loss is final (no more ball games!), and the wish to do whatever it takes to set things right. On the other hand, hope: the dream that we do survive death, that we can swing a bat or catch a curve in heaven's emerald fields (and, according to John's metaphysics, before the astonished eyes of moles and badgers under the earth as well).

Ambivalence colors all our encounters with death. Consider cryonics, the "science" of freezing the deceased in a bath of liquid hydrogen, transforming them into what one science-fiction writer calls "corpsicles," in the wild hope that some future civilization will thaw them out, cure whatever disease killed them, and give them, literally, a new lease on life. What do you think of this curious practice, which amounts, so far, to little more than a technological gloss on mummification? In my experience, it makes most of us jittery. We chuckle uneasily and crack jokes like "many are cold but few are frozen." Icing the dead seems undignified and most likely futile. Death, we sense, deserves better than this.

The great religions agree. None of them cheapens death. Death is a great, if baleful event, like the visit of a cruel emperor from across the seas. The religions may paint death as a devouring maw or a bleached skeleton or a frightful whirl-wind—but always they give death its due. They agree on this, too: that death is not the end. Death is a door disguised as a wall.

Even those non-religious teachings that reject an afterlife believe that death lends life meaning and savor. "A free man thinks of nothing less than death," said Spinoza, "and his wisdom is not a meditation upon death but upon life." Chuang Tzu takes the stoical attitude that

> life is the companion of death, death is the beginning of life. Who under-
> stands their workings? Man's life is a coming together of breath. If it
> comes together, there is life; if it scatters, there is death.

And yet, and yet . . . if we knew for certain that cryonics would work, how many millions would flock to the freezers, even at the going rate of $150,000 per corpsicle? "I don't want to achieve immortality through my work," said Woody Allen. "I want to achieve it through not dying." No one has expressed the horrors of the grave more vividly than Shakespeare:

> *Ay, but to die, and go we know not where,*
> *To lie in cold obstruction and to rot;*
> *This sensible warm motion to become*
> *A kneaded clod; and the delighted spirit*
> *To bathe in fiery floods, or to reside*
> *In thrilling region of thick-ribbed ice,*

To be imprisoned in the viewless winds
And blow with restless violence round about
The pendent world . . . 'tis too horrible!
The weariest and most loathed worldly life
That age, ache, penury, and imprisonment
Can lay on nature is a paradise
To what we fear of death.

Shakespeare, it has been observed, has no distinctive personality. His genius lies in his cold objectivity; he is, as Jorge Luis Borges puts it, "all men." He speaks for everyone, and nowhere more than here. Even for those who trust in an afterlife, death at times puts on a sinister air. Traditional tales of the origin of death often describe it as an accident, an error, a result of sin. The African "Two Messengers" story is typical: God sends two animal couriers to earth, the chameleon to announce that human beings will live forever, and the lizard to announce that human beings will die. The chameleon dallies on the path and the lizard arrives first. Because of this single act of tardiness, we are destined for the grave.

Most of the time, we keep death locked out of sight. Death is a mirage; death happens to others. But all this changes as we gray, wrinkle, and stoop with the passing years. Parents die; children die; companions die. We find that death—not just death in theory, death as the salt of life, death as spiritual exercise, but the flaccid skin and rattling breath of real death—surrounds us. We suddenly recognize, as the Buddha said, that "for the born there is no such thing as not dying." To realize this can be quite a shock. During my freshman year at Wesleyan University, I was bowled over when my English professor, a learned man in his late forties, described how, shortly after his mother's death, he had fled into his bed for several weeks when it dawned on him that he, too, would die. "I hadn't realized," he said, shaking his head in wonder, "I just hadn't realized. . . ."

Once death knocks at our consciousness, it becomes imperative to put it in perspective; to prepare, at least provisionally, for the demise of our loved ones and of ourselves. "Learning how to meet death," an elderly woman of high spiritual attainment once said to me, "is the most important task of all." Let us now examine a number of ways—some old, some new—to face this inescapable challenge.

Paul explores the extraordinary work of Therese Schroeder-Sheker.

CONTEMPLATIVE CLOSE-UP:
THERESE SCHROEDER-SHEKER

The Chalice of Repose

The Clark Fork River snakes its way through Montana's Bitterroot Valley, which is rimmed by the sharp peaks of the Rockies. Toward the end of this particular day, the brooding sky—a harbinger of the first snowfall—and the somber waters conspire to evoke aching remembrances of my loss. Six years ago, my father died in his hospital bed. Max died alone, sometime between midnight and dawn. His body, discovered by an attendant, was bagged and conveyed into the medical maw before I could reach the hospital in San Diego. The doctors had given no indication that Max's condition was critical. Quite the contrary.

Now there was my mother to care for, and so my rage at the ineptitude and cold indifference of the medical establishment went underground. At times, my anger surfaces and I burst into tears when my imagination puts me at his bedside, at the moment of his death. Did he slip gently into death? Was he conscious and afraid? Did he call for me? I would have crawled into bed and held him in my arms, as I had when he was sick.

A dying person is supposed to be physically embraced. This is the image from the movies I saw as a kid during World War II. The hero holds his buddy, comforting him with promises of remembrance, interspersed with oaths of vengeance, as the last inky trickle of blood runs from the corner of the dying man's mouth. Even on the chaotic battlefield, one died in the loving, unconditional presence of another. This is what I remember.

A few miles from the Clark Fork, in the university town of Missoula, lives a woman who uses music to embrace the physical and spiritual needs of the dying. Therese Schroeder-Sheker is the founder of the Chalice of Repose Project, a clinical practice at Missoula's St. Patrick Hospital that offers a loving presence to anyone who is dying. During the last four years Chalice workers have attended over 1,300 deathbed vigils, using music to support the physiological and interior processes of the dying person. When medical intervention can do nothing more, physicians at the hospital turn to Chalice's contemplative musicians to help alleviate the patient's physical pain and spiritual suffering.

Therese's home is a log house set among fir, poplar, and apple trees. Behind the house rise thick stands of trees; in front, a weather-beaten bench, once a church pew, faces out to the plains and the distant peaks. Inside, light pours in from windows open to the meadow and valley beyond. A handheld *shruti* box, an East Indian bellows instrument, sits atop a window ledge. A viola da gamba is propped against the wall.

Therese is tuning her harp. Her left hand turns the tuning pin, while with her right hand she thoughtfully plucks the strings. Her head presses close to the body of the harp as she listens. "I'm convinced," she muses, "that we don't choose the harp, but that it calls to us.

"My response to the harp was complete and total . . . the same way that people fall in love. Then, when I had to start to learn how to play it, and to tune it, I realized: my God, this thing called to me because it is a total curriculum in the interior life. The body of the harp, just like a chalice, has to be empty in order for us to draw out the sound. You have to go through the discipline and practice of tuning with minute hand gestures, every single day, several times a day. To tune and to stretch the strings is a metaphor for our own soul life. Every single one of us can do with reminders about how to be in tune with others and with ourselves. Is my thinking in tune with my feeling? Is my feeling in tune with my doing? All these relationships are taught, little by little by little, when you have constantly to tune and stretch and refine strings."

Twenty-five years ago, Therese was completing an undergraduate degree in music and working as a nurse's aide at a geriatric home in Colorado. When a resident died, she was instructed to get the corpse into a body bag right away so that it could be taken away to the morgue. Only then would the telephone calls to relatives be made. She was taught to clean and sterilize the room quickly so that the empty bed could be filled again as soon as possible. Young Therese never heard death discussed at the psychological or spiritual level. Death was an economic event: an empty bed meant a loss of revenue.

In the home, she watched the elderly sit day after day, hour after hour, often heavily sedated. Many had outlived their friends and families and they often died alone, some with the television set on. All of this disturbed Therese because she knew there was a better way. When she was growing up, death had been a natural part of life; a person's passing was mourned.

Checking in for duty one evening, she was told that one patient would probably die on her shift that night. He was an elderly man with advanced emphysema. Medically, nothing more could be done for him. To complicate the situation, he was a difficult resident, cantankerous and combative, someone who pushed people away.

"When I went into his room," Therese recalls, "I heard a tremendously loud and very frightening death rattle. He was thrashing from side to side, his lungs were filling up, and he was fulminating. It's like drowning. I closed the door and went over to his bedside. He was quite emaciated. I took his hand and called his name and said, 'I'm here . . . I'm here.' He held on and didn't push me away, so I knew he wanted me to stay. He was responding to my touch. He knew he was dying, and he was frightened. I didn't really think my way through this, but I just got into bed and held him. I positioned myself behind him in the midwifery position. I put my head behind his head, my heart behind his heart and held him, rocking him gently. Then, I began singing to him.

"I sang the Mass of the Angels, the *Adoro te devote* of Thomas Aquinas, the Ubi Caritas, the Salve Regina, the Mass of the Blessed Virgin Mary, only because they are beautiful and I knew them and they were totally with me and I could give them away easily. I knew nothing of his religious background, only that, as I sang, he began to breathe more evenly. I sang for about twenty minutes and as I sang softly and quietly in his ear, his breathing became less erratic and more synchronized with mine. He rested back into the music. I sang and held him, and then he died. I learned right then and there that touch and caring, being present and walking the final mile home was everything. Although the dying person's physical condition can't be changed, his interior condition can be supported. The dying need an unconditional presence if they are to let go and die in peace. That was the beginning."

After the death of the man in the geriatric home, Therese began attending deathbed vigils in Denver hospitals, hospices, and homes—not as a member of the regular medical staff, but informally, when friends would call and ask her to attend a family member. Therese would sing and play her harp. At the same time, she was pursuing her musical career with recordings and performances of medieval music. Then she attended a conference on medieval studies and heard the scholar Fred Paxton read a paper on "Liturgy and Anthropology."

Paxton's insights into the death rituals of Benedictine monasticism changed Therese's life, giving her intuitive work with dying persons a historical context and a grounding in anthropology. Paxton's scholarship illuminated for her the deep relationship between the dying person and the community, the mysterious symbolic bonds between the individual and the social group.

Paxton examined the customs set down for living and dying in the monastery of Cluny in Burgundy in the eleventh century, practices that reveal both the power and the subtle awareness of a contemplative approach to being and nonbeing.[1] When a monk feels that his death is near, he confesses it to the community, which immediately draws about him. "The monk will not die alone; at every step of his journey he will be surrounded by the good will, the prayers, and the physical presence of his fellow monks."

The dying monk is surrounded by his brethren who chant at his bedside. It is "a profound attempt to bring aid to the dying man, through the juxtaposition of action and contemplation in the expression of faith. In the ideal situation, the Credo will be chanted right at the moment of death, and that outpouring of faith, no doubt joined by the dying man if possible, will preserve the soul as it leaves the body."[2] To use music to help the dying person let go of the body, unbind from pain, and die peacefully remains the essential purpose of contemporary music thanatology and of practitioners like Therese Schroeder-Sheker.

The signage in the hallways of the hospital in Missoula is functional and generic—RADIOLOGY, ADMINISTRATION, SURGERY—and, aside from one or two strategically placed statues of saints, the ambiance is exactly what one would expect in any modern medical institution. But a few steps from the waiting room of the International Heart Institute are signs for the HARP ROOM and the sight of women lugging bulky instruments down the corridor.

A sacred pragmatism has emerged in Missoula. The medical doctor and the music thanatologist, the person wielding a scalpel and the person playing a harp, meet where science and the humanities encounter the Great Mystery. When families turn to their doctor and say, Do something! . . . this is my wife, or this is my husband, or this is my child . . . , the doctors can now say, We have something we can do for you. "When we come to the bedside," says Therese, "there is a very clear shift from exterior activity to more interior, contemplative activity."

When they are on duty, the Chalice workers travel with beepers and must arrive at the scene of an imminent death—a hospital room, a cardiology or intensive care unit, a hospice or a private home—emotionally and spiritually prepared. In Therese's words, they must come to the dying person "as open vessels," willing and able to be completely present to the dying person's pain. This state of preparation requires a daily reflective practice, an interior activity such as prayer, meditation, and silence that helps the Chalice worker to be open to the pain of another. The chalice, with its hollow interior and firm base, with its capacity to both receive and give, is model and metaphor for the work of the contemplative musician, a daily work of emptying in order to receive fullness. It is a state of interior readiness.

Chalice workers go to the bedside of the dying person in teams of two or three. The harpists sit on either side of the bed, so that the music anoints the person from head to foot. A typical vigil might last an hour; ideally, the musicians will be there at the moment of death. If death occurs while they are playing, they continue to play for as long as family or friends wish.

A Chalice of Repose vigil, Montana

The music is individually tailored to meet the needs of the dying person. Each vigil begins by taking the vital signs and by looking at the respiratory patterns. Five different people with the same or similar diagnoses of lung cancer would each receive different kinds of music and delivery. This prescriptive use of music is grounded in a body-systems phenomenology that posits a direct relationship between the melodic content of the music and the neurology of the person, between the harmonic content of the music and the state of the person's respiratory and circulatory systems. The music's rhythm engages the whole person, affecting thinking and feeling, metabolism and will.

Therese describes the process: "We begin in silence and we zero in, listening carefully for the breathing patterns, watching the rise and fall of the chest. It is ever so subtle. Then we begin to play. We synchronize our phrasing and cadencing of the music with the person's inhalation and exhalation. Then, we quietly begin to slow down. We may repeat something ten times, using sparsely delivered harmonic structures, and the closer to death the person comes the more open and spacious our playing becomes."

Therese recalls the first vigil she did in Missoula: "The dying man was in his early forties. He had a wife and two young sons so, by all normal accounts, he would be expected to live a great many more years, but he had advanced liver cancer.

"He was in agonizing physical pain, and no amount of morphine could relieve what he was experiencing. When I went in the room his wife was sobbing and calling his name: 'You said you'd never leave us. You said you'd always be with us. You told the boys you'd never leave them.' When I began to play it was hard for me not to get a lump in my own throat because her grief was so great. He had been passing in and out of consciousness, and she kept begging him to stay. 'You said you'd never leave us.' I kept on playing, and finally she fell onto the floor, sobbing and exhausted. At a certain point she lifted her head up. I was still playing, my eyes on him. He had been reclining all the way back on the bed and suddenly he quietly leaned up, as if he was seeing something that none of us could perceive. When she saw him, she changed completely. She said, 'It's okay, it's okay, you can go.' I kept playing, and in a matter of moments he leaned back and exhaled his last breath."

Many people are dying outside supportive communities and without an unconditional loving presence. Such was the unpredictable and ironic fate of my father, a man singularly dedicated to community. Yet, of late, I have had this fantasy: perhaps my father was not, strictly speaking, cold and alone in a hospital bed when he died. Perhaps he saw the radiant faces of well-wishers gathered around him. Their voices comforted him, telling Max that it was time and that it was okay. They were all there. Slum kids from the thirties and the refugee men and women that he cared for in Europe at the end of World War II. All the people that he had helped throughout his life. It was his luminous community, embracing him and welcoming him home.

DYING: A CONTEMPLATIVE HARVEST

Meeting Death

Like millions of other American schoolchildren, I was obliged during my high-school years to read Charles Dickens's *A Tale of Two Cities.* I cringed upon hearing the assignment, for I clerked part-time in the local library and knew well the chunky, leaden feel of Dickens's novels, more like paperweights than books with their 800-plus pages of tightly wound prose. When *Two Cities* turned out to be a slim, fast-paced read—about a revolution, to boot!—I was elated. Of its details I remember little, save cackling crones knitting funeral shrouds, the rumble of the guillotine as it fell toward the necks of countless victims—and the wonderful closing scene, stamped forever on my heart, of Sydney Carton striding through the rabid mob to his execution, where he utters those sublime last words: "It is a far, far better thing that I do, than I have ever done; it is a far, far better rest that I go to than I have ever known." In Carton's bearing, in his walk and in his words, I first encountered the idea of conscious death.

To die a collected death, to make one's farewells with grace, generosity, and even a dash of humor, to greet the afterlife as friend rather than foe: such is the aim of conscious dying in the world's religious traditions. This is no easy thing, and stories of dying masters are told and retold as examples for the living. Thus Gregory the Great's life of Benedict describes the saint's last minutes: "As he supported his weak limbs with the help of his disciples, he stood with hands raised to heaven and drew his last breath while praying."[3] A Jewish collection, the *Histalkut Hanefesh*, tells of the deaths of the Hasidic masters. When the Baal Shem Tov readied himself to die, he instructed his followers on how to care for his body, recited the Torah, meditated in solitude, and then prayed "until the syllables of his words could no longer be distinguished."[4] Rabbi Nachman of Bratzlav, "who already had achieved a rung so lofty that it seemed impossible to ascend higher while clothed with flesh," spent his last hours in similar fashion, counseling his followers, praying, and pondering "matters deep and most wonderful."[5]

From where, we wonder, comes the ability to die with such aplomb? Another Hasidic tale gives the answer: on his deathbed, Rabbi Simhah Bunam of Psyshcha, seeing his wife wracked with tears, said to her, "Be silent—why do you cry? My whole life was only that I might learn how to die."[6] A lifetime of prayers, devotions, sacrifices, fasts, Torah study, vigils, and teaching prepared the rabbi for this culminating act. As the following ancient Christian hymn suggests, God's presence in every aspect of daily life leads ineluctably to his presence at the moment of death:

> *God be in my hede*
> *And in my understandyng,*
> *God be in myne eyes*
> *And in my lokyng,*
> *God be in my mouth*
> *And in my speakyng,*
> *God be in my harte*
> *And in my thynkyng,*
> *God be in mine ende*
> *And at my departyng.*

Death, then, looks both forward and back. It mirrors the life that precedes it, compressing a lifetime of events into a single culminating moment. It also looks ahead to a new world, a new way of being: "I am not worried about myself, for I know clearly that I shall go from this door and immediately I shall enter another door," said the Baal Shem Tov on the very verge of death.[7]

Death is the pivot between two worlds, and as a result everything associated with the moment of death bears the stamp of the sacred and inflames our interest. The confessions of the dying carry special weight in court—not only because it is presumed that a dying person has no reason to lie but, more important, because a numinous glow surrounds every word spoken on the deathbed. Collections of last words abound. We relish both those that hint at a secret unveiled, such as Aldous Huxley's "I thought so!," and those that show the dying person's spunk, like Oscar Wilde's quip that "either this wallpaper goes, or I do." What we look for in last words is a combination of courage, integrity, and grit: the mark of a recollected death.

If our death summarizes our life, however, need those of us who have led wayward or barren lives expect a scattered, fruitless death? No, for death also looks forward into a new world, a new way of being. And in this rebirth, change is always possible. This explains the phenomenon of the deathbed conversion: not so much a cheap last-ditch attempt to avoid a hellish afterlife as a sense that now, at last, *I can make the effort, I can surrender my pride and obstinacy, I can change my life while I still have life to change.* In every tradition, the opportunity exists for a special effort at the time of death. Here are some examples:

ARS MORIENDI: THE CHRISTIAN ART OF DYING

In the late Middle Ages, Christian deathbed practices coalesced in the *ars moriendi* or "art of dying" literature. Initially presented in rough-hewn volumes illustrated by copious crude woodcuts, the Christian craft of dying reached its apogee in the seventeenth-century English Calvinist Jeremy Taylor's masterpiece, *Holy Dying.* Although nearly forgotten today, the *ars moriendi* material offers a complete guide to the hour of death, with precise advice on how to compose the soul, how to overcome postmortem dangers, and how family and friends can help the dying make a successful transition into the afterlife. Some of the recommendations include:

- *Education.* The dying person is instructed about what will befall him during death. According to the earliest texts, steeped in medieval imagery, he will face a horrific array of demons who will point to his sins and attempt to drag him into hell. The power of these fiends will be countered by the

Blessed Virgin Mary and the saints, who will intercede for his salvation before God.

We may take this description of postmortem struggle literally or figuratively. In either case, the dying person, now apprised of the coming battle for his soul, prepares himself accordingly. This is not so much a matter of steeling himself for war but of making of himself an apostle of peace, freeing his soul from its bondage to self-love and sin while he is still alive. He may take refuge in the compassionate intercession of the Virgin. He may gaze upon holy pictures, be sprinkled with holy water, depart the world by the light of specially blessed beeswax candles. A crucial stage of this preparation is:

- *Examination of conscience.* The dying person is urged to face himself without flinching in order to learn the state of his soul. Ideally, writes Taylor, this practice should be carried on throughout life as a safeguard against habit, for "by a daily examination of our actions we shall the easier cure a great sin, and prevent its arrival to become habitual." Such an examination will also make our "spirit tender and apt for religious impressions," and thus aid our search for wisdom and goodness.

- *Repentance and prayer.* The examination of conscience, to be complete, should include repentance, a declaration of sorrow for our sins—a sorrow felt with unbearable intensity, it is said, by those on the brink of death. Those familiar with Alcoholics Anonymous or other Twelve-Step programs may recognize, in this sequence of self-examination and repentance, Steps Four through Seven:

  4. Made a searching and fearless moral inventory of ourselves.
  5. Admitted to God, to ourselves and to another human being the exact nature of our wrongs.
  6. Were entirely ready to have God remove all these defects of character.
  7. Humbly asked him to remove our shortcomings.[8]

Repentance may take the form of sacramental confession and absolution, or it may be expressed through prayer. One lovely example of confessional verse, composed by Taylor, goes as follows:

> Support me with thy graces, strengthen me with thy spirit, soften my heart with the fire of thy love and the dew of heaven, with penitential showers; make my care prudent, and the remaining portion of my days like the perpetual watches of the night, full of caution and observance, strong and resolute, patient and severe. I remember, O Lord, that I did

sin with greediness and passion . . . let my hatred of sin be as great as my love to thee, and both as near to infinite as my proportion can receive.

And what of those who cluster around the deathbed, eager to help in any way that they can? Taylor suggests other prayers that may be said by companions of the dying. Here is one example:

Give thy servant patience in his sorrows, comfort in his sickness, and restore him to health, if it seems good to thee. . . . make his repentance perfect, and his passage safe, and his faith strong, and his hope modest and confident; that when thou shalt call his soul from the prison of the body, it may enter into the securities and rests of the sons of God in the bosom of blessedness and the custodies of Jesus. Amen.

THE *BARDO THODOL:* THE TIBETAN ART OF DYING

The most famous of all Tibetan texts, the Tibetan Book of the Dead, or *Bardo Thodol,* traditionally ascribed to the eighth-century Indian Buddhist master Padmasambhava, bears some close resemblances to the Christian *ars moriendi* literature. It too prepares the dying to meet their fate, offers abundant deathbed exercises, and envisions the immediate postmortem period as a time of perilous trial, in which one's behavior determines the outcome.

The *Bardo Thodol* describes the world of the dead with a vividness unmatched in any other religious literature. It is nothing less than a "Baedeker" of death, offering detailed maps of the three states, or *bardo*s, through which all of us will pass: the *chikai bardo,* or moment of death itself, with its glimpse of the Clear Light that bathes ultimate reality; the *chonyid bardo,* or intermediate state, with its revelations of peaceful and wrathful Buddhas; and the *sipai bardo,* or rebirth state, during which the dead prepare to rejoin the living.

The crux of dying, according to the *Bardo Thodol,* comes at the instant that the Clear Light is revealed. If the deceased can transfer consciousness into the Clear Light at this moment, then a favorable rebirth, or even final liberation, will be attained.

This transference of consciousness requires preparation. The first Dalai Lama (1391–1471) advised at least six months of training, and he warned of the terrible dangers of inexperience. Sogyal Rinpoche, a contemporary Tibetan teacher and author of *The Tibetan Book of Living and Dying,* counsels that practice in consciousness transference "must, always and in all circumstances, be carried out under the guidance of a qualified master."[9]

For obvious reasons, then, I won't provide a complete description of this technique. However, it is legitimate, I believe, to offer one variation on the practice, boiled to the bone and stripped of esoteric content. It entails three basic steps:

1. Meditate and pray until you achieve a state of tranquillity and collectedness.
2. Imagine the Buddha suspended in front of you, radiating compassion and splendor. Bathe yourself in his blissful presence.
3. Merge your consciousness with that of the Buddha.

Whether or not you choose to explore more deeply the practices of the *Bardo Thodol*, a vital lesson emerges: the importance of equanimity in the face of the death. The fourteenth Dalai Lama, discussing the complex meditations that prepare one for dying, has remarked that "the greatest obstacle of all is mental excitement."[10] In front of the perils of death, as both the *ars moriendi* literature and the *Bardo Thodol* teach, tranquillity will be our shield, recollection our armor, and kindness our banner.

ETHICAL WILLS: A JEWISH PREPARATION FOR DEATH

We can easily imagine ourselves hovering on the brink of death and pleading with God for just one more hour, one more minute, so that we may say to our loved ones what needs to be said. More often than not we would plead in vain, and the shroud would descend forever over our heartfelt, unheard advice.

Faced with this dilemma, Jewish tradition has developed the beautiful practice of writing an ethical will. This document, prepared anywhere from several decades to a day before death, generally takes the form of a personal letter to one's spouse, children, extended family, or the world at large. Like a legal last will and testament, it is read after the author's death. While an ethical will often contains detailed instructions about funeral arrangements, the main focus, as the title suggests, is on behavior. The author may offer maxims, memories, blessings, warnings, whatever imparts to his listeners the wisdom he wishes to leave behind.

Composing an ethical will raises vexing questions: How can I convey my understanding of life in a few brief paragraphs or pages? How can I give useful advice without bullying or browbeating? Should I be expansive or terse, jovial or solemn? Should I talk about myself or about my family? Is there anything that should go unsaid? *What do I really want to say?*

These questions prove to be a godsend. "Depend on it Sir, when a man knows he is to be hanged in a fortnight, it concentrates his mind wonderfully," observed Samuel Johnson. An ethical will, by forcing us to think about our death—and our legacy—has some of the same effect. It may teach the writer, as well as the readers, a lesson or two about how to live.

Paul writes about his mother, the suffering of caregivers, and the Buddhist response to death.

Upaya and the Contemplation of Death

"I'm not me." It was the first thing my mother had said in a long while. I was driving her to Encinitas on a weekend outing from the Alzheimer's facility where she lived. We were heading down California's Highway 101 to a retreat founded in the 1930s by Paramahansa Yogananda. The meditation garden there—open to the public—is an oasis of tranquillity in this land of baroque and outsized chain restaurants and buzzing freeways. Freedom from demons was what my mother needed.

A steep path led up through terraced gardens and pools filled with fat carp to a bluff with a view of the Pacific Ocean. Until recently, she had been able to nego- tiate the path, but this time I drove her to a point near the top from which she had only a short, level walk to a stone bench at the overlook. On the ocean below us, half a dozen surfers in their shiny wet suits sat on their boards, waiting for the next set of waves, exuding beach-boy insouciance, oblivious to the fact that, high above them, my mother also waited. Julia was ninety. She sat next to me on the bench and closed her eyes. I closed mine, and I was flooded by thoughts about her and wishes for her. She knew her mind had gone. I wanted nothing for her but peace.

My parents and their elderly neighbors had made a brave effort to shore up the dikes against the dark sea they knew would eventually envelop them. Yet the frequent visits to doctors and the daily jousts with the clanking monsters at the fitness center seemed—as much as they sustained physical life—to keep them at a distance from the resources of the inner life. They talked among themselves about illness and dis- ability, but the import and deeper meaning of death were rarely discussed. Yet death (like birth) is an intimate event with highly social consequences; it is veiled in personal mystery and ringed with cultural symbolism. It can lure us into embracing life more fully, with less judgment and with greater patience. Contemplation of death should help us to wake up among the living.

I have come to Upaya, a Buddhist center in New Mexico, to explore a contemplative approach to dying with its founder, Joan Halifax. And perhaps to begin healing a wound. Upaya, on

Cerro Gordo Temple at Upaya, New Mexico

the outskirts of Santa Fe, is a collection of low, rounded, Southwest-style buildings that include a main house and a *zendo*, where, this afternoon, Joan is to marry a young couple.

For thirty years, Joan has lived with death and dying as a research anthropologist and, more recently, as a priest in the Tiep Hien order. She regards death—with its mystery and inevitability—as an opportunity for growth and enlightenment. She shares Rilke's belief that death is a great gift "passed on unopened." "Dying," says Joan, "calls for truth in a more fundamental way than any other experience we human beings go though. The question is, How can we help this truth emerge?"

Mindfulness bell, Upaya

In Upaya's Project on Being with Dying, dying people and their caregivers gather at weekly meetings. Joan tells me about a woman named Jessica who, a few days before her death, attended one such meeting. She had burns on her neck from her radiation treatment. "There she is," Joan recalls, "sitting in an all-day meeting on Friday and she would die the following Tuesday. She was kind of transparent-looking, but she was there because she wanted to be there. At one point, Jessica turned to Sandra, one of our partners in the caregiving work, and said: 'You have sustained me. You have taught me to sustain myself in the face of my death.'"

Sustaining oneself in the face of death means coming to a more sublime understanding of death. Understanding—with its potential to liberate the dying from the cruelest fears and to ease suffering—is engendered by two complementary forms of practice.

The first is the practice of lovingkindness (*metta*), which fosters a sense of compassion toward self and other and toward the whole world. "You want to be friendly with death," says Joan, with a slight smile. "This friendliness requires that one practice cultivating a loving heart."

A second practice expands awareness of death itself. Death is inevitable, yet we do not know when it will come. While the impermanence of all things can seem like an abstraction, the truth of it appears vividly in a moment of pain and suffering. That moment inexorably flows into another moment, in the course of which the pain will change. "Death," says Joan, "becomes a gateway where you realize that in our life we are simply riding the waves of birth and death. From the deepest perspective: there is no birth, there is no death."

The work at Upaya aims at developing a greater stability of mind and cultivating an open heart toward oneself and others. The baseline for this is mindfulness and the emerging capacity for deep, reflective listening to another.

"This listening," says Joan, "means that we have stabilized our minds so completely that the person who is speaking can actually hear himself through our stillness. It is a quality of radiant listening, of luminous listening, of vibrant listening, but it is very still. It is listening with attention, with openheartedness, without prejudice. The quality of attention that we are invited to bring is as if the person who is speaking will not live another day, as if she were saying her last words. We listen with all our being. We offer our whole listening body."

I tell Joan that when I moved my mother to a care home, where she could be closer to my family, I expected (or hoped) that she would be pleased. But after taking one look at her new place and roommates, she exploded in anger. Although I was sensitive to her dementia, I was unprepared for the extent of her anguish and was devastated by her verbal onslaught.

Joan describes a practice for caregivers facing the desperation and rage of a loved one. The phrases are from Sharon Salzberg, Thich Nhat Hanh, and Joan Halifax.

"To begin, sit or lie down in as comfortable a position as possible. "Take a few deep, soft breaths as you let your body settle. Bring your attention to your breath and say the phrase you want to practice internally in such a way that it synchronizes with your inhalation and exhalation:"

"May I offer my care and presence unconditionally, knowing it may be met by gratitude, anger, or anguish.

"May I find the inner resources to truly be able to give."

"May I offer love, knowing that I cannot control the course of life, suffering, or death.

"May I remain in peace, and let go of expectations.

"May this experience be a heavenly messenger for me, helping me to open to the nature of life in all.

"May I see my limits compassionately, just as I view the suffering of others."

I ask Joan what she thinks happens at death when the conceptual, aware mind has already been destroyed by disease. "My hunch," she says, "is that the level of mind we are addressing is deeper than the conceptual level. And maybe

Doha: *a son's release ritual ten days after the death of his father, Assam, India*

being 'not me,' not having the ego fixations that construct a separate self-identity, is in fact a kind of strange gift, because we actually want to lose that fierce identity at the time of death." So although my mother's conceptual mind was broken up by Alzheimer's, that did not mean that her deepest nature—her Buddha nature, so to speak—had been disturbed. Whatever happens in our final days, whatever physical and mental ravages, there is, within us, liberation.

The sky is bright blue and patches of snow reflect the late afternoon sunlight on the distant hills. And, oh, yes, Joan has performed the wedding ceremony and the little party of guests has left the *zendo*. As the couple pose for snapshots, my thoughts are still about death and impermanence. I wonder what will happen to the couple when they leave this place. I hope that they treat each other with lovingkindness and pray that they will be fully present to each other's joys and suffering.

I am headed back to Northern California. I live on a bay where occasional violent storms with powerful winds churn up the water and uproot the trees. These storms can be truly frightening. But we geezers know that the storm is not the whole of reality. Above the storm, the sky is crystal-clear, free and spacious into infinity.

After Death

And what of death's aftermath? All religious traditions, and all stories grounded in life's natural rhythms, affirm that *from death comes life.* Perhaps you've seen *Bambi,* Walt Disney's most celebrated animated film, and have flinched, like most viewers, when the little deer's mother is shot by hunters. What in heaven, you wonder as you rise to snap off the television, is this brutal killing doing in a children's cartoon? But in an instant all is transformed: Bambi huddles in a snowbound glade, whimpering with terror, and the next moment spring has arrived, bluebirds soar, bunnies rustle in the grass, and Bambi, now an antlered buck, falls in love with a pretty faun. *From death comes life.*

I write these words on the anniversary of my father's death. Thaddeus Zaleski passed away at home in New York City on a cold February afternoon in 1991. I have just returned from weekday mass, where I prayed for the repose of his soul. *From death comes life.* My father's death, more than any single event, brought home to me the reality of the spirit and brought me home to a life of tradition. In the days after his passing, countless friends from various faiths—Buddhist, Methodist, Navajo, Muslim, and many more—prayed for his soul as it made its journey back to God. Each one prayed in a different way, responding to my father's death in the symbolic language that defined a given faith. I thanked them all. I thanked them for their outpouring of support and kindness—but that was the least of it. I thanked them for their prayers, for I was convinced, and I remain so today, that these petitions, whatever their form, helped my father and are helping him still. Death, I learned in those bitter weeks, brings all traditions together in prayer and worship, as it brings all people together in mourning and hope. Death, which tears families asunder, dividing baby from mother and sister from brother, leaving wounds that can take a lifetime to heal—old man Death, with his glittering scythe and gleaming skull—also binds us together with cords of love, woven by tradition and knotted by faith.

CONCLUSION

This book began with the epic voyages of Marco Polo, which so altered the cultural history of both East and West. Let us now imagine Marco as he returns home to Venice in 1295, after twenty-four years abroad, his boots stained with the soil of Afghanistan, Persia, India, Burma, and Cathay, his mind swarming with memories of Kublai Khan's imperial court, of the green waters of the South China Sea, of the squalid streets of Tu-Tu (modern Beijing), of courtiers and sages, scholars and slaves. Picture Marco in his ancestral home, the souvenirs of his travels spread around him. Perhaps he runs his hand along a thick roll of blue Chinese silk, or lifts a lacquered box filled with spices so exotic that they have no name in Western tongues, or idly examines for a moment an undeciphered parchment covered with Chinese characters. What, he wonders, should he do with this trove of materials and memories? Should he keep it for himself or give it to the world? And if the latter, how to accomplish it? How to tell his neighbors, his city, all the states of Europe about his discoveries, how to put to best use the manifold riches that have come his way?

Marco's musings are ours as well. Each of us is the heir to the wisdom of the ages, bequeathed to us as a sacred trust. Will we hoard it like a dragon nestled atop its treasure? Or will we allow it to multiply, like the man in Christ's parable who received five talents, turned them into ten, and "entered into joy"?

Our first task is to implant these teachings in our own minds and hearts. That has been the aim of this book: to display the depth and diversity of spiritual knowledge available to us today and to suggest ways in which it can make a difference in our everyday lives. But private work is only a beginning. Knowledge kept to oneself is a fire in a sealed box, which burns for an instant and then dies for lack of air. Knowledge spread abroad, by contrast, may warm the entire world. Or to put it another way, each of us has two roles to fulfill, that of student and that of teacher.

For over two decades Marco sat at the feet of the East, delving into its secrets, absorbing its knowledge, observing and learning its ways. Once home, Marco passed on his knowledge; he told of his adventures far and wide and wrote a book about his travels. We must do the same, passing on to others the bounty transmitted to us. To some extent this is a natural process, as we tell family and friends of our discoveries, and our enthusiasm ignites their own. In time, too, we may explore more organized ways of bringing contemplative practice into everyday life.

Drakes Bay, California

Marty Knapp

Whatever our efforts, personal or public, large or small, as teacher or student, parent or lover, through prayer or meditation, work or play, one truth prevails: that the life of the spirit, which we have called the contemplative life, opens to all who knock. No one beseeches the heavens in vain. But much depends on how we knock. If we hammer in a loud, imperious way, we may drown out the divine response and hear only the noise of our egotistical strivings. This, I suspect, lies behind so many of the sad stories of religious violence and cult madness that fill today's newspapers and the pages of history. Let us always remember the story of Elijah, which reminds us that God speaks in "a still small voice." That is the contemplative way: the way of stillness, silence, simplicity, surrender to the moment. In the contemplative life, we reject anger, anxiety, and self-love. We embrace clarity, collectedness, and service to others. We say no to haste, yes to calm; no to pride, yes to humility; no to taking, yes to giving; no to darkness, yes to light. "More light!" exclaimed Goethe on his deathbed, as he faced a new world. Let this call be always on our lips as we seek the gifts of the spirit and the new world they will bring: *More light!*

APPENDIX

The Future of Contemplation

As we enter the new millennium, we face the challenge of how to bring contemplative values and practices into everyday life. Here Jon Kabat-Zinn and Robert A. F. Thurman offer their thoughts on the future of contemplation:

MOVING TOWARD
A MORE CONTEMPLATIVE SOCIETY

by Jon Kabat-Zinn[1]

It is now time for society to turn attention to developing what we may call "inner technologies." The untapped potential of the human mind for individual and collective creativity and wisdom has to be intentionally cultivated.

An inner "technology," of which meditation in its most generic sense and most basic form (mindfulness) is the cardinal element, has the capacity to elevate our consciousness up to and beyond the challenges posed by our technological advances and harness them, as well as the power of the mind, for the greater good and harmony of all people and the planet. This capacity is built into a universal grammar of human psychology, I believe, just as our capacity for speech is built into our brain structure through a universal language instinct. Just as with language development, exposure and some training are needed to develop this capacity to its fullest extent. What is involved is basically a deep familiarity and intimacy with the activity and reactivity of one's own mind, and some competency in navigating through our mind moments and emotions with equanimity, clarity, and commitment.

From my work in the field over the past fifteen years, I see that more and more people are taking up or coming back to the practice of meditation and making it an integral part of their daily lives in a nonmechanical way. . . . It is important to point out that there should and can be no fixed form for this to happen. Meditative pathways, teachers, and programs cannot be cloned, although effective models might be adapted and modified, as has been the case in medical and educational settings with mindfulness-based stress reduction. Appropriate forms and vehicles need to develop out of individuals' personal contemplative experiences, meditation practices, and visions of what might be possible for those who undertake to bring the contemplative dimension into mainstream society. These forms will have to interface in appropriate ways with the social terrain and be sensitive to professional, institutional, generational, and ethnic cultures and their values.

Jon Kabat-Zinn is a best-selling author and director of the Stress Reduction Clinic at the University of Massachusetts Medical School.

THOUGHTS ON CONTEMPLATION AND ITS PLACE IN MODERN CULTURE

by Robert A. F. Thurman[2]

I think it is slightly misleading to speak of our culture as lacking contemplative mind. When we feel that, we are rather lamenting the deplorable contemplative states within which the common mind is absorbed. People's minds are absorbed in continuous reverie almost all the time. When they sleep, they experience a withdrawal from sensory stimuli, though they identify that as a state of unconsciousness. Education in any particular culture builds up a world picture, constantly reinforced by symbols and images and contemplated lifelong. Television, modern culture's peculiar contemplative shrine, supplies a contemplative trance to millions of people, for hours on end, day after day, year in and year out. It is, unfortunately, a trance in which sensory dissatisfaction is constantly reinforced, anger and violence are imprinted, and confusion and the delusion of materialism are constructed and maintained.

Thus, when we talk about seeking to increase and intensify contemplative mind in our culture, we may really be talking about methods of transferring contemplative energies from one focus to another. We want people to contemplate disidentification, detachment, and contentment, to cheer themselves up by becoming less greedy and needy. We want them to contemplate tolerance, patience, nonviolence, and compassion, to unstress themselves by feeling less angry, irritated, and paranoid. We want them to develop more wisdom, more freedom, more capacity for responsibility and creativity, by seeing through the constructed realities in which the materialist culture has us enmeshed. It is important that we recognize the value choices implicit in our esteem for contemplation. Only by doing so can we understand the opposition we are encountering. . . .

There are many ways to make our society more contemplative. Joyce wrote *Finnegans Wake* to make unthinking embeddedness in words more difficult. Maharishi Mahesh Yogi, the founder of Transcendental Meditation, tried to organize contemplative SWAT teams to travel to trouble spots and send out mass-meditation waves to calm groups caught in the flames of fury and violence. Contemplation is taught in thriving Eastern-based centers, Cistercian monasteries, and hospitals, and should be taught more widely through every available medium.

Robert A. F. Thurman is professor of Indo-Tibetan studies in the Department of Religion at Columbia University.

NOTES

Introduction

1. Josef Pieper, *A Brief Reader on the Virtues of the Human Heart*, trans. by Paul C. Duggan (San Francisco: Ignatius Press, 1991), 21.

2. Simone Weil, *Waiting on God* (London: Fontana Books, 1959), 72.

3. Quoted in Siegel, Richard, *The Jewish Catalog*. Compiled and edited by Richard Siegel, Michael Strassfeld and Sharon Strassfeld (Philadelphia: Jewish Publication Society of America, 1973), 150.

4. Quoted in Frithjof Schuon, *The Feathered Sun: Plains Indians in Art and Philosophy* (Bloomington: World Wisdom Books, 1990), 50.

5. Weil, *Waiting on God*, 67.

PART I: DAY

Chapter 1. Day: Introduction

1. Quoted in James G. Needham, *The Biology of Mayflies* (Ithaca: Comstock Publishing Company, 1935), xv.

2. George Appleton, ed., *The Oxford Book of Prayer* (Oxford and New York: Oxford University Press, 1985), 185.

3. Thomas Kelly, *A Testament of Devotion* (New York: Harper and Brothers, 1941), 89 *et passim*.

4. Edward Conze, *Buddhist Texts Through the Ages* (New York and Evanston: Harper & Row, 1964), 56.

5. Glenn H. Mullin, *Death and Dying: The Tibetan Tradition* (Boston, London, and Henley: Arkana, 1986), 6.

6. Quoted in Carol Zaleski, *The Life of the World to Come: Near-Death Experience and Christian Hope* (New York and Oxford: Oxford University Press, 1996), 16.

7. Al-Ghazali, *The Remembrance of Death and the Afterlife*, trans. by T. J. Winter (Cambridge: Islamic Texts Society, 1989), 10.

8. D. S. Roberts, *Islam: A Concise Introduction* (San Francisco: Harper & Row, 1981), 37.

Chapter 2. Waking Up

1. This morning sitting is adapted from material presented in *The Recollected Heart* by Philip Zaleski (San Francisco: HarperSanFrancisco, 1995).

2. St. Benedict, *RB 80* (Collegeville: The Liturgical Press, 1981), 15–16.

3. St. Benedict, *RB 80*, 95.

4. St. Benedict, *RB 80*, 47.

5. Raymond DeMallie, ed., *The Sixth Grandfather* (Lincoln and London: University of Nebraska Press, 1984), 226.

6. DeMallie, *The Sixth Grandfather*, 28.

7. James Darmester and L. H. Mills, translators, *The Zend-Avesta*, in *Sacred Books of the East*, Volume XXXI (Oxford: Oxford University Press, 1887), 292.

8. John S. Mbiti, *African Religions and Philosophy* (Oxford and Portsmouth, N. H.: Heinemann, 1990), 62.

9. F. Max Muller, translator, *The Larger Sukhavati-vyuha*, in *Sacred Books of the East*, Volume XLIX (Oxford: Oxford University Press, 1894), 55.

10. Nishimura, Eshin, *Unsui: A Diary of Zen Monastic Life* (Honolulu: University of Hawaii Press, 1973), entry 12.

11. Jiyu Kennett, *Selling Water by the River: A Manual of Zen Training* (New York: Pantheon Books, 1972), 239.

12. Quoted in D.S. Roberts, *Islam*, 102.

13. Kennett, *Selling Water by the River*, 238.

14. Mrs. Sinclair Stevenson, *The Rites of the Twice-Born* (London: Oxford University Press, 1920), 227.

Chapter 3. Eating

1. John Lame Deer and Richard Erdoes, *Lame Deer: Seeker of Visions* (New York: Simon & Schuster, 1972).

2. Shunryu Suzuki, *The Training of the Zen Buddhist Monk* (New York: University Books 1959), 137.

3. David Scott and Tony Doubleday, *The Elements of Zen* (Rockport, MA: 1992), 82.

4. Daisetz Teitaro Suzuki, *The Training of the Zen Buddhist Monk* (New York: University Books 1959), 147.

5. Stevenson, *The Rites of the Twice-Born*, 242 *et passim*.

6. Zen Master Dogen and Kosho Uchiyama, *From the Zen Kitchen to Enlightenment*, trans. by Thomas Wright (New York: Weatherhill, 1983), 7, 8.

7. Mohammed Marmaduke Pickthall, *The Meaning of the Glorious Koran* (New York: New American Library, 1963), 49.

Chapter 4. Working

1. Weil, *Waiting on God*, 125.

2. Quoted in Richard M. Hogan and John M. LeVoir, *Covenant of Love: Pope John Paul II on Sexuality, Marriage, and Family in the Modern World* (San Francisco: Ignatius Press, 1992).

3. Weil, *Waiting on God*, 75–6.

4. James T. Baily, ed., *A Crafts Anthology* (London: Cassell & Company, 1953), 17.

5. Baily, *A Crafts Anthology*, 1–2.

6. M.K. Gandhi, *Man v. Machine* (Bombay: Bharatiya Vidya Bhavan, 1966), 36–7.

7. Wm. Hepworth Dixon, in Mark Holloway, *Heavens on Earth: Utopian Communities in America 1680–1880* (New York: Dover Publications, 1966), 70.

8. Theodore Parker, in Edward Deming Andrews, *The People Called Shakers* (New York: Dover Publications, 1963), 104.

9. R.K. Prahbhu and U.R. Rao, ed., *The Mind of Mahatma Gandhi* (London: Oxford University Press, 1945), 132.

10. Prahbhu and Rao, *The Mind of Mahatma Gandhi*, 136.

11. Mohini M. Chatterji, translator, *The Bhagavad Gita or The Lord's Lay* (Boston: Houghton Mifflin Co., 1887), 64.

12. Chatterji, *The Bhagavad Gita or The Lord's Lay*, 66 et passim.

13. Arthur Braverman, ed., *Warrior of Zen: The Diamond-hard Wisdom Mind of Suzuki Shosan*, 59.

14. Gene Logsdon, "The Barn Raising," in John A. Hostetler, *Amish Roots: A Treasury of History, Wisdom, and Lore* (Baltimore: The Johns Hopkins University Press, 1989), 78.

15. Brother Lawrence of the Resurrection, O.C.D., *Writings and Conversations on the Practice of the Presence of God*. Critical Edition by Conrad De Meester, O.C.D., trans. by Salvatore Sciurba, O.C.D. (Washington, DC: ICS Publications, 1994), 12–13.

Chapter 5. Simple Pleasures

1. *Tao Te Ching, 43*, in James Legge, translator, *The Sacred Books of the East*, Volume XXXIX (London: Oxford University Press, 1891), 87.

2. Bede Griffiths, *The Golden String* (Springfield, IL: Templegate Publishers, 1980), 9.

Chapter 6. Being with Others

1. Quoted in Sophy Burnham, *A Book of Angels* (New York: Ballantine Books, 1990), 41–2.

2. C.S. Lewis, *The Lion, the Witch, and the Wardrobe* (Harmondsworth: Penguin Books, 1959), 19.

3. Quoted in D.S. Roberts, *Islam*, 101.

4. Alois Musil, *The Manners and Customs of the Rwala Bedouin* (New York: American Geographical Society Oriental Explorations and Studies No.6, 1928), 459.

5. H.R.P. Dickson, *The Arab of the Desert* (London: George Allen & Unwin Ltd., 1949), 118.

6. Joseph Chelhod, "Islands of Welcome in a Sea of Sand," in *The Unesco Courier*, February, 1990, 13.

7. Quoted in Tzvi Rabinowicz, ed., *The Encyclopedia of Hasidism* (Northvale, N.J.: Jason Aronson, 1996), 225.

8. Mother Teresa, *My Life for the Poor*, ed. by Jose Luis Gonzalez-Balado and Janet N. Playfoot (New York: Harper & Row, 1985), 95.

9. Mother Teresa, *My Life for the Poor*, 97 et passim.

10. Mother Teresa, "The Nobel Prize Speech," in Robert Serrou, *Teresa of Calcutta* (New York: McGraw Hill Book Company, 1980), 109.

11. Quoted in Rabinowicz, ed., *The Encyclopedia of Hasidism*, 65.

12. Cicero, "De Amicitia," in Michael Pakaluk, ed., *Other Selves: Philosophers on Friendship* (Indianapolis: Hackett Publishing Company, 1991), 87.

13. Joseph Epes Brown, *The Sacred Pipe: Black Elk's Account of the Seven Rites of the Oglala Sioux* (Harmondsworth: Penguin Books, 1971), xiv.

14. Joseph Epes Brown, *The Spiritual Legacy of the American Indian* (New York: The Crossroad Publishing Company, 1982), 17.

15. Brown, *The Spiritual Legacy of the American Indian*, 44.

Chapter 7. Words

1. Quoted in *Parabola* VIII:3, 68.

2. N. Scott Momaday, "The Man Made of Words," in *Indian Voices: The First Convocation of American Indian Scholars* (San Francisco: The Indian Historian Press, 1970), 49.

3. Knud Rasmussen, *The Netsilik Eskimos: Social Life and Spiritual Cultures, Report of the Fifth Thule Expedition, 1921–1924*, vol. 8 (Copenhagen: Gyldendalske Boghandel, 1931), 16, 321.

4. Louis I. Newman, *The Hasidic Anthology: Tales and Teachings of the Hasidim* (New York: Schoken Books, 1963), 509.

5. Newman, *The Hasidic Anthology*, 511.

6. Mani-bhak-hbum, quoted in Edward Rice, *Eastern Definitions* (New York: Anchor Books, 1980), 279.

7. Pickthall, *The Meaning of the Glorious Koran*, 185.

8. Pickthall, *The Meaning of the Glorious Koran*, 211.

9. Anonymous, *The Way of a Pilgrim*, trans. by R.M. French (2nd ed., New York: Harper, 1954; reprint ed., New York: HarperCollins, 1991), 38.

10. This piece appeared originally in *Praying Magazine*. It appears here with the kind permission of Brother David Steindl-Rast, O.S.B.

11. Quoted in Ruth Tooze, *Storytelling* (Englewood Cliffs, N.J.: Prentice-Hall, 1959), xv.

12. N. Scott Momaday, "The Man Made of Words," in *Indian Voices: The First Convocation of American Indian Scholars* (San Francisco: The Indian Historian Press, 1970).

13. Chu Hsi, *Learning to Be A Sage: Selections from the Conversations of Master Chu, Arranged Topically*, trans. with a commentary by Daniel K. Gardner (Berkeley: University of California Press, 1990), 146.

14. Chu Hsi, *Learning to Be a Sage*, 129.

15. Chu Hsi, *Learning to be a Sage*, 135.

16. Chu Hsi, *Learning to be a Sage*, 135.

17. Chu Hsi, *Learning to be a Sage*, 132.

18. Chu His, *Learning to be a Sage*, 147.

19. Jean Leclercq, *The Love of Learning and the Desire for God* (New York: Mentor Omega Books, 1962), 24.

20. Benedict, Saint, *The Rule of St. Benedict*, trans. with introduction and notes by Anthony C. Meisel and M.L. del Mastro (Garden City: Image Books, 1975), 87.

21. Quoted in Maurus Wolter, OSB, *The Principles of Monasticism* (St. Louis: B. Herder Book Company, 1962), 215.

22. Jonathan Omer-Man, "Study of the Torah as Awakening," *Parabola* VII: 1 (Sleep), 58.

23. George Steiner, "The Retreat from the Word," in *Language and Silence: Essays on Language, Literature, and the Inhuman* (New York: Atheneum, 1967).

24. Mother Teresa, *A Gift for God: Prayers and Meditations* (San Francisco: Harper & Row, 1975), 68–9.

25. John Climacus, *The Ladder of Divine Ascent*, trans. by Colm Luibheid and Norman Russell (New York: Paulist Press, 1982), 158.

26. Quoted in Elizabeth McCumsey, C.H.M., "Silence," in *The Encyclopedia of Religion*, Mircea Eliade, editor-in-chief (New York: Macmillan, 1987), Vol. XIII, 323.

27. John Climacus, *The Ladder of Divine Ascent*, 159.

Chapter 8. Movement

1. Thomas Merton, *The Asian Journal of Thomas Merton*, edited from the original notebooks by Naomi Burton Stone, Brother Patrick Hart, and James Laughlin (New York: New Directions, 1973), 233, 235–6.

Chapter 9. Going to Sleep

1. Newman, *The Hasidic Anthology*, 447.

2. Suzuki, *The Training of the Zen Buddhist Monk*, 95.

3. Quoted in Annemarie Schimmel, *Mystical Dimensions of Islam* (Chapel Hill: The University of North Carolina Press, 1975), 114.

4. Schimmel, *Mystical Dimensions of Islam*, 115.

5. Saint Benedict, *The Rule of St. Benedict*, 69.

6. Saint Benedict, *The Rule of St. Benedict*, 82.

7. W. Montgomery Watt, *The Faith and Practice of Al-Ghazali* (London: George Allen and Unwin Ltd., 1953), 118.

8. Adapted form Isaac Lesser, editor, *The Book of Daily Prayers* (Philadelphia, 1848), 221.

9. Patricia Garfield, *Creative Dreaming* (New York: Ballantine Books, 1974), 80.

10. "Beaver Dreaming and Singing" in "Pilot Not Commander: Essays in Memory of Diamond Jenness," ed. Pat and Jim Lotz, *Anthropologica*, Special Issue n.s. #1 and 2 (1971).

PART II: LIFE

Chapter 10. Life: Introduction

1. *Pirke Aboth* V:24, in *The Ethics of the Talmud: Sayings of the Fathers*, edited with introduction, translation, and commentary by R. Travers Herford (New York: Schocken Books, 1962), 144.

2. *Alcoholics Anonymous Comes of Age: A Brief History of A.A.* (New York: Alcoholics Anonymous World Services, Inc., 1957), 50.

Chapter 11 Birth

1. *Buddhacarita*, in *Buddhist Scriptures*, selected and translated by Edward Conze (Harmondsworth: Penguin Books, 1959), 36.

2. Grantly Dick-Read, M.D., *Childbirth Without Fear*, revised and edited by Helen Wessel and Harlan F. Ellis (New York: Harper & Row, 1985), 247 ff.

3. Everard im Thrun, *Indians of Guiana*, 217, quoted in James Hastings, *Encyclopedia of Religion*

and Ethics (Edinburgh: T. & T. Clark, 1928), Vol. II, 635.

4. N. Scott Momaday, *The Names: A Memoir* (New York: Harper & Row, 1976).

Chapter 12. Childhood

1. John Stratton Hawley, "The Thief In Krishna," in *Parabola* IX: 2, "Theft," 11–12.

2. Weil, *Waiting on God*, 75.

3. Eberhard Arnold, in *Children in Community* (Woodcrest, N.Y.: The Plough Publishing House, 1963), 3.

4. Arnold, in *Children in Community*, 3.

5. Arnold, in *Children in Community*, 4.

6. Arnold, in *Children in Community*, 4.

7. Arnold, "Thoughts Taken from Eberhard Arnold," in *Children in Community*, 6.

8. Quoted in Walter Joseph Homan, *Children and Quakerism* (Berkeley: Gillick Press, 1939), 23.

9. Quoted in Homan, *Children and Quakerism*, 31.

10. Quoted in Homan, *Children and Quakerism*, 31.

11. Quoted in Thomas Buckley, "Doing Your Thinking," *Parabola* IV: 4, "Storytelling and Education," 32.

12. Buckley, "Doing Your Thinking," 35.

13. Drawn from Hayim Halevy Donin, *To Be a Jew: A Guide to Jewish Observance in Contemporary Life* (New York: Basic Books, 1972), 130.

14. Donin, *To Be A Jew*, 113.

15. *Pirke Aboth* III:8 in Charles Taylor, ed., *Sayings of the Jewish Fathers* (Cambridge: Cambridge University Press, 1897), 45–46.

16. Patricia Ebrey, translator and editor, "The Classic of Filial Piety," in *Chinese Civilization: A Sourcebook* (New York: The Free Press, 1993), 64.

17. Ebrey, "The Classic of Filial Piety," in *Chinese Civilization*, 65.

18. Cheng Duanli, "A Schedule for Learning," trans. by Clara Yu, in Ebrey, *Chinese Civilization*, 197.

19. Cheng Duanli, "A Schedule For Learning," in Ebrey, *Chinese Civilization*, 197.

20. *Li Ki*, trans. by James Legge in *Sacred Books of the East: The Texts of Confucianism* Vol. XXVIII, (Oxford: Oxford University Press. 1885), 425.

21. *Li Ki*, in *Sacred Books of the East*, Vol. XXVIII, 82.

22. Cheng Duanli, "A Schedule for Learning," in Ebrey, *Chinese Civilization*, 198.

23. The text can be found in English translation as "Disobedient Children," in John A. Hostetler, editor, *Amish Roots: A Treasury of History, Wisdom, and Lore* (Baltimore: The John Hopkins University Press, 1989), 111–12.

24. Elchaninov, Aleksandr, *The Diary of a Russian Priest*, trans. by Helen Iswolsky (London: Faber, 1957).

Chapter 13. Coming of Age

1. Arthur Amiotte, "Eagles Fly Over," *Parabola* I: 3, 29.

2. Brown, *The Sacred Pipe*, 47.

3. Brown, *The Sacred Pipe*, 57.

4. Brown, *The Sacred Pipe*, 58.

5. Brown, *The Sacred Pipe*, 66.

6. Quoted in Charlotte Frisbie, *Kinaalda: A Study of the Navaho Girl's Puberty Ceremony* (Middletown, CT: Wesleyan University Press, 1967), 11.

7. Frisbie, *Kinaalda*, 12.

8. This pattern is based on the field work of Charlotte Frisbie, as described Frisbie, *Kinaalda*.

Chapter 14. Marriage and Family

1. "Orangutan Love," CNN Interactive Website, November 8, 1996.

2. "Married Orangutan Couple Takes Next Step," CNN Interactive Website, January 23, 1997.

3. "Married Orangutan Couple Takes Next Step," CNN Interactive Website, January 23, 1997.

4. See Alan Unterman, "Judaism," in Jean Holm, editor, *Rites of Passage* (London: Pinter Publishers, 1994), 127.

5. Quoted in John Meyendorff, *Marriage: An Orthodox Perspective* (St. Vladimir's Seminary Press, 1975), 109.

6. Quoted in Meyendorff, *Marriage*, 111.

7. Quoted in Meyendorff, *Marriage*, 113.

8. Clifford Geertz, *The Religions of Java* (Glencoe, IL: The Free Press, 1960), 55.

9. Mrs. Sinclair Stevenson, *The Rites of the Twice-Born* (London: Oxford University Press, 1920), 90.

10. Paraphrased, in modern idiom, from Stevenson, *Rites of the Twice-Born*, 91.

11. John S. Mbiti, *African Religions & Philosophy*, Second Revised and Enlarged Edition (Oxford: Heinemann International Literature and Textbooks, 1969), 131.

12. *Zohar* 1:89a, in Louis I. Newman and Samuel Spitz, editors, *The Talmudic Anthology* (New York: Behrman House, 1945), 271–72.

13. G.K. Chesterton, *Heretics* (New York: John Lane, 1906), 191–92.

14. "Family Instructions," trans. by Clara Yu, in Ebrey, *Chinese Civilization*, 243.

15. "Family Instructions," trans. by Clara Yu, in Ebrey, *Chinese Civilization*, 243.

Chapter 15. Aging

1. *The Laws of Manu*, trans. by Georg Buhler, in *The Sacred Books of the East*, Vol. XXV (London: Oxford University Press, 1888), 198.

2. *The Laws of Manu*, 199.

3. *The Laws of Manu*, 202.

4. *The Laws of Manu*, 202.

5. *The Laws of Manu*, 204.

6. *The Laws of Manu*, 206.

7. *The Laws of Manu*, 199–200, 207.

8. Athanasius, *The Life of Antony*, trans. by Robert C. Gregg (New York: Paulist Press, 1980), 42.

9. Pamela T. Amoss, "Coast Salish Elders," in Pamela T. Amoss and Stevan Harrell, *Other Ways of Growing Old* (Stanford: Stanford University Press, 1981), 232.

10. John Neihardt, *All Is But a Beginning*, quoted in *Songs of Experience*, compiled and edited by Margaret Fowler and Priscilla McCutcheon (New York: Ballantine Books, 1991), 56.

11. Quoted in Ronald Blythe, *The View in Winter* (New York: Harcourt Brace Jovanovich, 1979), 243.

12. George Congreve, "Treasure of Hope for the Evening of Life," quoted in Blythe, *The View in Winter*, 239.

Chapter 16. Dying

1. Frederick S. Paxton, translator and commentator, *A Medieval Latin Death Ritual: The Monastic Customaries of Bernard and Ulrich of Cluny* (Missoula: St. Dunstan's Press, 1993), 20.

2. Paxton, *A Medieval Latin Death Ritual: The Monastic Customaries of Bernard and Ulrich of Cluny*, 20.

3. Gregory the Great, *Dialogues, Book II: Saint Benedict*, trans. by Myra L. Uhlfelder (Indianapolis: The Library of Liberal Arts, 1967), 47.

4. "The Death of the Hasidic Masters," trans. by Samuel H. Dresner, in Jack Riemer, ed., *Jewish Reflections on Death* (New York: Schocken Books, 1976), 27.

5. "The Deaths of the Hasidic Masters," trans. by Dresner, in Riemer, *Jewish Reflections on Death*, 29–30.

6. "The Deaths of the Hasidic Masters," trans. by Dresner, in Riemer, *Jewish Reflections on Death*, 24.

7. "The Deaths of the Hasidic Masters," trans. by Dresner, in Riemer, *Jewish Reflections on Death*, 27.

8. *Alcoholics Anonymous Comes of Age*, 50.

9. Sogyal Rinpoche, *The Tibetan Book of Living and Dying* (San Francisco: HarperSanFrancisco, 1992), 233.

10. Tenzin Gyatso, *The World of Tibetan Buddhism: An Overview of Its Philosophy and Practice*, translated, edited, and annotated by Geshe Thupten Jinpa (Boston: Wisdom Publications, 1995), 138.

Conclusion

1. From Jon Kabat-Zinn, "Catalyzing Movement Toward a More Contemplative/Sacred-Appreciating/Non-Dualistic Society" (The Contemplative Mind in Society, 1996). Reprinted by permission.

2. From Robert A.F. Thurman, "Meditation and Education: Buddhist India, Tibet and Modern America" (The Contemplative Mind in Society, 1996). Reprinted by permission.

ACKNOWLEDGMENTS

Our gratitude to Charles Halpern of the Nathan Cummings Foundation and to Rob Lehman of the Fetzer Institute for their steadfast support of contemplative practices in everyday life.

We also wish to thank the following people for their many contributions to this project: Bill Aron, Rev. Dom Anselm Atkinson, O.S.B., Nora Bateson, Tara Bennett-Goleman, Linda Blachman, Richard Blair, Elizabeth Block, Paul Blankenheim, Norman Boucher, Jeffrey Brooks, Edward Espe Brown, Joseph Bruchac, Shira Burstein, Mirabai Bush, Robert Bussewitz, Leonie Caldecott, Stratford Caldecott, Priscilla Carrasco, Tracy Cochran, Anders Cole, Max Cole, John and Mary Collier, Linda Connor, Sr. Scholastica Crilly, O.S.B., Andrew DeLisle, Susan DeLisle, Shendl Diamond, Lois Dubin, Daniel Gardner, Rt. Rev. Dom Hugh Gilbert, O.S.B., Daniel Goleman, Nancy Graeff, Philip L. Greene, Barbara F. Gundle, Joan Halifax, Kabir Helminski, Linda Hess, Jamie Hubbard, Lawrence Hudetz, Lynn Johnson, William Johnston, Jon Kabat-Zinn, Jennifer Kaufman, Rev. Dom Bede Kierney, O.S.B., Sr., Mary Elizabeth Kloss, O.S.B., Marty Knapp, Christine Knodt, Miles Krassen, Dechen Latshang, Eileen Latshang, George Leonard, Barbara Leslie, Richard Lewis, Parvati Markus, Rohana McLaughlin, Richard Millington, John Ockenga, Rabbi Jonathan Omer-Man, Dr. Dean Ornish, Ram Dass, Claire Renkin, Meridel Rubenstein, Therese Schroeder-Sheker, Rabia Seidel, Vera Shevzov, Br. David Steindl-Rast, O.S.B., Brian Stock, Jean Sulzberger, Kazuaki Tanahashi, Robert A. F. Thurman, Taitetsu Unno, Very Rev. Mother Mary Clare Vincent, O.S.B., Frank Ward, Jan Watson, Lewis Watts, Petroc Willey, Sr. Mary Frances Wynn, O.S.B., Jeff Zaleski.

Many thanks to our agents, Barbara Lowenstein and Eileen Cope, for sterling efforts on our behalf, and to our editor, John Loudon, and his assistant, Karen Levine, for invaluable advice and support.

Finally, a special thanks to Libby Colman for her editorial contributions on childbirth and her endless patience; to Carol Zaleski for ideas and editorial improvements beyond counting; and to Carol, Kriston, John, and Andy for being such perfect gifts of the spirit.

ABOUT THE AUTHORS

Jean Zaleski

PHILIP ZALESKI is senior editor of *Parabola* magazine, author of *The Recollected Heart: A Monastic Retreat,* and editor of *The Best Spiritual Writing 1998.* He teaches religion at Smith College and literature at Wesleyan University. His writings on religion and culture appear regularly in national publications including the *New York Times, Parabola, First Things,* and *Reader's Digest.*

Marty Knapp

PAUL KAUFMAN is coauthor, with Daniel Goleman and Michael Ray, of *The Creative Spirit.* A former visiting research associate at Harvard University, he shares a George Foster Peabody award with Bill Moyers for his work on *The Public Mind.*